THE
PATTERN MAKER'S ASSISTANT

INCLUDING

**The Preparation and Use of Tools;
Lathe, Core, Branch, and Sweep Work;
and Practical Gear Construction**

**SIXTH EDITION, 1889
WITH 250 ILLUSTRATIONS**

BY

JOSHUA ROSE, M.E.
Author of "Complete Practical Machinist"

ASTRAGAL PRESS
Mendham, New Jersey

Reprinted in cooperation with the
Early American Industries Association
from the copy in its collection at
the Spruance Library of the
Bucks County Historical Society,
Doylestown, Pennsylvania.

Library of Congress Catalog Card Number 95-74288
International Standard Book Number 1-879335-59-X

Published by
THE ASTRAGAL PRESS
5 Cold Hill Road, Suite #12
Mendham, New Jersey 07945-0239

Printed in the United States of America

PREFACE.

THE object of this book is to impart a knowledge of Pattern Making that shall be useful to apprentice Pattern Makers, and also to practical machinists, because the drawings of the designer do not as a rule give any instructions as to the construction of the patterns, while at the same time that construction may affect to a considerable degree, the manipulations of the machinist.

Furthermore, it often occurs in the experience of a general machinist, that he is required to make a pattern either in iron or wood, and the complete isolation which usually exists between the pattern shop and the machine shop, is an effective bar to the acquisition of knowledge by observation.

The information is given from actual pattern shop practice, and in the ordinary workshop parlance.

The tables have been selected with a view to a collection comprising all that the Pattern Maker of the widest experience requires; arranged for his convenience, although in as compact a form as possible.

CONTENTS.

THE
PATTERN MAKER'S ASSISTANT.

CHAPTER I.

PATTERN MAKING.

THOSE savans who have read our old earth's unwritten history in and from its strata, tell us that, in ages far remote, men made tools and contrivances of bronze, which, being an alloy, necessitated the fusion and casting of the metal. This casting involves the use of patterns, and pattern making may therefore lay claim to the highest antiquity. But the modern idea of the division of labor has exalted it to be a distinctive art ; in the last generation, for instance, a good machinist (or rather engineer or millwright, for those terms were then applied to builders of machinery,) was required to be alike expert in working upon both wood and metal. He constructed his framing of wood, and made the patterns for his cast metal work ; he was to-day a lathe hand, to-morrow a vise hand.

As, however, the present age of iron dawned, it became apparent that working in wood and in metal must be separated, not only because the handiwork could be more cheaply produced by reason of the increased skill arising from continuous practice, but also because the amount of knowledge required to make an artisan skillful in either the manufacture of wood or of iron, was too great to be thoroughly mastered in the working lifetime of an ordinary, or even an unusually expert workman. Hence modern intelligence soon discovered that better as well as cheaper work could be obtained by a practical education in one particular branch of usefulness, and hence pattern making has taken its place as a specialty. The field of usefulness of cast iron has developed to a remarkable extent during the last twenty years, and the same remark applies to cast steel during the last ten years; both of these materials are steadily encroaching upon the domain of usefulness of wrought iron, stone, and bricks and mortar. So that the field of application for pattern making is stretching outward and onward, to the discomfiture of its rivals. From these considerations, we may readily perceive that a real proficiency in pattern making will exercise to the utmost the skill of the workman, on account of the unceasing variety of the patterns, in form and in the purposes for which they are designed; and the advantage of a retentive memory is evident when we consider that years may elapse ere the same pattern maker may be called upon to exercise his skill upon the same or a similar piece of work. In this art, there are to be considered many details that are seldom or never shown in drawings; such, for instance, as the amount necessary to allow on the pattern for finishing certain parts of a casting, and on what part such allowance is required; and the method which has been proved by experience to be the safest and most expeditious in molding from a certain kind of pattern. But above all these considerations lies the fact that drawings merely show the shape which the finished pattern is required to have, leaving it entirely to the judgment of the pattern maker to elect in what way the various pieces of wood (of which the pattern is constructed) shall have the grain lie, and how they shall be fastened or held together. There is, it is true, an unwritten practice which has obtained universal observance in particular branches of pattern making; but in the newer fields into which the art has advanced and is advancing, this unwritten practice is merely in the process of formation, which state of things must continue so long as casting is discovered to have new arenas of application. A goodly store of well remembered experience is therefore invaluable to the pattern maker; and this being so, the quicker it is obtained the better. Hence the learner should always keep a record of the work which falls under his observation, in which record the sizes and proportions of the work, the method of putting it together, the time taken in its production, and (if possible) whether the castings were satisfactory, noting the defects in the latter, if any, together with suggestions for the remedy of those defects. A pen and ink sketch of the pattern made in the margin will add to the usefulness of the record, besides accustoming the hand to making correct sketches and elucidating the explanation. The operative's intelligence will be much exercised in the shaping and building-up of patterns, depending as this does on the strength of the material of which the casting is to be made, the strength of the pattern itself, and the desirability of its molding well. Dr. Andrews has well said (in the *English Mechanic*): "The correct forms to be given to the materials employed in the construction of tools or machinery depend entirely upon natural principles. Natural form consists in giving to each part the exact proportion that will enable it to fulfill its assigned duty with the smallest expenditure of material, and in placing each portion of the materials under the most favorable conditions of position that the circumstances will admit of. Such natural form is not only the most economical, but, strange to say, it is always correct in every respect, and is invariably beautiful and lovely in its outlines."

I may now mention the qualifications necessary to enable an artisan to become a good pattern maker: First: As the idea of the size and contour of the article or work required will be conveyed to him by drawings, it is necessary that he should be conversant with the principles of mechanical and architectural drawing; and it may be of great advantage to him, though it is not absolutely neces- sary, to be able to make such drawings. It is too often the case that the apprentice pattern maker gains his knowl- edge of drawing from the drawings from which he operates, which, being simple in the first case, and becoming compli- cated only after the lapse of two or three years, makes the acquisition of a knowledge of drawing possible without either study or application; but the result is that, so soon as he is called upon in a new field of action, upon a descrip- tion of work different from that to which he has been ac- customed, he becomes timid, gets confused, finds it neces- sary to ask many questions upon and concerning various parts of the drawings, and then does not obtain credit for the amount of ability to which his skill in handling his tools perhaps entitles him. Furthermore, a knowledge of draw- ing will enable him to learn his trade in a comparatively short space of time, and give him confidence in, and a re- tention of, that which he has already learned. Secondly: He should be perfectly familiar with the operations of the brass and iron founder, as it is by him that patterns will be used to produce the required forms. The pattern must be so made that a mold can be made from it, and that it may be made in the most expeditious manner. The pattern maker, it must be remembered, determines how the mold- er is to mold the pattern, so that the latter is controlled in his operations by the former. For the benefit of those who have been unable to devote sufficient time to the work of the foundery, it will be necessary, as we proceed, to explain the operations of molding different kinds of pat- terns, selecting those which will best serve as a key to the whole. Thirdly: The pattern maker must be acquainted with some, at least, of the properties of the metals of which the castings from his patterns are to be made; such, for instance, as how they behave in passing from the fluid, to the solid state, the strains to which a casting is subject during this transition, to what extent those strains may be modified by alterations of proportion or shape in the pattern, the shrinkage of castings, and the alteration in **form** which takes place in the cooling of castings of various sizes and shapes. Fourthly: He should, if possible, add to the above qualifications a general knowledge of the manner of fitting up the different kinds of work for which patterns are used.

With regard to the first requirement, it is not my purpose to enter into the subject of mechanical drawing, which is treated of in books devoted exclusively to that subject. With regard to the second, I shall, as already stated, refer to it hereafter. The third I shall consider after I have treated upon timber, and tools; and the fourth can only be obtained by watchfulness on the part of the student as to what is being done in the workshop in which he is engaged. This latter may seem a trivial matter; but I have on several occasions, by watching where certain castings required to be most operated upon in the machine or vise, had a pattern altered, making it apparently of an incorrect form, with the result that the time necessary to fit the work was reduced by one half. This subject, however, will be treated upon in its proper place.

Of the different kinds of wood serviceable to the pattern maker, pine is, for many reasons, usually employed. It should be of the best quality, straight-grained, and free from knots; it is then easy to work in any direction, possessing at the same time sufficient strength for all but the most delicate kinds of work, and having besides the quality of cheapness to recommend it. Care taken in its selection at the lumber yard will be amply repaid in the workshop. When it is straight-grained, the marks left by the saw will show an **even roughness** throughout the whole length of the plank;

and the rougher the appearance, the softer the **plank.**
That which is sawn comparatively smooth will be found
hard and troublesome to work. If the plank has an uneven appearance—that is to say, if it is rough in some parts
and smooth in others—the grain is crooked. Such timber
is known to the trade as catfaced. In planing it, the
grain tears up, and a nice smooth surface cannot be obtained. Before purchasing timber, it is well to note, what convenience the yard possesses for storing. Lumber on the
pile, though it be out in all weathers, does not deteriorate,
but becomes seasoned; nevertheless its value is much increased if it has an extemporized roof to protect it from
the sun and rain; but as it is not convenient to visit the
pile for every customer, quantities are usually taken down
to await sale, and for such, a shelter must be provided,
otherwise it will be impossible to insure that the lumber is
dry, sound, and fit for pattern making ; it being obvious that
the foregoing remarks on the storage of lumber apply to
all woods.

The superiority of pine for pattern making is not, however, maintained when we come to fine delicate patterns or
patterns requiring great durability. When patterns for
fine work, from which a great many castings are to be made,
are required, a pattern wherefrom to cast an iron pattern
is improvised, because, if pine were employed, it would not
only become rapidly worn out, but would soon warp and become useless. It is true that a pine pattern will straight-
en more easily than one made of a hard wood ; but its
sphere of usefulness in fine patterns is, for the above reasons, somewhat limited. Iron patterns are very desirable
on account of their durability, and because they leave the
sand easily and cleanly, and because they not only do not
warp, but are also less liable than wooden ones to give way
to the sand, while the latter is being rammed around them
by the molder—a defect that is often experienced with light

patterns, especially if they are made of pine. Iron patterns, however, are expensive things to make, and therefore it is that mahogany is extensively employed for fine or durable pattern work. Other woods are sometimes employed, because they stand the rough usage of the molding shop better and retain the sharp corners, which, if pine be used, in time become rounded, impairing the appearance of the casting. Mahogany is not liable to warp, nor subject to decay; and is for these reasons the most desirable of all woods employed in pattern making, providing that first cost is not a primary consideration. There are various kinds of this beautiful wood, that known as South American mahogany being chiefly used for patterns.

Next to mahogany we may rank cherry, which is a very durable wood, but more liable to twist or warp than mahogany, and it is a little harsh to the tool edge. If, however, it is stored in the workshop for a length of time before being used, reliable patterns may be made from it. In addition to these woods, walnut, beech, and teak are sometimes employed in pattern making.

The one property in all timber to be specially guarded against is its tendency to warp, bend, expand, and contract, according to the amount of humidity in the atmosphere. Under ordinary conditions, we shall be right in supposing a moisture to be constantly given off from all the exposed surfaces of timber; therefore planks stored in the shop should be placed in a rack so contrived that they do not touch one another, so that the air may circulate between the planks, and dry all surfaces as nearly alike as possible. If a plank newly planed be lying on the bench on its flat side, the moisture will be given off freely from the upper surface, but will, on the under surface, be confined between the bench and the plank: the result being that a plank, planed straight and left lying as described, will be found, even in an hour, to be curved, from the contraction of the upper surface due to its extra exposure; and therefore it is that lumber newly planed should be stored on end or placed on edge. Lumber expands and contracts with considerable force across the grain; hence if a piece even of a dry plank, be rigidly held and confined at the edges, it will shrink and rend in twain, often with a loud report. There is no appreciable alteration lengthwise in timber from the above causes; and if two pieces be glued together so that the grain of one crosses that of the other, they can never safely be relied upon to hold. Hence they had better be screwed, so that there will be a little liberty for the operation or play of the above forces, while the screws retain their hold. The shrinkage, expansion, and warping of timber may perhaps be better understood by considering as follows: The pores of wood run lengthwise, or with its grain, and hence the moisture contained in these passes off more readily endwise or from any surface on which the pores terminate. Then again the wood shrinks precisely in proportion in which the moisture leaves it; and if we have full knowledge of the direction of the grain, and of the position in which a piece of timber stands or lies, we can (all other things being equal, that is to say, supposing there to be no artificial heat or other disturbing cause operating on one more than on another side of it) predicate in what direction it will warp. Thus, let A, Fig. 1, be a piece of timber having the direction

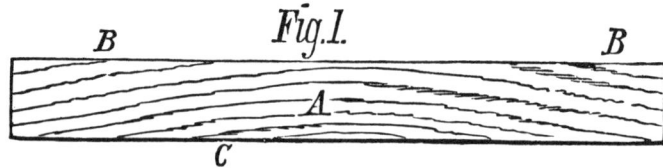

of its grain as denoted by the lines; then its surface, B B, which has the grain and pores terminating upon it, would allow free exit of the moisture, and that face would dry first (especially if it lay uppermost) and would contract the most, so that after a time the shape of the piece would be curved, as shown in Fig. 2. Now if it had been placed to lay with the face, C, uppermost, the warping would have been much less, because the extra porosity of the face, B B, would have been counteracted by the lack of circulation of air. If, on the oth-

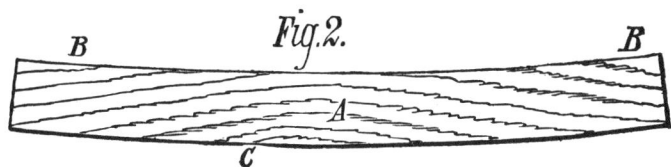

Fig. 2.

er hand, it was placed endwise, the warping, though it would have taken place, would have been appreciably less. It must not be supposed that thoroughly seasoning the timber will remove the tendency to warp, for timber, however long and carefully it has been dried or seasoned, undergoes considerable transformation of shape so soon as much of its outer surface is removed, making it appear that the seasoning or drying process takes place mainly at and near the outer surfaces, and is renewed every time an entirely new surface is presented to the action of the atmosphere. Thus, if we take a thoroughly seasoned piece of wood 3 inches square and 1 foot long, and cut it into strips 1 inch square and 1 foot long, the pieces will warp in a day or so; and if, after a few days, we take those inch strips and cut them into strips $\frac{1}{4}$ inch square and 1 foot long, these latter will again warp; and no matter what pains might be taken with these last strips to season them and let them assume their new shape, were we to cut them into thin veneers the warping process would again set in. It is well, therefore, in particular work, to cut out roughly the various parts of the pattern, so that, while some parts are being operated upon, the others may be assuming their new shape, and thus become not so liable to warp after being worked up in the pattern.

TOOLS, ETC.

One of our first requisites in the way of tools and appliances will be a carpenter's bench, which may be made as follows: Three pieces of stuff, 2x5 inches and 3 feet long, will serve for supports for the top. Two 12 inch boards, 12 feet long and 1 inch thick, will do for the sides. Nail these side boards firmly to the 2x5 inch cross pieces, and put on a top of suitable material, and the bench is ready for the legs. Now take four pieces of stuff, 2x5 inches, and of the requisite hight for the legs, and frame a piece 1x3 inches across each pair of legs, about 6 inches from the bottom, placing the legs at the distance apart necessary for the width of the bench. Then cut a fork or slit in the top end of each leg, so as to straddle the cross piece at the ends, and put a bolt 3½x⅜ inches through each leg and through the side boards, and the bench will be complete; and it will possess the advantage that it can be taken down in a few minutes by removing the bolts from the legs.

The jack plane is employed for roughing off the surface timber; the stock is made of beech and the blade of cast steel. The blade acts most effectively when it is ground well away toward the corners, thus producing a curved edge, as shown in Fig. 3. When the blade is placed in the stock,

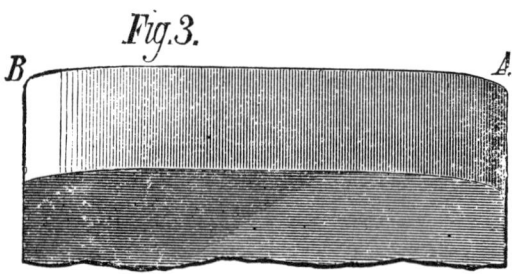

Fig.3.

and in position to cut off the largest amount of stuff, its cutting edge should protrude through the face of the stock about a sixteenth of an inch, while the corners, A B, are about level with the face of the stock. The beveled face should stand at about an angle of 50° to the flat face. The grindstone should be kept true and liberally supplied with water; the straight face should not be ground away, nor indeed touched upon the stone. The pressure with which the blade is held against the grindstone should be slight at and toward the finishing part of the grinding process, so as not to leave a long ragged burr on the end of the blade, as is sure to be the case if much pressure is applied; and it will occur to a slight extent even with the greatest of care. The blade should not be held still upon the grindstone, no matter how true, flat, or smooth the latter may be; but it should be moved back and forth across the width of the stone, which will not only grind the blade bevel even and level, but will also tend to keep the grindstone in good order.

If a grindstone is in excellent condition (that is, true, flat, and level, or slightly rounding), as it should be, it tempts the workman to grind the plane blade with the stone running toward him, as shown in Fig. 4, for the following reasons: If the stone, A, travels in the direction of the arrow, C, the plane blade, B, will relieve the abrasion of the stone

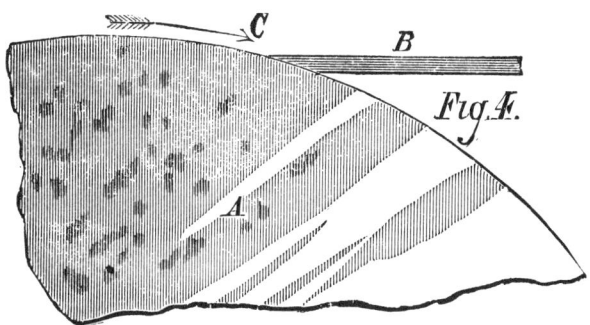

at the cutting edge first, thus leaving it clean and with no tendency to leave a long ragged edge; but if the blade were held on the other side of the stone, that is to say, with the stone running from the operator, as shown in Fig. 5, the result will be a long ragged edge on the plane blade, especially if much pressure be placed on the blade.

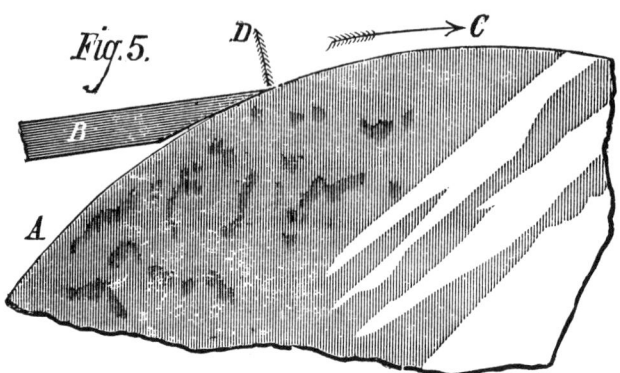

Fig. 5.

In Fig. 5, A represents the grindstone, B the plane blade, and C the direction in which the grindstone is supposed to revolve: in which case it becomes evident that the plane blade will receive at its edge some pressure in the direction of the arrow, D; and the metal at the cutting edge of the blade, being very thin, gives way to this pressure and bends back instead of abrading off, leaving a long feather edge, as shown in Fig. 6, from A to B. This edge breaks off in many cases further back than it should do, and inevitably breaks off when the blade is applied to the oilstone, leaving upon the face of the oilstone particles of steel which must be removed before a good edge can be secured

Fig. 6.

to the tool. As a rule, however, this feather edge is broken off by tapping the blade on the palm of the hand, or it may be removed by passing the edge lengthwise on a piece of wood. It is, however, better to hold the blade as shown in Fig. 4; but there are other considerations which sometimes render this impracticable. For instance, if the stone is out of true, the high spots will strike against the cutting edge, and render it impossible to hold the blade steadily, and hence impossible to grind it true. If the stone has soft spots in it, as most stones have, the blade will dig in those soft spots, and will also be thrown off the stone when encountering an unusually hard spot. If, in consequence of digging in a soft spot, the blade catches, the cutting edge will be ground completely off; so that it is only under exceptional and unusual circumstances that the blade can be ground in the position shown in Fig. 4. It is better, therefore, to grind it in the position shown in Fig. 5, which is safer and surer. In oilstoning a plane blade, the straight face should be held quite level with the face of the oilstone, so that the cutting edge may not be beveled off. Not much application to the oilstone is necessary to the straight face, because that face is not ground upon the grindstone, and it only requires to have the wire edge or burr removed, leaving an oilstone polish all along the cutting edge. The oilstoning should be performed alternately on the flat and beveled faces, the blade being pressed very lightly on the oilstone toward the last part of the operation, so as to leave as fine a wire edge as possible. The wire is the edge or burr which bends or turns over at the extreme edge of the tool, in consequence of that extreme edge giving way to the pressure of the abrading tool, be it a grindstone or an oilstone. This wire edge is reduced to a minimum by the oilstone, and is then so fine that it is practically of but little account; to remove it, however, the plane blade or iron may be buffed backwards and forwards on the palm of the hand.

The iron being sharpened, we may screw the cover on, adjusting it so that its edge stands a shade below the corners of the iron, and then screwing it tight; the blade or iron and the cover must now be placed in the mouth of the plane stock, and adjusted in the following manner: The plane iron should be passed through the mouth of the stock until as much in depth of it is seen to protrude from the bottom face of the stock as is equal to the thickness of shaving it is intended to cut: to estimate which, place the back end of the plane upon the bench, holding the stock in the left hand with the thumb in the plane mouth, so as to retain the iron and wedge in position, the wedge being turned toward the workman. A glance down the face of the stock will be sufficient to inform the operator how much or how little the cutting edge of the iron protrudes from the face of the plane stock, and hence how thick his shaving will be. When the distance is adjusted as nearly as possible, the wedge may be tightened by a few light blows of the hammer. If, after tightening the wedge, the blade is found to protrude too much, a light blow on the fore end of the top face of the plane will cause it to retire. The wedge should be tightened by a light blow after it is finally adjusted.

In using a jack plane, we commence each stroke by exerting a pressure mostly on the fore part of the plane, commencing at the end and towards the edge of the board, and taking off a shaving as long as the arms can conveniently reach. If the board is longer than can be reached without moving, we pass across the board, planing it all across at one standing; then we step sufficiently forward, and carry the planing forward, repeating this until the jack planing is completed. To try the level of the board, the edge or corner of the plane may be employed; and if the plane is moved back and forth on the corner or edge, it will indent, and so point out the high place.

The fore plane (or truing plane, as it is sometimes called) is made large, so as to cover more surface, and therefore to cut more truly. It is ground and set in the same manner as the jack plane, with the exception that the corners of the iron or blade, for about one eighth inch only, should be ground to a very little below the level of the rest of the cutting edge, the latter being made perfectly straight (or as near so as practically attainable) and square with the edge of the iron. If the end edge of the cover is made square with the side edge, and the iron is ground with the cover on, the latter will form a guide whereby to grind the iron edge true and square; but in such case the cover should be set back so that there will be no danger of the grindstone touching it. The oilstoning should be performed in the manner described for the jack plane, bearing in mind that the object to be aimed at is to be able to make as broad and fine a shaving as possible without the corners of the plane iron digging into the work. The plane iron should be so set that its cutting edge can only just be seen projecting evenly through the stock. In using the fore or truing plane, it is usual, on the back stroke, to twist the body of the plane so that it will slide along the board on its edge, there being no contact between the cutting edge of the plane iron and the face of the board, which is to preserve the cutting edge of the plane iron from abrasion by the wood; as it is obvious that such abrasion would be much more destructive to the edge than the cutting duty performed during the front stroke would be. The face of the fore plane must be kept perfectly flat on the under side, which should be square with the sides of the plane. If the under side be hollow, the plane iron edge will have to protrude further through the plane face to compensate for the hollowness of the latter; and in that case it will be impossible to take fine shavings off thin stuff, because the blade or iron will protrude too much, and as a consequence there will be an unnecessary amount of labor incurred in setting and resetting the plane iron. The reason that the under surface should be square, that is to say, at a right angle to the sides of the body of the plane, is because the plane is sometimes used on its side on a shooting board.

When the under surface of the plane is worn out of true, let the iron be wedged in the plane mouth, but let the cutting edge of the iron be well below the surface of the plane stock. Then, with another fore plane, freshly sharpened and set very fine, true up the surface, and be sure the surface does not wind, which may be ascertained by the application of a pair of winding strips, the manner of applying which will be explained hereafter. If the mouth of a fore plane wears too wide, as it is apt in time to do, short little shavings, tightly curled up, will fall half in and half out of the mouth, and prevent the iron from cutting, and will cause it to leave scores in the work, entailing a great loss of time, in removing them at every few strokes. The smoothing plane is used for smoothing rather than truing work, and is made shorter than the truing plane, so as to be handier in using. It is sometimes impracticable to make a surface as smooth as desirable with a truing plane, because of the direction of the grain of the wood. Thus in Fig. 7, let E represent a piece of stuff requiring to be planed on

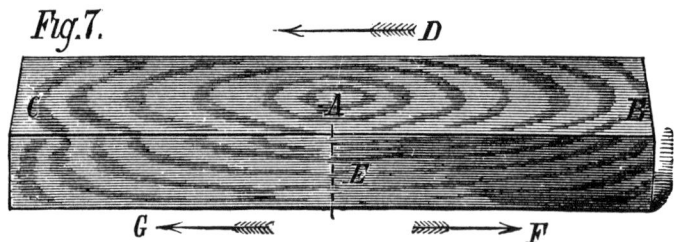

Fig. 7.

the upper surface, and let us plane it, cutting in the direction of the arrow, D. It is evident that the edge of the plane iron, when cutting the surface from B to A, will strike against the edge or end of the grain of the wood, tending to rough it up; whereas, while passing from A to C, the tendency of the pressure of the iron edge would be to smooth the grain of the wood downwards, the difference between the two tendencies being sufficient to make it necessary in many cases to use a smoothing plane, cutting in both directions, as shown in Fig. 7, first from A to B, cutting in the direction of the arrow, F, and then from A to C, cutting in the direction of the arrow, G. Thus the cutting will be at all times performed in the direction tending to smooth down and not rough up the grain of the wood. That this method of planing is necessary is demonstrated in planing across the end grain of wood, for which purpose the smoothing plane is almost indispensable, and in which operation it is necessary to use it, on small surfaces, with a side as well as with a forward sweep, thus producing a curved motion, the most desirable direction of which is determined by the direction of the grain of the wood.

Fig. 8 represents an ordinary compass plane, which is a necessary and very useful tool for planing the surfaces of

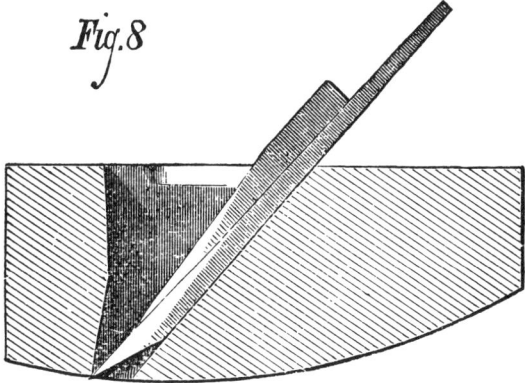

Fig. 8

hollow sweeps. This tool is sometimes made adjustable by means of a piece dovetailed in the front end of the plane, as shown in Fig. 9, at A; which, by being lowered, alters the sweep and finally converts it from a convex to a concave. There is now, however, in the market a compass plane, the body of which is made of malleable iron with a sole made of a blade of spring steel, which, by the operation of two screws, can be set to any curvature, either concave or convex, within the capacity of the instrument.

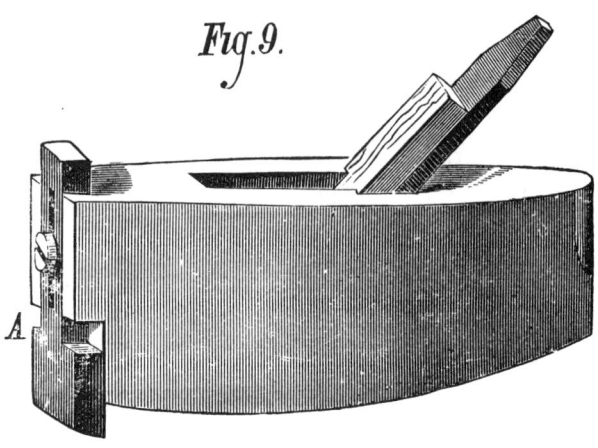

Fig.9.

Another very useful species of plane is the router, shown in Fig. 10, which represents one of these planes in opera-

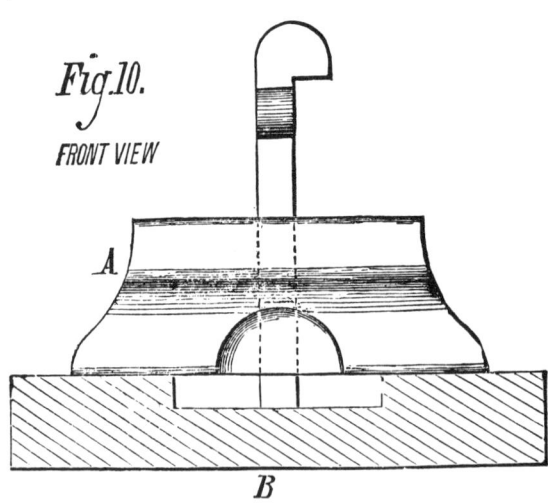

Fig.10.

FRONT VIEW

tion, A being the router, and B the work. The use of this tool is to plane out recesses (exactly to any given depth) such as are required to receive rapping plates. The wood in the plane stock is cut away just over the edge of the iron, to give clearance for the shavings, and so that the cutter may be seen at work.

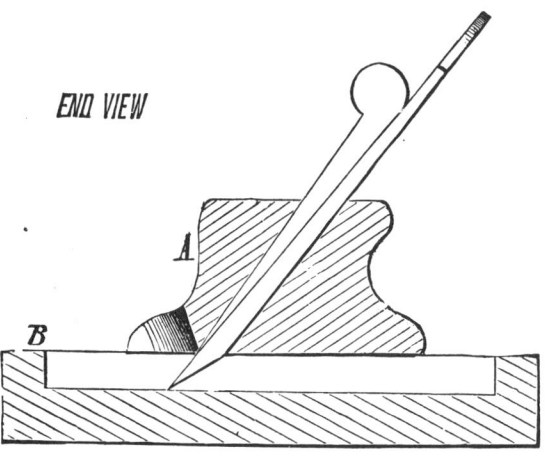

END VIEW

Rabbet planes are narrow planes having the sole or side of a conformation to suit the work. Fig. 11 represents a rab-

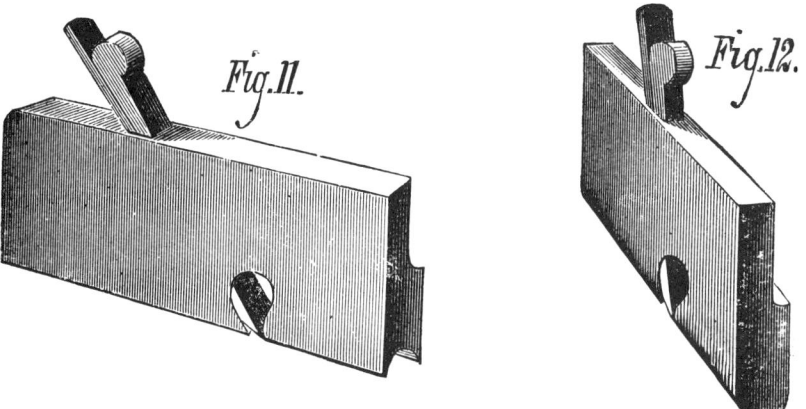

Fig. 11.

Fig. 12.

bet plane to suit a round edge, Fig. 12, a similar plane for a groove, and Fig. 13 a side rabbet plane. The latter is, however, very seldom used, but is especially useful in planing hard wood cogs fitted to iron wheels, or the teeth of wheel patterns, or other similar work. One or two flat bottomed ones will also be required. Small thumb rabbet planes,

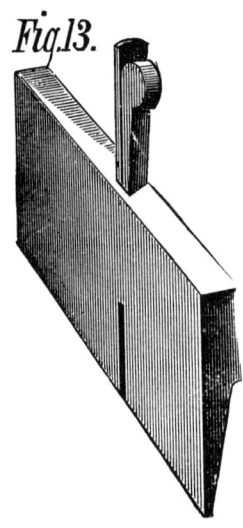

Fig.13.

having an iron stock, with the blade near the front end, are now supplied, and are very useful for cutting out half checks that are not cut right across the stuff.

Fig. 14 is an end, and Fig. 15 a side, view of a core box plane, suitable for planing semicircular grooves out of the solid. The principle of its construction and use is that the angle in a semicircle is a right angle. Suppose, for example, that Fig. 16 represents a piece of wood having a semicircular groove in it, and we mark off on the groove the points, *a*, *b*, *c*, *d*, *e*, and strike from each of these a line direct to each corner of the groove. We shall thus find that the two lines struck will be at a right angle to each other, the two lines, A A, meeting at the point, *a*, being at a right angle. The two side faces, CC, of the plane in Fig. 14 are made to stand at a right angle to each other; and while the plane is in position (as shown in Fig. 14) to bear against the corners of the core

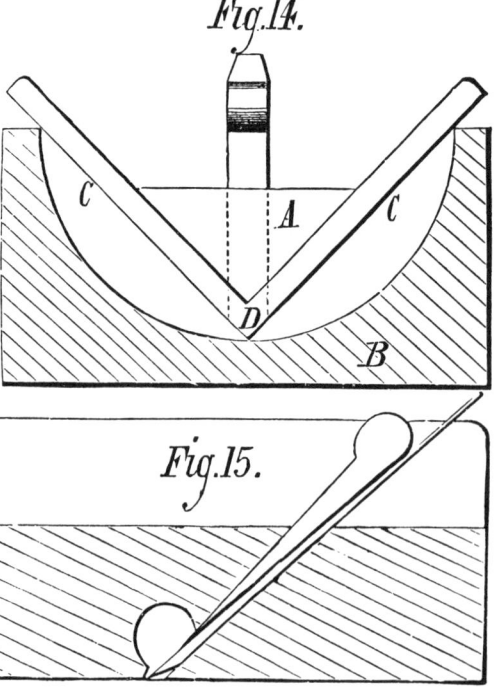

Fig.14.

Fig.15.

box, a semicircle (the apex of the plane, D, in Fig. 14) must be in the semicircle, and will only cut away the wood in the form of the circle, no matter in what position

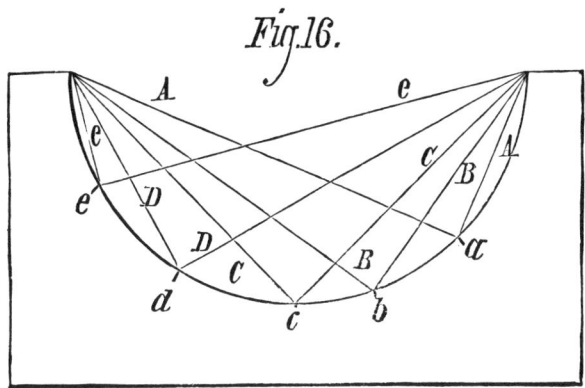

Fig.16.

the plane stands, so long as its sides touch the corners of the semicircle. This being the case, the first operation in using this plane is to cut out the required semicircle to the necessary width, which may be done with a rabbet plane. The core box plane may thus be employed to cut out the semicircle, commencing at each of the corners and planing on each side down to the center of the depth of the

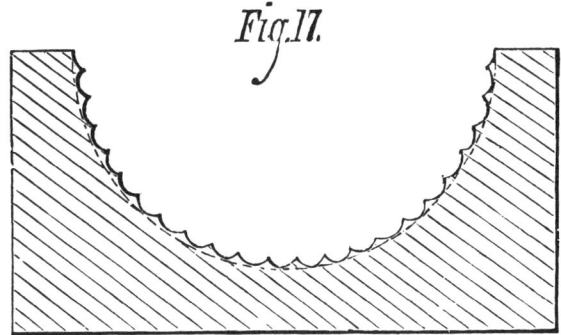

Fig.17.

semicircle. As this plane is intended to finish the work, it is desirable to cut away as much of the stuff as possible before employing it, the work appearing as shown in Fig. 17. These planes have one disadvantage. They are apt to abrade the corners of the work; hence great care should be exercised in their use, and care must also be taken that the extreme point of the plane iron stands just at the apex of the angle of the body of the plane; for if it be in advance or not up to it, the work will not be semicircular.

Of late years there have been introduced planes having a stock of iron, the advantage being that the mouth does

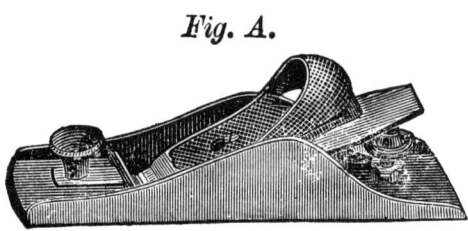

Fig. A.

not wear larger, the soles keep true, and all parts are interchangeable. The blade of the block plane, shown in Fig. A, is set at a greater angle, as is necessary for planing the end grain of wood. The circular plane, shown in Fig. B, is an especially desirable tool, because the sole can be set to any desired curve, either concave or convex, and the plane can be used clear up to the edge of the curve;

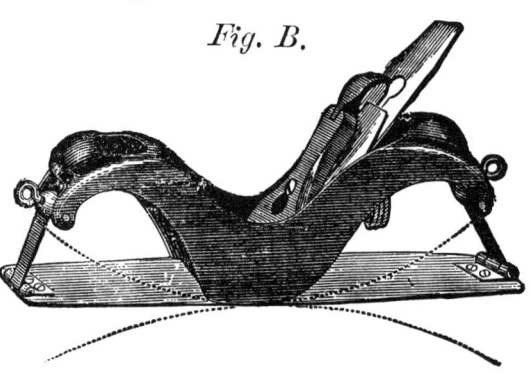

Fig. B.

in which respect it possesses an advantage over the plane shown in Figs. 8 and 9.

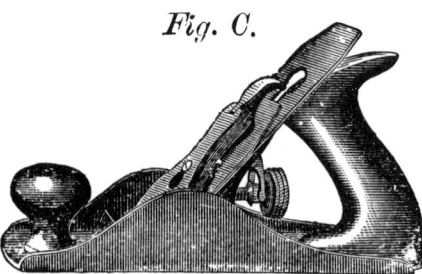

Fig. C.

In Figs. C and D are smoothing and jointer planes of this class; and it may be mentioned that the blades can be altered in adjustment while the plane is being operated.

There is a sense of flatness in using these planes, that is

very desirable for true work. The manner in which the iron fits to the blade is shown in Fig. E, the iron being

Fig. D

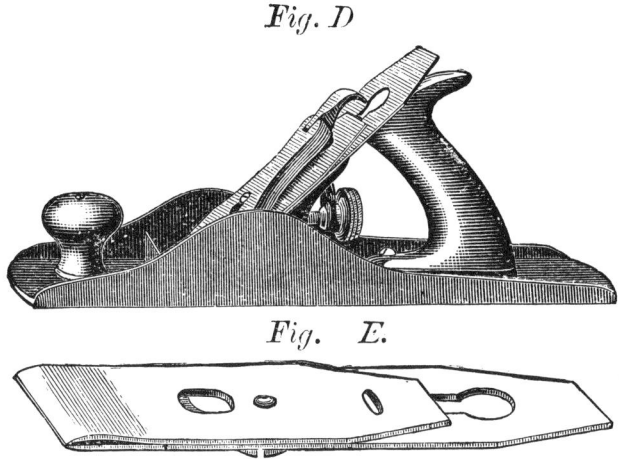

Fig. E.

curved to insure that it shall touch the blade close to the cutting edge, supporting and stiffening it so that thinner blades can be used, the latter being easier to grind and oilstone.

Of chisels, the principal kinds used are the paring chisel, used entirely by hand pressure, and the firmer chisel, for use with the mallet. The difference between the two is that the paring chisel is the longer. A paring chisel, worn to half its original length, will however answer for use as a firmer chisel, because, when so worn, it is sufficiently long for the duty. A chisel should not, however, be used indiscriminately as a paring and firmer chisel, for the reason that the paring chisel requires to be kept in much better order than the firmer chisel does. It is necessary to have several sizes of chisels, varying in width from an eighth of an inch to an inch and a half. A paring chisel for general use is shown in Fig. 18. Its width is about one and a half inch, and its handle should be exactly of the form shown in the engraving; the total length of handle

2*

being six inches, from A to B being one and a half inch, and the diameter at C, and from B upwards, being one and a half inch. The hollow below B is of three-eighths inch

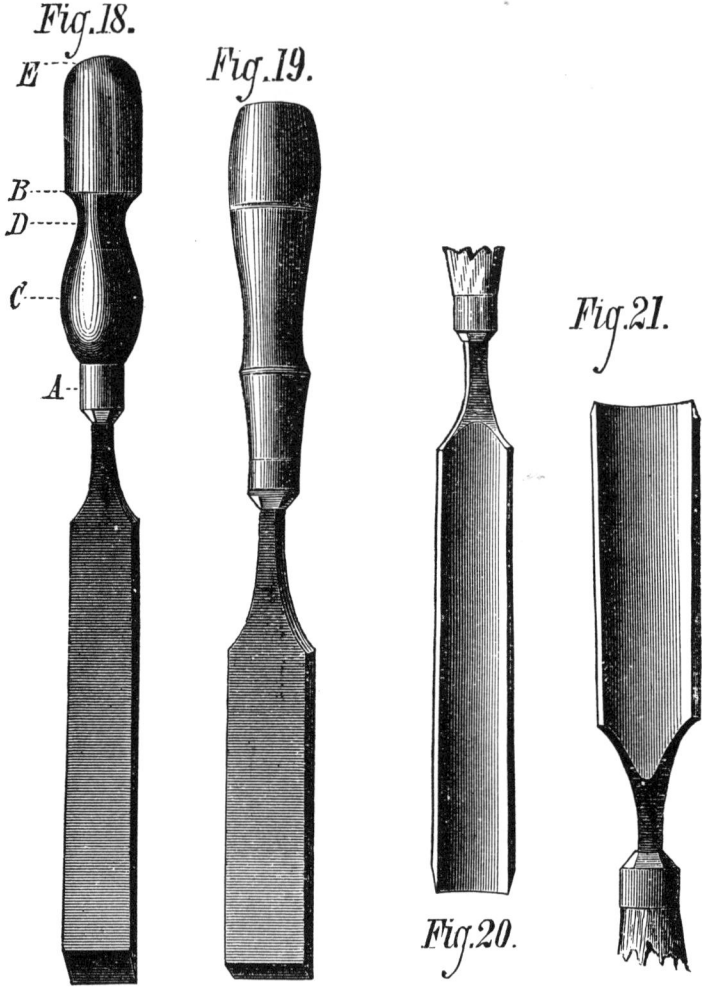

radius, and the diameter at D is one inch. This shape and size gives a good purchase, especially from A to B, where the hand is most often applied, the end, E, being against the operator's shoulder. A firmer chisel having a handle of the ordinary pattern is shown in Fig. 19.

Chisels are sharpened in the same manner as plane irons; but being usually narrower, they require special attention in the grinding, as they should be held against the grindstone with an amount of pressure proportionate to their width. In describing Figs. 5 and 6, it was explained how a long feather edge may be given to a tool in the grinding; and these remarks apply especially to chisels. Hence, towards the finishing part of the grinding operation, the chisel should be held very lightly against the stone; the flat face of the chisel should never be ground, but should be kept straight and even, otherwise the whole value of the tool will be impaired. In setting the edge of a chisel upon an oilstone, it is necessary to exercise great care that the hands are not elevated so as to oilstone the blade at a different bevel to that at which it was ground, and not to allow the movement of the hands to be such as to round off the bevel face at and near the cutting edge—an error which, from lack of experience, is very apt to occur. The position in which the bevel of the chisel should be pressed to the oilstone should be such that the marks made by the oilstone will lie from the back of the bevel to the cutting edge, but be shown more strongly at and towards the cutting edge. The motion of the hands of the operator should not be simply back and forth, parallel with the length of the oilstone, but partly diagonal, which will greatly assist in keeping the bevel level with the oilstone. Very little pressure should be applied to the chisel during the latter part of the process of oilstoning; and the flat face of the chisel should be held level with the face of the oilstone, and moved diagonally under a light pressure, sufficient only to remove the wire edge. After the setting is complete, the chisel should be lapped upon the hand, to remove the fine wire edge left by the oilstone.

The next tool is the gouge, of which there are several kinds. Those having the bevel on the concave side are termed inside gouges; and when the bevel is on the convex side, they are called outside gouges. Gouges, like chisels, are also classed into firmer and paring gouges, the distinction between the two being the same as in the case of chisels. It is not necessary to possess a full set of each kind of gouges; half a set each of inside and outside will suffice. Fig. 20 represents a paring, and Fig. 21 a firmer, outside gouge.

The inside gouge may be ground a little keener than the chisel or plane iron, and requires care in the operation, since it has generally to be ground on the corner of the grindstone, which is rarely of the same curve as the gouge requires. In oilstoning a gouge, what is called a slip is employed. Slips are wedge-shaped pieces of oilstone, of various curves and shapes, to suit the purposes for which they are applied. The gouge should be held in the left hand, and the slip in the right, the latter being supplied with clean oil. The back or convex side of the gouge must be laid level on the face of the oilstone, and the handle worked to and from the workman, who must roll it at the same time, so as to bring every part of the curve of the gouge in contact with the face of the oilstone. All the remarks upon grinding and oilstoning chisels apply with greater force to gouges, because the small amount of the surface of the gouge, in contact with either the grindstone or oilstone, renders it extremely liable to the formation of a feather edge in grinding, and a wire edge in oilstoning. In grinding outside gouges, a new feature steps in; for if the gouge be kept at the same inclination throughout the grinding, as in the case of all the tools heretofore mentioned, the center of the gouge will be keener than the corners; to avoid which the gouge is given a rolling motion to bring every part against the action of the grindstone, while at the same time lowering the back hand as the corners of the gouge approach the stone. This if evenly performed, gives an equal keenness to all parts of the cutting edge. The same rising and falling motion of the back hand is necessary in oilstoning the convex side of the gouge. The concave side is to be rubbed with an oilstone slip, taking care to let the slip be flat in the trough of the gouge and not elevated at the near end; for if once a habit of beveling, however slightly, the flat faces of tools is contracted, it tends to increase, so that the tools finally lose their characteristics, and are in fact ruined, so far as their application to good work is concerned.

Several sizes of squares are necessary to the pattern maker, because his work necessitates in many cases that the blade be short, in order to admit of its application to the

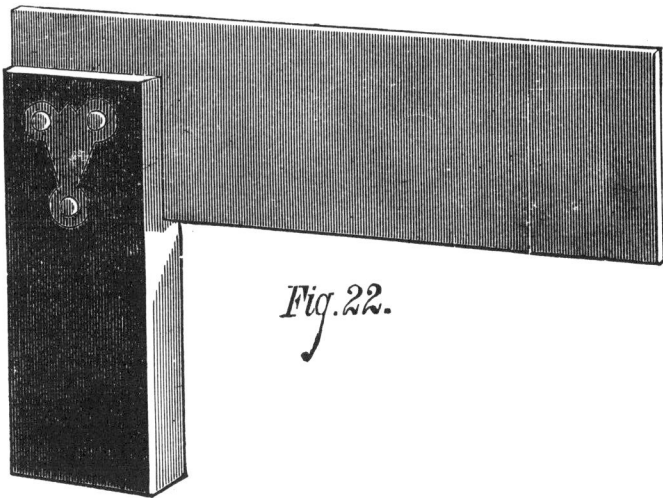

Fig. 22.

work. Fig. 22 represents an ordinary try square; the blade should be of sawblade, and the back of hard wood, the inside and outside edges of the back being covered with sheet metal, to prevent undue wear.

In Fig. F is shown a try square which can be used as a simple square or as a mitre square. By simply changing the position of the handle, and bringing the mitred face at the top of the handle against one edge of the work in **hand,** a perfect mitre, or angle of forty-five degrees, can be struck from either edge of the blade.

Fig. F.

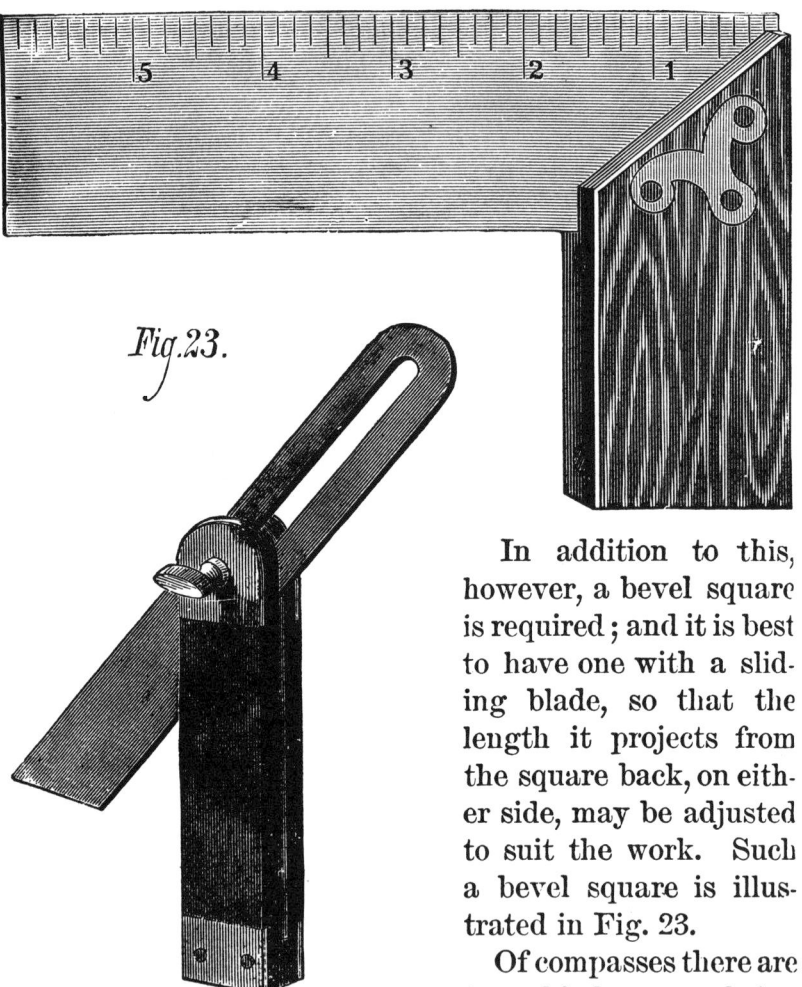

Fig. 23.

In addition to this, however, a bevel square is required; and it is best to have one with a slid-ing blade, so that the length it projects from the square back, on eith-er side, may be adjusted to suit the work. Such a bevel square is illus-trated in Fig. 23.

Of compasses there are two kinds, one being plain, and having no means of permanent adjustment, as shown in Fig. 24. This is used for casual measurements or marking. The other has an attachment by which it may be permanently set, as shown in Fig. 25, in which A represents a thumb screw employed to set one leg firmly against the radius piece, C, and B being an adjusting screw for finally adjusting the compass points after the thumb screw, A, is fastened, the spring, D, operating to keep the leg, E, firmly against the face of the screw, B ; so that, when the adjustment of the compass points is once properly made, the compasses may be laid upon the bench and used from time

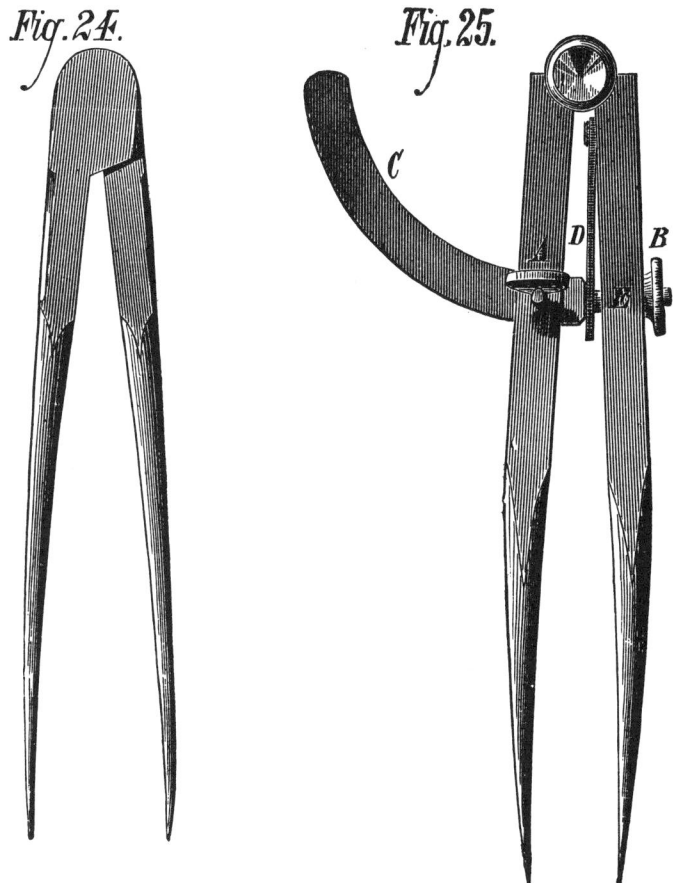

Fig. 24. Fig. 25.

to time without danger of the adjustment being altered by handling or by a slight blow.

An excellent attachment for compass points has lately come into use; it is for the purpose of fastening to the marking leg a pencil, to avoid scratching the surface of the work with the compass point.   This device and its mode of application are shown in Fig. 26, in which A represents a thin tube with the feet, G G, on it, and provided with the split, B.   C is a clamp, provided with a thumbscrew, E.

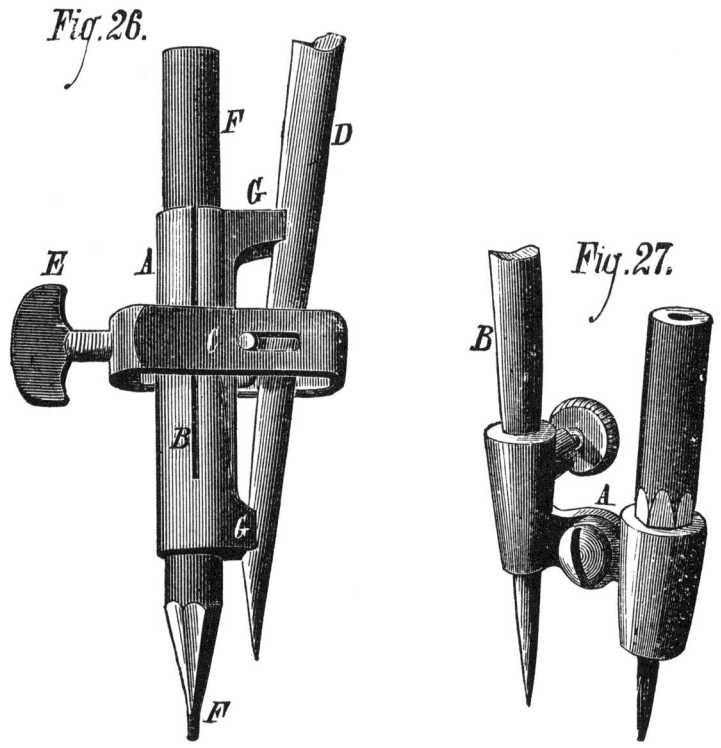

Fig. 26.

Fig. 27.

D represents one of the compass legs.   F is a piece of lead pencil which passes through the tube, A.   The attachment is slipped on the compass leg, and the screw is tightened up, clamping that leg to the feet, G G, and clamping at the same time the pencil in the tube.   Another of these attachments, in which the pencil point is adjustable in a direction

other than that in which the compass point stands, is
shown in Fig. 27, the pencil tube being swiveled at A, and
B representing the compass leg.

Fig.28.

The points of compasses should
be forged out when they get thick
from wearing short, and they
should be tempered to a blue
color. For marking small holes,
compasses are too cumbersome for
fine work, and spring dividers are
preferable. A recent improvement
in these tools consists in making
the spring helical, as shown in
Fig. 20, instead of making it broad,
flat, and thin, as formerly.

Of gages for drawing marking
lines at any regulated distance
from the finished edge or edges
of the work, there are several
kinds. First we have that shown in Fig. 29, which
is the kind ordinarily sold; others have, instead of the

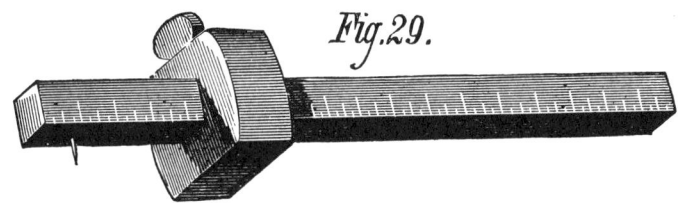

Fig.29.

set screw, a wedge running lengthwise, as shown in Fig.
30. A better gage, however, than either of these is that
shown in Fig. 31, in which A represents the tightening
wedge, standing at a right angle to the rod of the gage.
The advantage of this design is that it requires only one
hand to work it, inasmuch as the wedge may be loosened
or tightened by striking it, as if it were a hammer, against

2**

anything that may happen to lie on the bench. Thus the gage may be set and adjusted with one hand, while the other is holding the work, as is often necessary when marking small work. The marking point should be a piece of steel

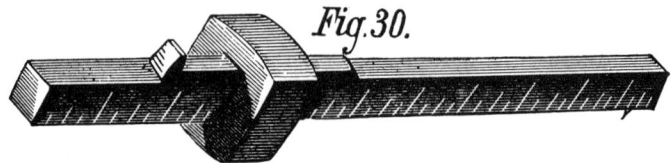

Fig. 30.

wire fitted tightly in the stem, the protruding part being ground or filed to a wedge, with the two facets slightly rounding, and whose broad faces stand at a right angle to the stem of the gage ; the point or edge only projecting sufficiently to produce a line clear enough to work by ; other-

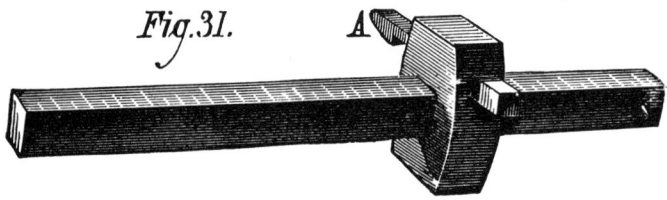

Fig. 31.

wise it will not be suitable for accurate work. The mortise gage is similar to the above as regards the stem and sliding piece, but it is provided with two marking points, their distance apart being adjustable. Fig. 32 represents the gage referred to, the head screw working in brass nuts.

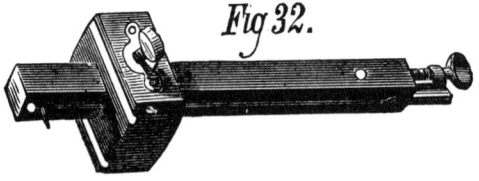

Fig 32.

On account of the narrowness of the base afforded by the sliding piece on the common gage, there is not sufficient steadiness to gage to any great width, so that for widths above ten or eleven inches we must have recourse to the gage shown in Fig. 33. It is called the panel gage; its sliding piece may be seven inches long, and the stem two

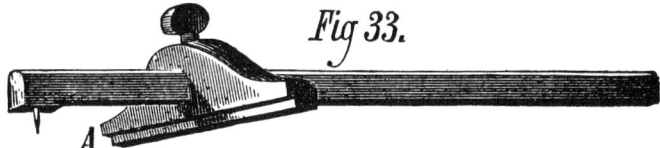

Fig 33.

feet; the rabbeting at A forms a steadying base, the part of the rod about the marking point being raised to corre· spond with the distance from the rabbet to the stem nut. Next we have the cutting gage, shown in Fig. 34, in which a steel cutter takes the place of the marking point, being

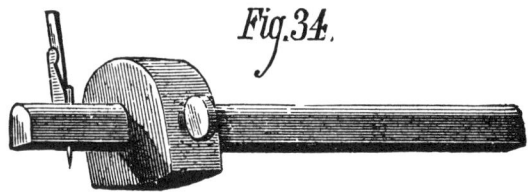

Fig.34.

wedged in position. It is employed to cut thin strips of wood; that is to say, of thicknesses up to about a quarter of an inch. The cutter point should be tempered to a dark straw color.

In Fig. G is shown a gage in which one side has a fixed

Fig. G.

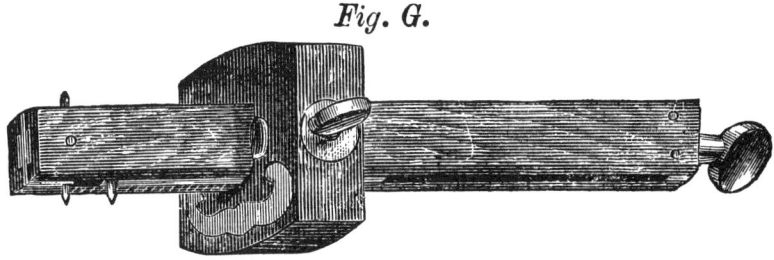

point, and the other an adjustable one for mortise and oth- er similar work, the movable point being operated by the thumbscrew shown at the end.

For marking off curves or large circles, we require a pair of beam compasses or trammels, as shown in Fig. 35. They are composed of two sliding sockets, made of either wood or metal, fitted, at a sliding fit, to a staff. They are made of various designs, to suit the taste of the maker, and are often made by the pattern maker himself during his term of probation. The style shown in Fig. 35 is one very easily made. A A represents a staff of any desired length, composed of common pine. B and C are the two sliding sockets or holders; the mortises in them are made to fit the

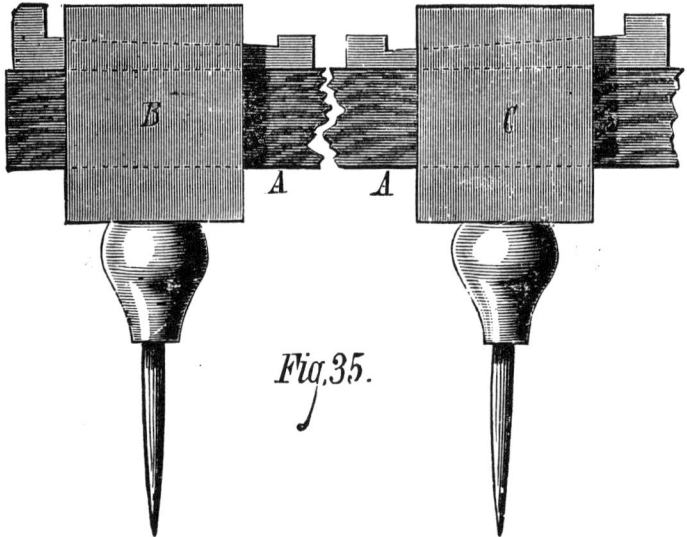

Fig. 35.

thickness of the staff, but they are longer than they are wide, to admit of the fastening wedge. They may be made of some hard wood, such as maple. The lower parts being turned and fitted with brass ferrules, a small hole is then drilled up the turned end of each, into which bradawls of large size are driven; they are then pointed on a grindstone. The wedges are made with a gib head on the small end, so as to prevent them from flying out when tapped back to loosen the sliding sockets from the staff, for adjustment. If maple be used for the sockets, then the wedges may be made of a dark colored wood, sandpapered and varnished two or three times, which will give them a neat appearance. Made as above described, the trammels will be light and almost everlasting; and as the materials are always at hand, the cost is a minimum.

Fig. 36.

In place of the wedge, a screw may be, and sometimes is used, in which case a packing piece of either wood or sheet brass should be inserted, as shown in Fig. 36, at A, which will protect the staff from being indented by the end of the screw when the latter is tightened up.

Our next requirement is the straight edge, which, for small work, is better of steel than of wood. A straight edge is a piece of stuff whose edges are straight and parallel to each other, which is necessary because they are sometimes used in conjunction with the square. A pair of straight edges, termed winding strips, are indispensable; their use is shown in Fig. 37, in which A is a piece of work requiring to have its edge true; B B are the winding strips, placed on the work as shown, so that by casting the eye along the upper edge of one strip, and leveling the head so that the edge of one strip will be brought nearly horizontally level with the other, it will readily be perceived whether the two are level one with the other, and hence whether the face of the work is true. Winding strips are simply

pieces, of wood made parallel and true, and generally
about two feet long, three or four inches wide, and about
five-eighths of an inch thick.   When the edges have been
made as straight as possible with the truing plane, one of
these should be lightly chalked on its edge face and laid
upon the other, and then moved back and forth through
a distance of about one-half inch.   The upper one should
not be pressed to the lower, but allowed to lie of its own
weight; otherwise it will spring to suit the outline of the
lower one, or bear upon it at the points pressed by the
hands.   Before separating the two, take a blacklead pen-

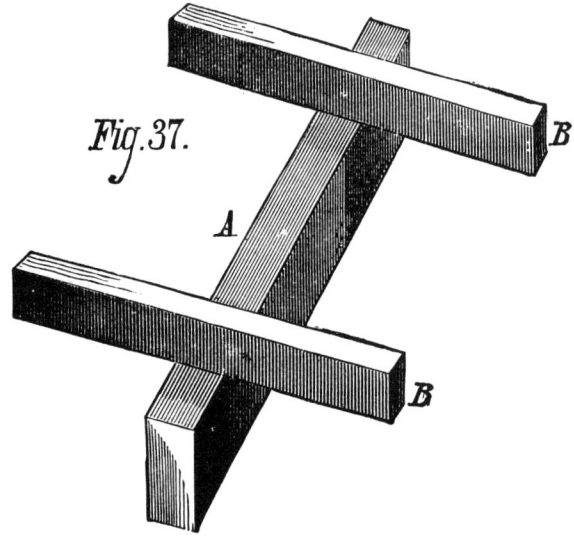

Fig. 37.

cil and make a mark on one side of each, so as always to
be able to bring the pieces together in the same way.
Then separate them and ease away the high places, continuing the truing operation until they bear all over.   In
placing them upon the work, be careful that they stand
parallel to each other; that is to say, that the distance
between them is about the same at each end, otherwise
the eye will be misled in sighting them when on the work.

In Fig. 38, we have an ordinary screwdriver, the point of which should be shaped as shown at A, in Fig. 39, and not as shown at B, as is usually the case, because if the part entering the screw head is tapered, it not only raises a burr on the screw head, but it is liable to slip out, even from a screw that drives easily, and much more from one that drives hard. To grind it to the shape shown at A, it should be ground on that side of the stone in which the latter is running toward you, the length of the screwdriver being at a right angle to the plane of the stone and the handle held in one hand, while the driving end is held in the other, which should be supported by the grindstone rest. If the stone is a small one, the screwdriver, while being ground in this position, should be moved a little, so that first one corner and then the other will approach the stone, so as to prevent the grinding from being hollow, which would weaken the screwdriver point by thinning it in the middle. Screwdrivers should be made of cast steel, and tempered at the point to a blue color.

The mallets should be of hickory, and of the form shown in Fig. 40; the sizes being, one $2\frac{1}{2}$x3x5 inches long, and another about 3x$3\frac{1}{2}$x$5\frac{1}{2}$ inches long, the handles being mortised and properly wedged to the head.

Of oilstones there should properly be two, one for roughing and one for finishing. Wichita or Arkansas stones are even in grain and cut well, and are the best for our purpose. In addition to the large oilstone, a number of slips of oilstone are necessary, some being flat, others half round and flat, with round edges, their uses being for gouges and other tools in which the cutting edges are hollow or curved. The general oilstone should be kept with a flat face, otherwise it will be impossible to properly set plane blades, firmer and paring chisels, and other similar tools upon it. With this object in view, the workman should set small tools upon the ends, so as to prevent the stone from becoming hollow in the middle. When it becomes necessary to grind the face of the oilstone, it may be done upon the grindstone; but a better plan is to take a flat board and liberally supply it with clean sand and water, and then grind the oilstone on it by hand, leaving the face a little rounding in its length, by easing it off at each end, but

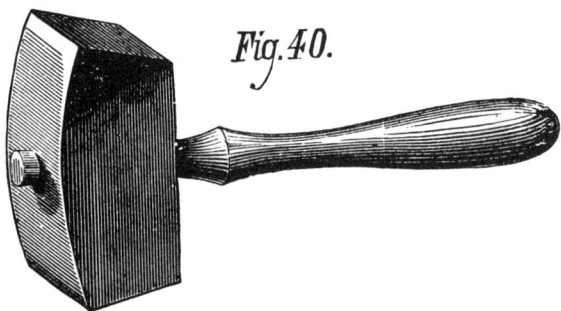

Fig. 40.

leaving it flat across the face, by which means it will last longer without regrinding. There are some stones which are used with water instead of oil; they do not cut, as a rule, very freely, but the finer grades of them will cut unusually smooth. These are the descriptions used by the Japanese workmen, who use two stones, one to rough cut, which cuts very freely; the other to finish, which seems to grip the metal firmly, rendering it easy to keep the tool at the necessary angle and level, while at the same time it cuts very finely indeed. The first is a bright yellow stone, the latter is of a green slate color—hot water being used on both of them. Aside from those already mentioned, we have the Turkey **stone, a close-grained and amber-colored stone, which cuts**

freely or fine, according to the grade of the stone. For all
ordinary purposes the Arkansas stone will suffice, and it
is obtaianble at almost every hardware store. The oilstone for general use should be fitted into a block of wood,
having a margin outside of the stone of one half inch on
each side, and about an inch at each end, the block being
hollowed on the bottom face so that it will stand firmly and
not rock when in use. It should also be provided with a
cover, to prevent dust and dirt from accumulating upon it.

Two pairs of inside and three pairs of outside calipers
are necessary to the pattern maker, the smallest of each
pair being large enough to take in diameter up to four
inches, the largest from four up to about ten inches. The
other pair of outside calipers may be large enough to use
upon diameters from ten to eighteen inches. For bores
above ten inches a wire gage may
be used, by bending a piece of wire
as shown in Fig. 41, which may be
shortened by being bent more, or
lengthened by being straightened.

Fig. 41.

It is preferable to make an adjustable gage, such as shown
in Fig. 42, in which A and B represent two sliding pieces
of steel, and C and D screws and nuts. It is obvious that,

Fig. 42.

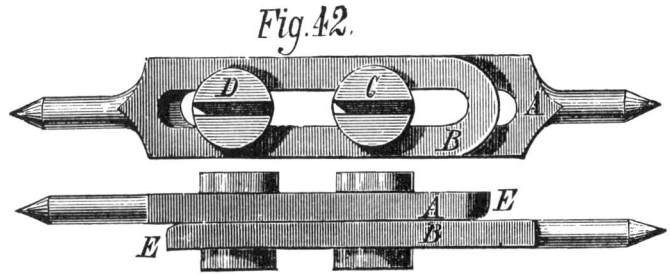

when the screws are loosened sufficiently to just let the
sliding pieces move by a slight tap, the gage may be extended by striking the ends, E, or either of them, their in-

3

side edges being rounded off to prevent them from burring. It is better to set them at first a little below the required size, and to perform the adjustment by opening them, so as not to require to strike the point at all. The points should, however, in any event, be tempered to a blue. It is an excellent plan to file away the screw heads on two sides, a little, say $\frac{1}{32}$ inch, thus forming a sliding piece under each head to fit into the slot of the gage, which will prevent the screws from turning when screwed or unscrewed, and in the end save much annoyance. A small machinist's square and a steel rule are also necessary for small fine work, the wooden ones being too clumsy. The edges of the rule should be trued so that it may be used as a straight edge.

CHAPTER II.

LATHE — LATHE CHUCKS, AND LATHE TOOLS.

To give the required form to various patterns, recourse must frequently be had to that useful machine, the lathe. The lathe adapted for pattern work is strong and steady in the framework, to avoid the tremor resulting from the high speed at which it is driven. It should be of good and durable workmanship, and should also be handy; that is to say, the parts requiring frequent adjustment should be provided with the readiest means for accomplishing that end; and especially is this the case with the hand rest and the manner of holding it to the lathe bed, as it is, in the

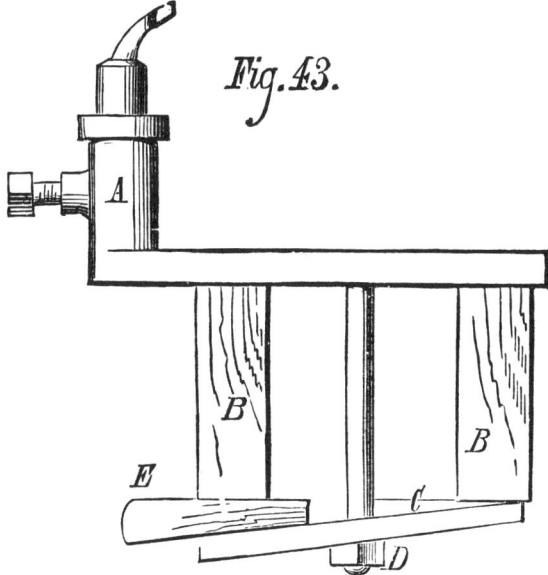

Fig.43.

progress of a piece of work, almost constantly changed in position. Fig. 43 shows the method, still followed by many wood turners, of holding the hand rest; it is a primitive arrangement, but the tightening and loosening of the wedge, E, is found to take less time than screwing up the nut D.   In Fig. 43, A is the hand rest, B B the lathe shears, C the clamp, and D the nut upon the bolt, E, the head of which slides in a groove running along the foot of the hand rest.   It will be observed that the nut, being beneath the lathe shears, is somewhat unhandy to get at, and the wrench may not perhaps at the moment be at hand; while, in any event, screwing up a nut with a wrench is a slow process.   In some cases there is substituted, for the nut, a wheel with a tapped hole in its center; but it is still not perfect, because the workman, in slacking it off, gives the wheel a twist; and while his attention is absorbed in the intricacy of his work, the momentum of the rim of the wheel has kept it turning, so that it either unscrews itself altogether and falls off, or runs so far back that it requires handling twice to bring it home when refastening it.   A much better method is now in many cases adopted; it is shown in Fig. 44, in which A A represents the lathe shears, B the hand rest, C the fastening bolt, D a piece hinged at each end and having through its center a hole to receive the fastening bolt, and a countersink or recess to receive the nut and prevent it unscrewing.   E represents a hinged plate, and F a lever having a cam at its pivoted end.   A slot for the fastening bolt to pass through is provided in the plate, E.   In this arrangement, a very moderate amount of force applied to bring up the cam lever will cause the plate, D, to be pressed down, carrying with it the nut.   This arrangement is simple, cheap, durable, and very handy, and may be applied on any existing lathe to the hand rest, slide rest, or tail stock.   There are other simple and useful contrivances devised for the same purpose; but generally speaking, the lathe requires to be designed to accommodate them, and they are not superior in action to the system above described.

The running head of the lathe requires particular mention. The mandrel should always be of steel, turned true, hardened, and trued by an emery wheel, after the hardening process. It should be well fitted to its bearing; for if it is not, an unpleasant jarring noise will be produced when the latter is set in motion.

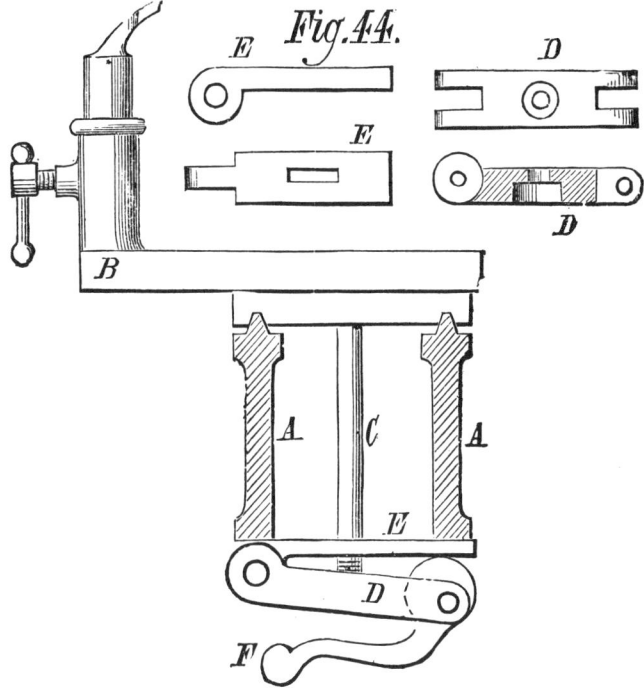

Fig. 44.

Hard steel coned bearings are very desirable, and will work perfectly when properly made, lasting practically unimpaired for years. They are, however, expensive to make; and in view of the present active competition in producing cheaply, most mechanics, knowing the difficulty attending the proper fitting of this style of mandrel, feel more or less dubious as to the perfection of such lathes until they have been well tried. Next to a hard steel coned bearing, we should prefer a cylindrical one of hard brass; that is to say, a mixture of five parts copper, one part tin, and one quarter part zinc. The length of the journal should be three times its diameter; the brasses should be made in halves, and adjusted so that the faces of the brasses are butted when the cap screws are tightened home, and the journal is at a neat working fit in the bearings. It will then be a long time before the brasses will require letting together for adjustment. If, however, the joint faces of the brasses are left open, the cap screws are apt to slack back, there being no pressure on them, to retain them in their places. It is an advantage to have the mandrel bored nearly through its length, say within one inch of the tail pin or screw, whose coned end forms the bearing for that end of the mandrel. The size of the hole referred to should be as large as consistent with the strength of the mandrel. This arrangement is shown in Fig. 45.

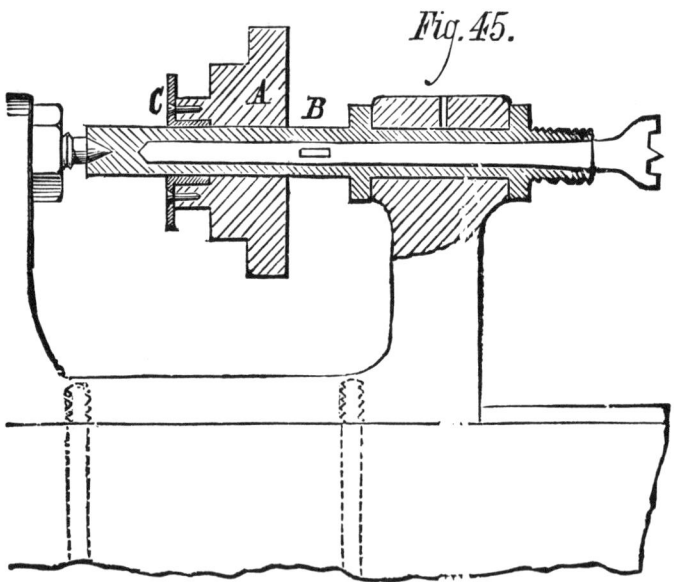

Fig. 45.

The usefulness of this bore or hole is that when a number of small pieces require to be turned, a nipping chuck can be screwed on the mandrel, and a long piece of stuff can be pushed up the hole, and the projecting end to be operated upon nipped in the chuck ; then, when a piece is finished, all we have to do is to advance our long piece of stuff and proceed again.

The method ordinarily employed is to drive a plug into the mandrel, and form the projecting end to the shape required. By this plan more stuff is lost than is used ; and if the plug is not well fitted and driven, it loosens while being operated upon, to say nothing of the trouble of extracting the stub from the mandrel when the work is cut off. Another purpose served by the long bore is that it will form a guide for a boring bar.

The cone pulleys should be as light as possible for a power lathe. Hard wood is very suitable for them, the manner of fastening to the mandrel being shown in Fig. 45. The cone pulley, A, is bored to fit the mandrel, B, tightly, and secured at the end to receive the light brass bush, C, which is keyed to the mandrel and screwed to the pulley. The reason for making the cone pulley of wood is that, if it were of iron, and consequently heavy, it would, fròm its weight, require time to get up to its full speed ; and from its momentum, it would take some little time to stop in both cases, especially if the work were heavy. The tail stock should, in addition to the hand wheel be provided with an arm ; and a lever, to give rapid motion to the spindle when used for boring purposes, should be added, the arrangement being as illustrated in Fig. 46, in which A represents the arm or fulcrum, and B the lever, which is applied after the hand wheel is removed. The end of the screw must be cut like a double eye. The long hole or slot in the middle of the line is to allow for the difference in the direction of the motion, since the lever moves from its end as a center, while the tail stock spindle moves in a straight line. The supporting frames of the lathe need not be very heavy, but should be well braced to the shears or bed, and screwed fast to the floor. It is not an uncommon thing, when an unusually large job is being done in the lathe, to

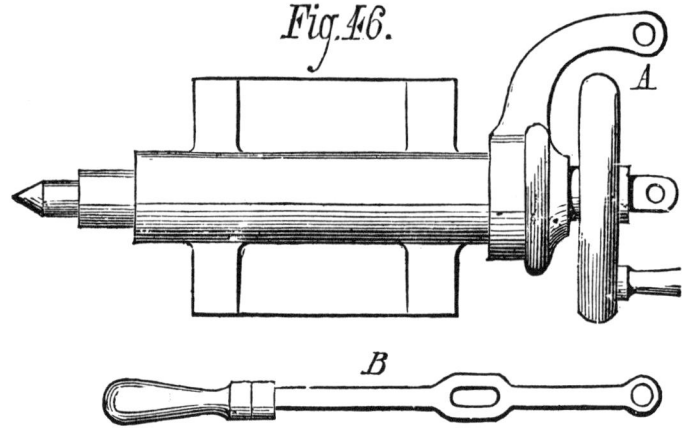

Fig. 46.

brace or shore the lathe by means of braces placed between the lathe shears and the floor, wall, and ceiling. Of this arrangement it is sufficient to say that it is merely a make-shift, and is only resorted to when the floor is springy. In cases where it is necessary to use one lathe for both large and small work, the countershaft overhead should be so placed that the belt will run quarter-cross when the lathe head is placed across the bed, in which position there will be full swing for large work from floor to ceiling.

It remains now to provide, for large work, a means of supporting the hand rest. The handiest is the portable tripod rest shown in Fig. 47. The legs, A A A, are curved so as to get the rest close up to a large chuck. Heavy weights, in the form of a U, as shown at B B B, may be clamped, by means of the set screw, to the legs, to give additional steadiness if required; but if good spread be given to the legs, so that they may form an angle of about 60° to the floor (taken from the point of the foot to where the leg joins the hub), the weights may be dispensed with; and at the same time more space will be occupied, so that it may not be possible at all times, on account of surround-ing objects, to get such a broadly spread rest in-to the position required; hence a narrower spread in conjunction with the weights, is, under such condition, the most desi-rable.

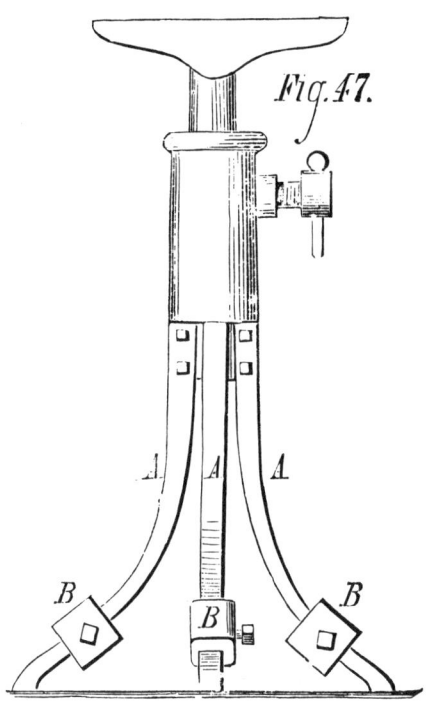

Fig. 47.

We come now to the various chucking contriv-ances employed by the pattern maker. In Fig. 48, A represents a fork center, the taper part of which fits into the lathe mandrel in place of a center, the extreme end, B, being a flat projection, providing that there is a recess in the mandrel to receive it, as there should be.

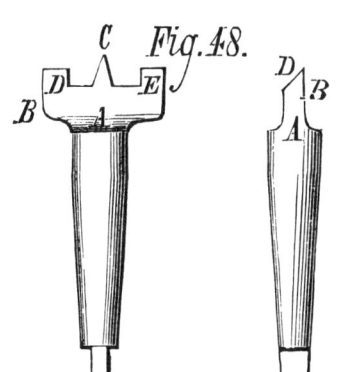

Fig. 48.

But if the lathe mandrel is bored up a great distance, then the extra length which may be given to the conical part of the fork will cause adhesion suf-cient to drive the work. The broad part is wedge-shaped on the edge view, the center point, C, being turned conical, similar to a common center. The cen-ter, C, acts to keep the work true, and as a guide in taking the work in and out of the lathe, while the prongs, D and E, drive it. This tool,

3*

however, is only to be depended upon for small work; for larger work, center plates are used. They are made of metal and screwed firmly to the work. Of these center plates, one has a slot in it, so that it may be used in conjunction with the fork; while another has a conical hole in the center, which hole is made to fit the back center of the lathe. They may be made of hard wood,

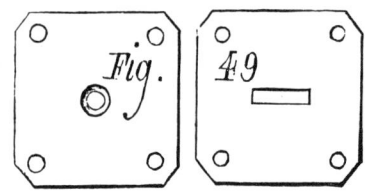

screwed to a small iron face plate; such plates are made useful for a variety of purposes. A pair of such center plates are shown in Fig. 49 — A being that to receive the back center, and B that for the fork center. Another driving chuck for small work is shown in Fig. 50, the part, A, having an internal screw to fit the driving screw on the lathe spindle, and the point, B, being a coarse screw intended to screw into the work; which latter should have a small hole bored up it to prevent (especially in the case of hard woods) the pressure of the screw from splitting the work.

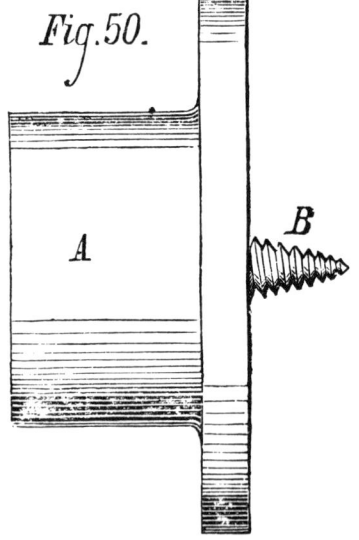

Fig. 50.

From the appliances for turning work between the centers, we pass to those for holding work independent of the back center of the lathe by means of chucks, the name by which such appliances are generally known. Fig. 51 is a back view of a face plate, to which work may be held by screws; the usual method, however, is to screw to the face plate a disk of wood, and then to true the wood across the face and on the diameter. The work is then fixed to the new surface thus obtained. Many good purposes are served by the intervention of the disk of wood (or chuck, as it is usually termed) between the metal plate and the work. For instance, it is a guard which effectually prevents the turning tools from touching the metal of the face plate. It supports the work (being nearly of the same size) when required, and obviates the necessity of having more than three or four face plates of metal. Its surface is readily made to conform to the shape of the work, and furthermore it is very readily trued up. When we have to deal with large sizes, a mere disk of wood will not serve, as it will be too weak across the grain: and here it may be remarked that the work often supports the chuck, and therefore we should always,

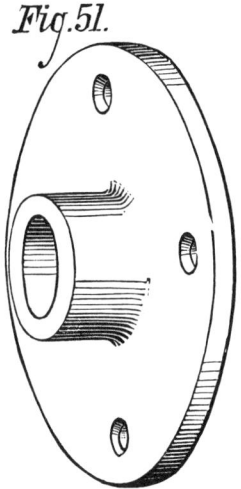

Fig. 51.

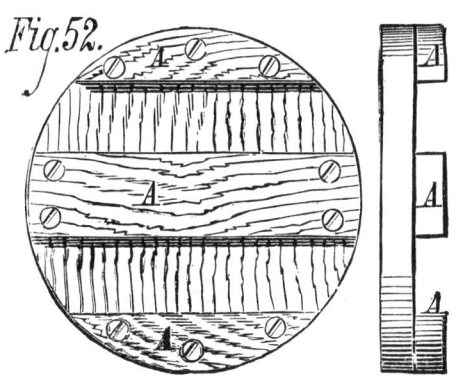

Fig. 52.

in fixing, make the grain of the work cross that of the chuck, because the centrifugal force due to the high velocity is so great that both the chuck and the work have before now been rent asunder by reason of the non-observance of this apparently small matter. When it is considered that the chuck has not sufficient strength across the grain, battens should be screwed on at the back; but a chuck so strengthened will require truing frequently, on account of the strains to which its fibers will be subjected from the unequal expansion or contraction of its component parts. Fig. 52 shows the back of a chuck strengthened by the battens, A A A.

Another method of making a chuck is shown in Fig. 53. It is considered superior to the former, from its greater ability to resist outward strains in every direction, while the strains to which it must necessarily be subject, from variations of temperature and humidity, are less than in the former. It will also be found that it can be trued with greater facility, especially on the diameter, as the turning tool will not be exposed to the end grain of the wood. To make one of these chucks about 2 feet in diameter, we proceed as follows: Procuring two bars for the back, say 4x2

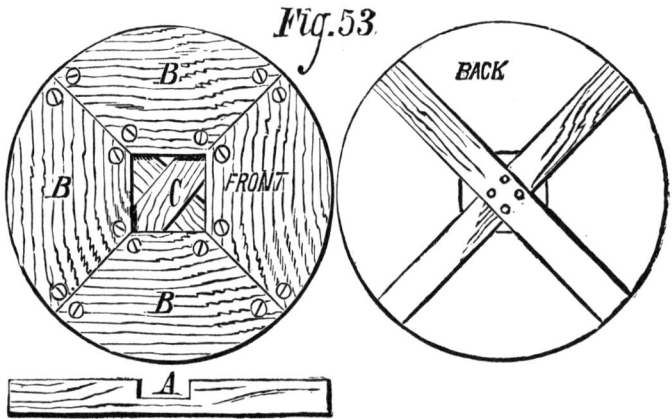

inches and 2 feet long, we plane them all over; then in the middle of each we cut out the recess (shown at A in Fig. 53) to a depth equal to half the thickness, the width of the recess being equal to that of the bar; this process is termed half checking. We next fasten these bars together by gluing and screwing them at the center, driving the screws thightly home while the glue is warm. Upon the cross thus formed, we superpose the segments shown in the front view of Fig. 53, at B B B; these may be of almost any thickness, say from $\frac{7}{8}$ to $1\frac{1}{2}$ inch. They should be planed on the back, and should not extend to the center, but leave an open space (as shown in Fig. 53, at C) of about 4 or 5 inches. This opening can be filled, if desired, by screwing on a square piece. If the segments were carried to the center, they would be too weak to bear a screw near that point; and again, in large chucks we very seldom require to use the part about the center. Chucks of very large size — that is to say, from 4 feet upwards — will require more support than is afforded by the four arms of the cross. Three bars can be put together, so as to give six arms, which will answer probably for a 6 or 7 feet chuck. For still larger sizes, it is necessary to cast a strong circular plate to form the middle of the chuck, and to then bolt the requisite number of arms to it. The strength of the chuck will of course depend upon the number of arms and their depths; and unless the chuck is very substantial, a difficulty will be experienced in turning, on account of the tremor. A chuck having the middle of iron and the outside of wood, supported by arms, is shown in Fig. 54.

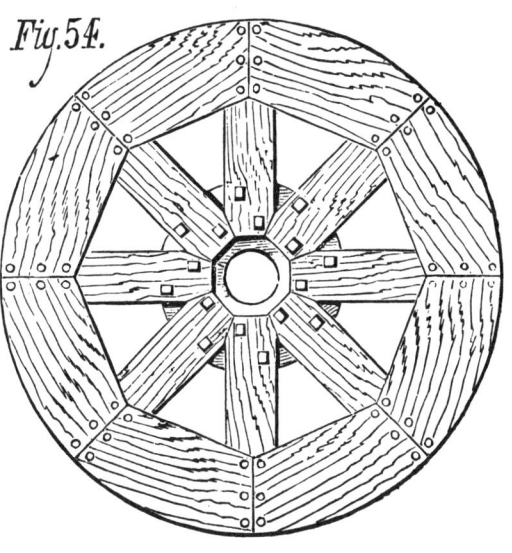

Fig. 54.

In shops where the size of the work necessitates the employment of chucks of so large a diameter, a special lathe is of great advantage, because a lathe having an elevated bed is so tremulous and shaky; while those having large solid heads are too cumbersome, and are not belted to run at a sufficiently high rate of speed. In such cases, the arrange-

ment shown in Fig. 55 is an excellent one. **A** represents
a lathe head bolted firmly to two uprights, B B, which are
firmly fixed to the joists, C, and to the flooring at D, right
over and upon the joists supporting the flooring, or else

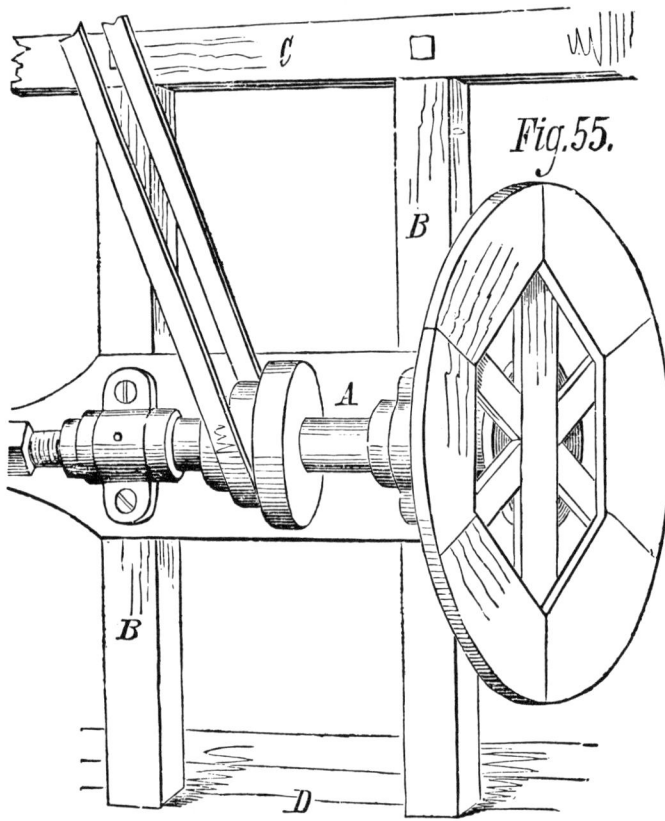

upon beams provided for the purpose.   By this **means the**
work may, if the lathe head is fixed midway upon the posts,
B B, be as large as the space between the ceiling and the
flooring will admit, a movable tripod rest, such as shown
in Fig. 47, being employed for a tool rest.

Fig. 56 represents a side and face view of a very useful
chuck, suitable for holding core boxes while boring them.
It is shown attached to one of the metal plates that fit the

mandrel of the lathe, and is usually made of hard wood;
but for a large sized one, say 15 or more inches in diameter,
the disk portion, A, may be made of pine wood.   The

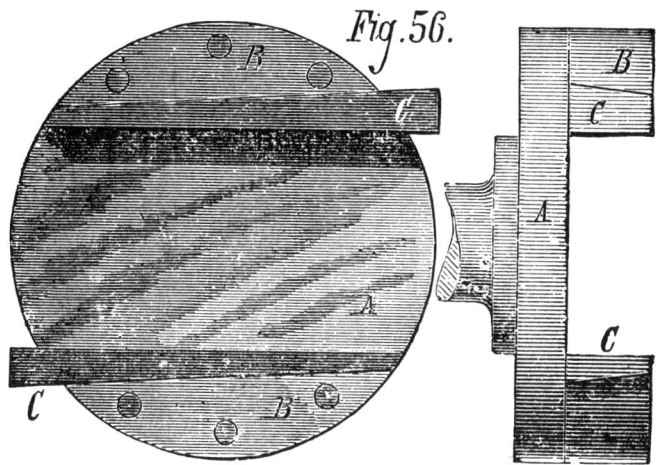

Fig. 56.

two sides, B B, are firmly fixed to the disk, their inner
edges being planed at an acute angle to it.   The work is
held by driving the wedges, C C, and may be truly chucked by them in a comparatively short space of time.

Another very useful chuck is shown in Fig. 57.   It will
answer the same purposes as that shown in Fig. 56.   It
is, however, made entirely of metal, somewhat similar to a
machinist's dog chuck, but much lighter.   Pieces of wood
may be screwed on the jaws at A A, and bored to the curvature of any round piece of wood — an advantage which
the chuck shown in Fig. 56 does not possess.   Or the jaws
may be turned round in their places, so that the faces, A
A, will stand outwards, and the wooden pieces screwed
thereon may be made to fit a hole.   This chuck will be
found to save much time over the plan of screwing work
to the common face plate.   V pieces of wood may be fixed to
the jaws, and a piece of work in the rough held by them
during the process of facing, boring, and turning the pro-

jecting part. The work can then be reversed in the chuck, and similar operations performed on the opposite end ; and the work can be taken from the lathe and tried as to either

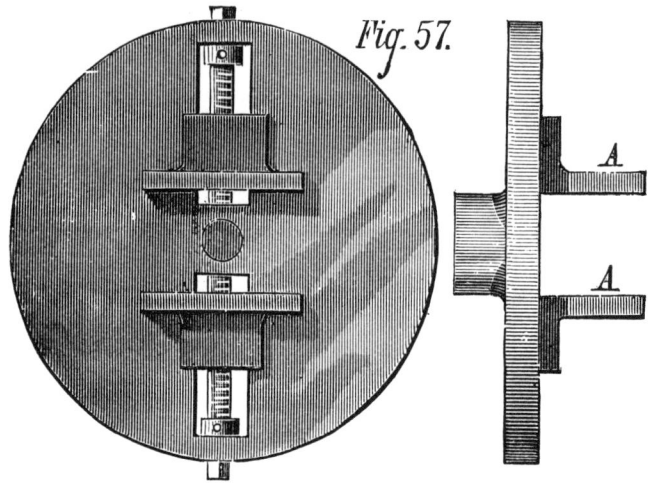

Fig. 57.

fit or conformation, and, if necessary, restored in a moment to its original position in the chuck, so as to run quite true ; but at the same time, for first class work, it is better not to use the V's on finished surfaces. For holding bits and small work, neat little chucks may be purchased at the hardware stores, and they act similarly to the nipping arrangements applied to boring braces. These chucks can be supplied to screw on the lathe mandrel ; or they will, with a taper shank, fit into the taper holes provided to fit the lathe centers. It is well to have one of each, so as to be able to use one of them in place of the still lathe center, to operate upon work already chucked on the face plate of the lathe.

A simple and very useful chuck still remains to be described, being what is known as the cement chuck, which is made as follows : A disk of hard wood is screwed to a metal plate, where it should remain permanently ; but if the face plate cannot be spared, bore a slightly taper hole through the disk, a little smaller than the diameter of the screw of the lathe mandrel, and partly through the disk. Then screw the disk on the mandrel, working the disk backwards and forwards to form a thread in the bore of the disk, and then turn and face it perfectly true. Then bore a small hole in its center, and drive in a piece of soft steel wire, leaving a short length projecting from the face, and turn it to a point, as shown in Fig. 58.

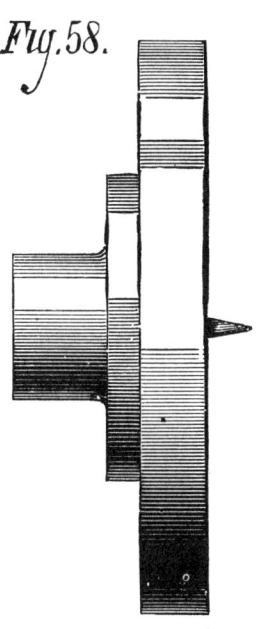

Fig. 58.

The object of this chuck is to drive thin, delicate work, which it would be difficult to screw or clamp by adhesion, and this is accomplished as follows: We first prepare a wax, composed of 8 parts of resin to 1 of the best beeswax, melted and well stirred together, and run into tubes of paper or other suitable molds. To chuck the work, we take a stick of the wax, and press its end against the face of the chuck while the lathe is running, and then place the center of the piece of work on the steel point, applying sufficient pressure to cause the steel point to force its way into the work. Just before the work touches the wax surface, we throw the lathe belt on to the loose pulley; and the momentum of the lathe, combined with a moderately heavy pressure, will generate, by friction, sufficient heat to melt the wax and cause the work to adhere to the chuck. The work may be detached, when necessary, by inserting behind it a thin wedge or blade.

TURNING TOOLS.

The turning work necessary in making patterns is usually done by hand; although on small and plain work.

3**

such as simple boring and facing, slide rest tools may be used to advantage, inasmuch as they will operate quicker than hand tools. Since, however, pattern lathes are not usually provided with slide rests, we shall confine our remarks to hand tools. For roughing out, the turning gouge, shown in Fig. 59, is used. In grinding this gouge, it is necessary to lower the back hand when grinding at and towards the outside corners, so that the cutting edges may be formed, by the junction of two faces, at as acute an angle as those forming the cutting edge in the centre of the width of the tool.

Fig. 59.

It is always the custom to reduce the work in the lathe to nearly the required form by this tool, the finishing tools being (with one exception) simply scraping tools, and not, properly speaking, cutting tools; hence it is evidently inadvisable to leave much for them to take off. The manner of holding the gouge is shown in Fig. 60. One hand grasps the handle near the end, while the other grasps the gouge near the cutting point, that is to say, as near as the hand rest will permit. It is sometimes, however, necessary to slightly vary the manner of holding, by passing the forefinger of one hand around the hand rest while the gouge is confined between the thumb and forefinger, thus gripping the gouge end to the rest. This is advisable when turning a piece of work that is not completely round, as, for instance, tipping off the teeth of a gear wheel, in which case gripping the gouge

to the hand rest will steady it and prevent it from digging into the work. The gouge is shown, in Fig. 60, to be cut-

ting from right to left; it will, however, cut equally well if used from left to right, in which case the position of the hands must be reversed, the left hand gripping the gouge near the cutting edge. In either case, however, the gouge is not held horizontally level, but is tilted to one side, the lower side being the cutting one, otherwise the tool would rip into the work.

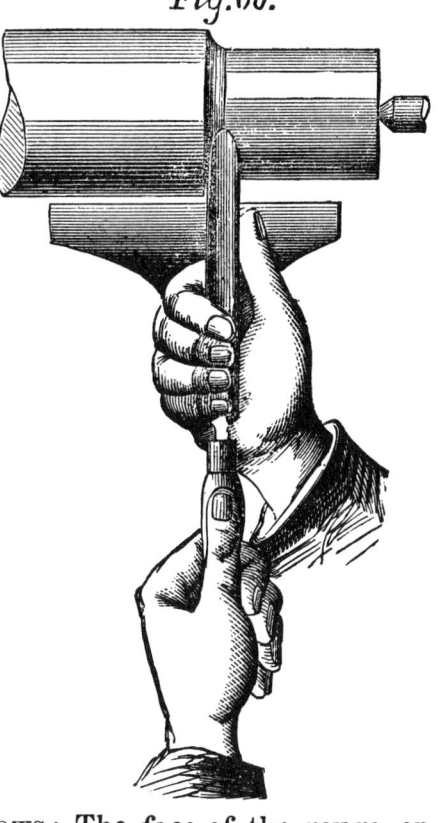

Fig. 60.

Fig. 61 shows the section of the tool and the tilt of the tool when cutting from right to left; while that of the tool, A, shows tilt when cutting from left to right. The reasons for this are as follows: **The face of the gouge, on**

its hollow side and near the cutting edge, receives the strain which is necessary to curl the shaving, that is to say, which is necessary to force it **out of** the straight

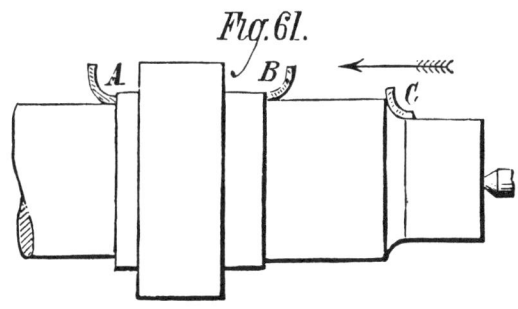

Fig. 61.

line. But if we were to place the gouge in the position shown in Fig. 61, at C, the whole of this strain would be placed upon the gouge, tending to force it forward and into the cut, as denoted by the direction of the arrow ; and as a consequence, the gouge would run forward and dig into the work, in spite of all endeavors to prevent it. When, however, the gouge is held in the positions relative to its line of travel to its **cut,** shown in Fig. 61, at A and B, there is but little tendency for it to run forward, and it can be fed easily to its cut. In addition to its use as a roughing tool,

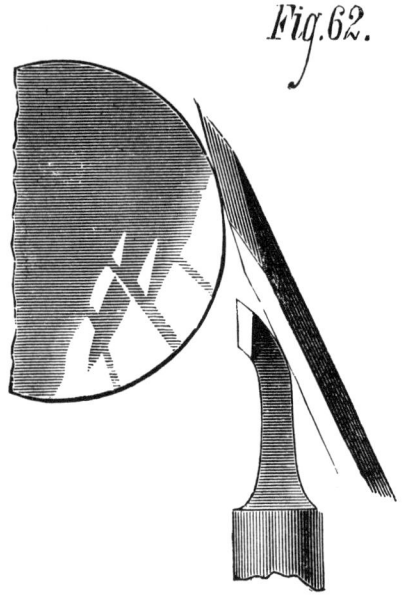

Fig.62.

the gouge makes a very efficient finishing tool for hollows, though it is not often employed as such by pattern makers. In this case, however, great care must be taken in controlling its position to the work, as shown in Fig. 61.

For finishing plain work, we have the tool shown in Fig. 62, which is the exception noted previously as being a finishing and, at the same time, a cutting tool. It is called a skew chisel, because its cutting edge is ground at an angle or askew to the center line of its length. Furthermore, it is beveled at the cutting end on both sides (as shown in the edge view), being ground very keen. It is employed for finishing straight or parallel surfaces, and for dressing down the ends or down the sides of a collar or shoulder. When used for finishing straight or parallel surfaces, it performs its cutting in the center of the length of its cutting edge only, as shown at A, in Fig. 63, and is held in the position relative to the work shown in Fig. 62. When nicely sharpened it leaves a polish. unlike other finishing tools; but with these advantages, it has a drawback (and a serious one) to learners, as it seems to have a terrible propensity for tearing into the work, whether it is used upon the circumference or facing the shoulders of the work. This difficulty can only be overcome by practice, and the reason lies in the difficulty of learning how to handle the tool with dexterity. It must be held almost flat

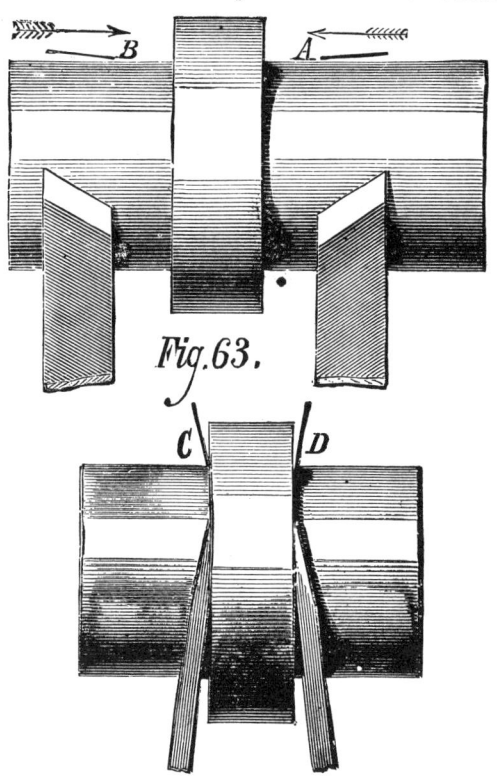

Fig. 63.

to the work; and yet, if it should get quite flat against the work, the cutting edge would cut along its whole length, and the pressure of the cut would be sufficient to force the tool edge deeper into the work than is intended, which process would continue, causing the tool to rip in and spoil the work. The face of the chisel nearest to the face of the work being operated upon, stands almost parallel, with just sufficient tilt of the tool to let the cutting **edge meet** the work in advance of the inside face of the tool; or in other words, the amount of the tilt should be about that of the intended depth of the cut; so that, when the cutting edge of the tool has entered the wood to the requisite depth, the flat face will bear against the work and form a guide to the cutting edge. The corner of the chisel which is not cutting must be kept clear of the work. Fig. 63 will convey the idea, the arrows showing the direction in which the chisel is, in each case, supposed to be traveling.

The short lines, A and B, under the arrows, and those touching the collar, at C and D, show the tilt or incline of

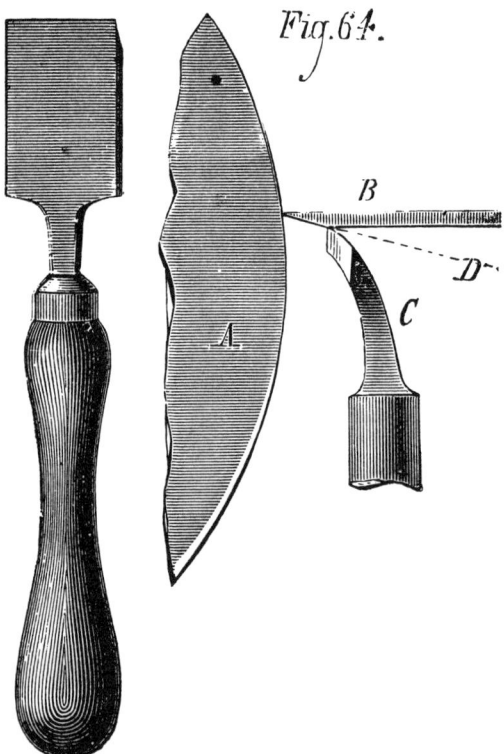

Fig. 64.

the chisel to the work. In turning the circumference, the obtuse corner of the chisel is the cutting one; while in turning down a side face, it is the acute angle. Most pattern makers, however, do not often use the skew chisel for finishing straight cylindrical work, because it is liable to make the surface of the work more or less wavy. It is, however, almost always used for cutting off and for cutting down shoulders, for which purpose it is highly advantageous. For circumferential work on cylindrical surfaces, an ordinary chisel is mostly employed, the position in which it is held to the work causing it to scrape rather than cut. A worn-out paring chisel is as good as any. Such a chisel is shown in Fig. 64, the position in which it is held being illustrated by A, which represents a section of a piece of cylindrical work; B representing the chisel, and C the hand rest. Some pattern makers prefer to increase the keenness of this tool by holding it so that the plane of its length lies in the direction denoted by the dotted line, D; this, however, renders it more likely to rip into the work, and the position shown is all that is necessary, providing the cutting edge be kept properly sharpened. This chisel is also used on side faces.

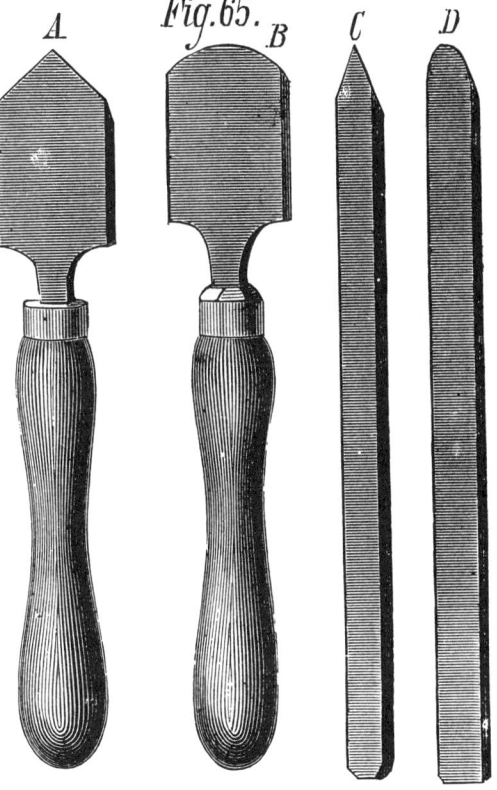

Fig.65.

Still another tool, sometimes used for finishing plain cylindrical surfaces and side faces, is that shown in Fig. 65, at A. It is used in the same manner and relative position as the chisel shown above, in Fig. 64.

For finishing hollows, which should first be roughed out with the gouge, the form of tool shown at B, in Fig. 65, should be used. Several of these tools, of various sizes, should be kept; they are used in the same position as the finishing chisel, shown in Fig. 64. The tool shown at C, in Fig. 65, is used upon large work, and is advantageous because it presents less surface of cutting edge in proportion to the depth of the cut than the gouge; and, in consequence, it is less liable to cause the work to jar or tremble. It is usually made about 2 feet long, which enables the operator to hold it very firmly and steadily. It is used with its top face lying horizontally, and should be kept keen.

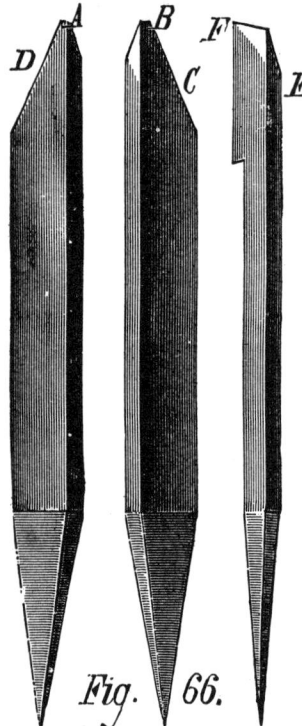

Fig. 66.

D, in the same figure, represents a similar tool, with a round nose; this latter is not, however, made long, and may be used in a handle.

For boring and shouldering purposes, the tools shown in Fig. 66 are employed; those shown at A and B, having their cutting edges at C and D, are therefore right and left hand tools. When, however, the hole is too small to admit of those tools being used, that shown at E may be employed, its cutting edge being at F.

The temper of all these tools should be drawn to a light brown color, and the instruction given for grinding bench tools should be rigidly observed in grinding and oilstoning these turning tools.

CHAPTER III.

THE FOUNDRY.

HOW A PATTERN IS MOLDED.

IT has been already remarked that the operations of the molder are, to a large extent, predetermined by the pattern maker; hence it becomes necessary that the latter shall have a knowledge of foundry work, otherwise he is likely to make the patterns very expensive and awkward to mold. In learning the trade, an apprentice is usually put to work and distinctly instructed as to the required form of his work, without knowing anything of the reasons therefor. In this way he attains a practical knowledge of how different classes of patterns should be, or are, usually made; but it takes him years to become an expert mechanic, for the reason that, having learned by rote, he is incapable of meeting new conditions to the best advantage, until his experience has included both observations in the foundry and, in some cases, consultations with foundrymen. Before entering, therefore, into the method of putting together different kinds of pattern work, it will be well to take a glance at the foundry, and examine the contrivances and the operations of the workmen, so that our operations in pattern work may be intelligently made from the beginning.

The floor of the foundry first demands our attention. It is composed of a layer of molding sand of sufficient depth to imbed patterns of the size usually cast in that foundry. For exceptionally large work, there is usually a place where the natural earth has been excavated to a greater depth; the cavity is filled with molding sand. This place is usually within easy reach of the crane (which commands

4

almost every part of the floor) and the threshold of the melting furnace or cupola. We next observe the capacious oven for baking cores and drying molds for such special work as may require these operations; but the particular contrivance with which the pattern maker has now to concern himself is represented in Fig. 67. It is called a flask, and is composed of two or more parts (two only being shown in the engraving). The lower part is

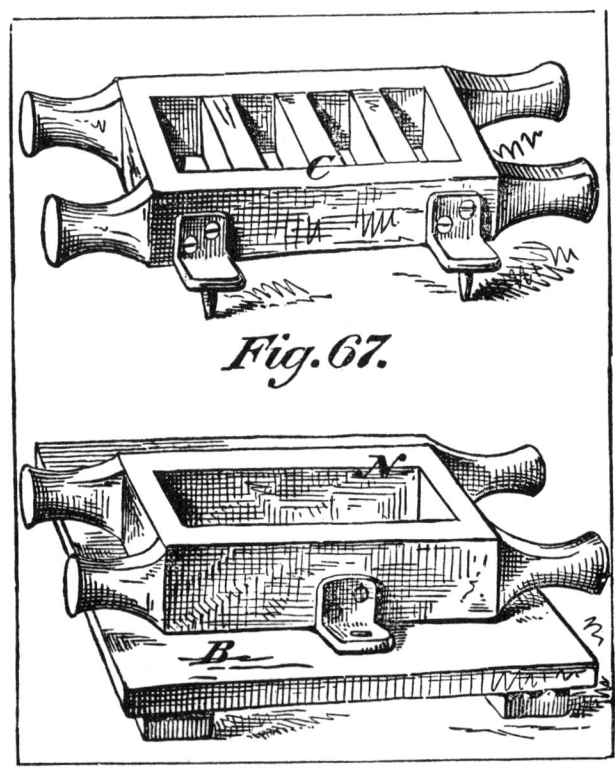

Fig. 67.

called the nowel, and the upper the cope. Each part is simply a strong rectangular frame of wood or iron. The sides, being continued past the rectangles, are roughly shaped for use as handles. The cope is provided with several crossbars, which embrace the pattern, as it were, being roughly shaped like it in contour and approaching it in size, being about half an inch larger all round. These bars, by their adhesion, support the body of the sand in the cope, and in this they are frequently assisted by nails driven nearly half way into them. When an intermediate part is used with the two parts shown in Fig. 67, the contrivance is called a three-part flask; with two intermediates it is called a four-part flask, and so on. As the cope is provided with crossbars, so also the intermediates, having to lift a ring of sand, are provided with wings; that is to say, as much crossbar as will extend from the sides to within about half an inch of the pattern. The parts are guided, in their position one to the other, by taper pins on one part fitting into eyes fixed to the other part, as shown in Fig. 67, in which the cope is shown with the side having the two pins exposed to view, while the opposite side of the nowel, having one eye, is visible. In many cases, and for large work, the nowel is dispensed with, and the foundry floor is used in its stead, in which case the cope is guided to, and retained in, its place by stakes driven into the floor sand, as shown in Fig. 68, so that, when lifted to admit of the pattern being drawn from the mold, the cope may be returned to its exact proper and former position. In Fig. 68, A represents the pattern whose impression in the floor sand, at M, forms a part of the mold. B represents the cope; for the word cope is usually applied to the upper part of the mold as well as to that portion of the flask which contains it. The top print, C, of the pattern, has formed its impression in the cope at P. R is a round taper peg, which leaves a hole in the cope at r, through which hole the molten metal is poured. It also leaves an indentation at r'; and from this latter a gutter is made by the molder to communicate with the mold, M, as shown. The stakes referred to above are marked S. The dots, shown around the impression of the top pattern print, C, in the cope, are small holes made in the sand (after the molding is finished) by a piece of fine wire, and are for the purpose of giving vent to the air and gases which must escape when the metal is poured in.

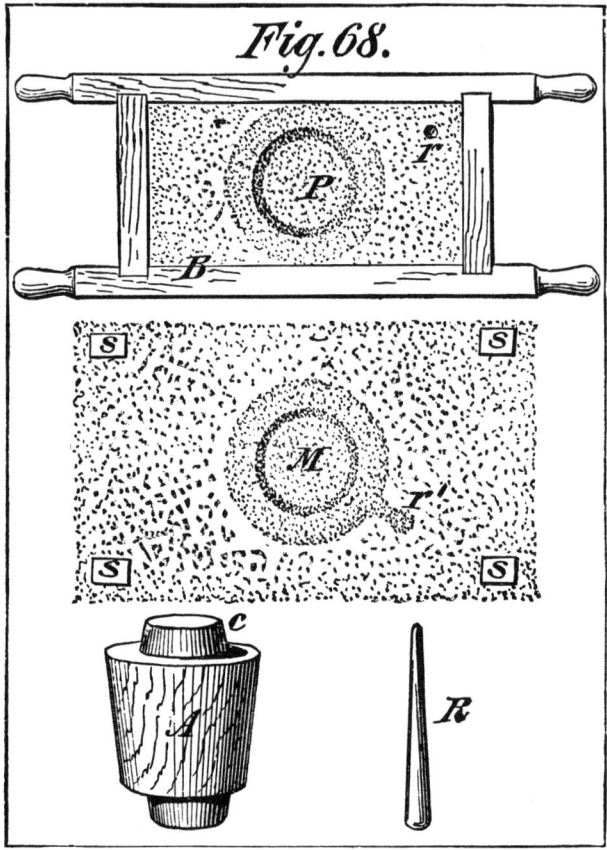

It will be seen that, when a mold is made in the flask we have described, it can perform no further duty until the casting has been made; for every mold, therefore, we require a flask, and hence the pile of these appliances we always see in a foundry. For light work, however, a comparatively modern and greatly improved device has come into general use. It is termed a snap flask, each part having a hinge at one corner and a latch at the diagonally opposite one; so that, after the mold is made, it can be detached from the perfected mold and can be used to make another. Sometimes, though rarely, it happens that a casting is required of such form that the patterns cannot be constructed so as to be molded with a flask of the ordinary kind. The flask requires to come to pieces and the mold to be parted sidewise; this adds greatly to the labor of the molder, and the pattern maker should so construct the pattern as to avoid this, whenever he can devise any means of so doing. Even when the pattern is molded in the floor, the mold is sometimes of necessity made to part on one or more of its sides, and these partings are termed drawbacks.

By watching the operations of a molder, we shall observe that, in the case of a solid pattern—that is to say, a pattern not made in halves—he always endeavors to have as little of the pattern in the cope as possible, and in this respect the pattern maker should supplement his efforts. The reason is obvious: the cope has to be lifted while as yet there has been no opportunity to loosen the pattern in the mold. It is true that, in some cases, a bar is passed through the cope and driven into the pattern, and by rapping it the loosening is accomplished; but it is not well to have recourse to such an expedient, because, wherever the bar passes, the cope is damaged, and must be mended; and when a mold has to be mended, it is doubtful if the correct form, such as the pattern would have given it, will be left. Furthermore, it is all work in the dark; for the effect or extent of the rapping cannot be scrutinized, and it may therefore produce an undue distortion in one direction, while in another it may not have been effectual. Perhaps the bar may have descended at a place in the pattern where it is comparatively weak, from crossgrain of the wood or from some other cause. This measure is, therefore, on account of these difficulties, seldom resorted to; and it may be generally disregarded in the calculations of the pattern maker. The cope, then, being, as we may say, a dead lift, and with nothing to guide the operator in moving it, either horizontally or vertically, any part of the

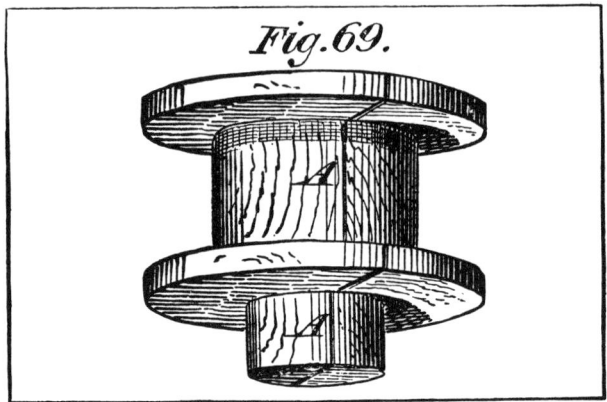

mold contained in it is much more liable to break down than is the other part of the mold. In extracting the pattern from the lower part of the mold, the eye lends to the molder great assistance. The pattern can be loosened in

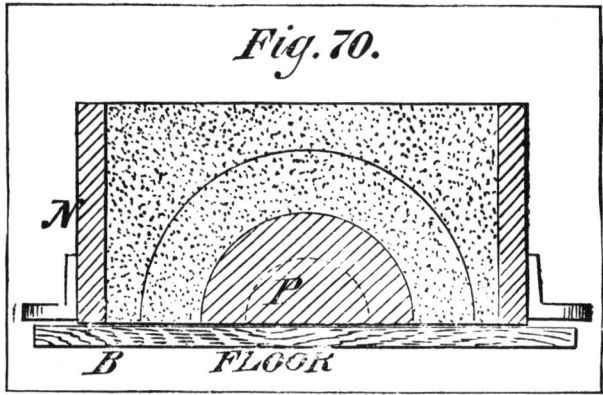

the sand before extraction, and is furthermore less cumbersome to handle than is the cope: all of which circumstances tend to preserve the lower part of the mold from damage during the extraction of the pattern. Rapping a pattern tends to alter the form of the mold from that calculated upon. A circle becomes slightly oval, a square becomes an oblong, and so on: and this cannot in most cases be avoided, because it is necessary to rap the pattern so as to enable the molder to extract the pattern without drawing out the sand with it; all that can be done in this direction is to rap the pattern as little as possible, and equally in all directions.

When a flask nowel is used, the labor involved in making a parting of the mold is facilitated. Fig. 67 shows a board cope and nowel for an ordinary straight parting; but it is evident that the parts of the flask may be made to show a crooked, a curved, or irregular line at the joint, if it is required, in which case the bed board must be made of similar conformation. The process of molding with a flask independently of the floor, is illustrated in Figs. 70 and 71. If it be required to mold the pattern illustrated in Fig. 69, which is made in halves, the joint being denoted by the line, A A, one of the halves is taken and laid with its flat face upon the molding board, B, shown in Fig. 70. The nowel, N, is then placed upon the board, so that the half of the pattern will be in about the middle of the flask nowel. Sand is then rammed tightly in the nowel; and when the latter is filled with the sand, it is turned upside down, showing the flat face of the half pattern, the rest of the half pattern being imbedded in the sand. The other half of the pattern is then placed upon the one in the sand, its proper position being determined and regulated by pegs fitting into holes, provided in the first part, to receive them. The next operation is to put on the cope, as shown in Fig. 71, the taper pins being fast to the cope lugs shown on the sides, fitting into holes provided in the nowel lugs, similarly shown, serving to hold the cope in position and prevent it from moving. The cope is then filled with sand, lightly rammed, the taper pin, R, Fig. 68, being inserted to leave in the mold the hole, R, Fig. 71, through which to pour the melted metal. The cope is now lifted vertically; and as the pattern is made in halves, the top half lifts with the sand in the cope. In some cases a

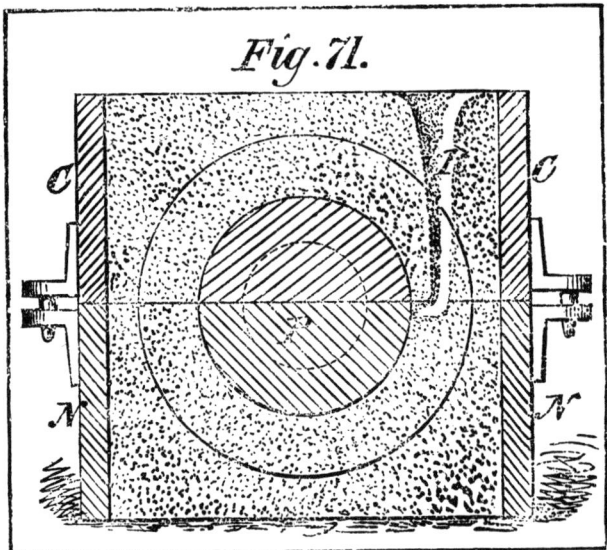

Fig. 71.

screw is fixed into the top half of the pattern, the head of the screw projecting into the cope: the object being to insure that the top half of the pattern shall lift with the cope. The next procedure is to extract the two halves

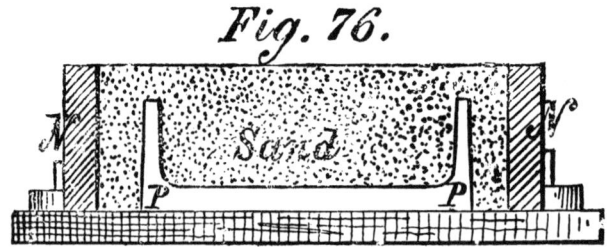

Fig. 76.

of the patterns from the molds, and perform any trimming or repairing that the mold may require, after which the cope is again placed upon the nowel, and the mold is complete, ready to have the metal poured in.

In Figs. 76 and 77, we have another example of flask molding, but for a pattern of different shape to our previous one. The pattern is, in this case, not made in halves, its flanges on one side being left loose. In Fig. 76, one half of the pattern is shown on the molding board, and the nowel placed thereon and rammed with sand;

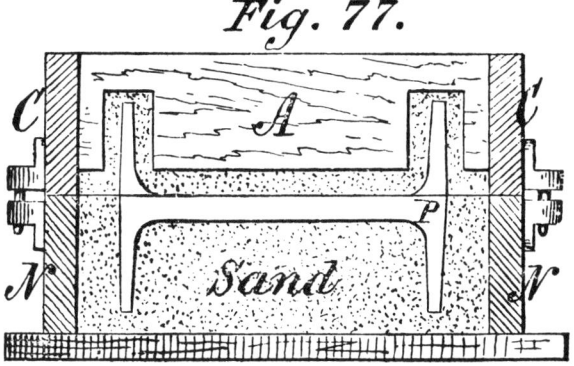

Fig. 77.

while in Fig. 77, the pattern is shown molded and ready to have the cope taken off, A representing one of the crossbars fitted into the cope, and following the outline of the pattern.

CHAPTER IV.

THE FOUNDRY.

ON CORES.

CORES are projecting bodies of sand, either left in the mold by the pattern itself or else made in a separate device called a core box. They are placed, after being dried, in position in the mold. The purpose of a core of the latter description is to leave a hole or recess of such a peculiar shape or in such a position that it is impracticable to make the mold of the necessary conformation by the use of the pattern alone. The use of these cores also permits us to modify the shape of a pattern that would otherwise be difficult to mold. For example, Fig. 78 represents

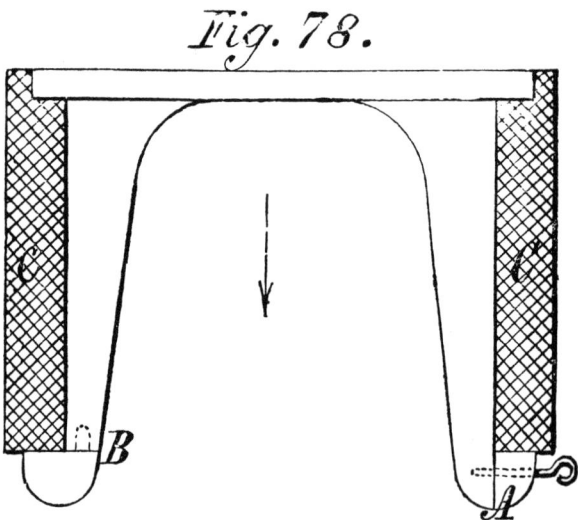

Fig. 78.

a plate of such length that it is necessary to mold it in the direction indicated by the arrow; as the pendants, which are long and narrow, with their projections at the extremities, would lock the pattern in the mold. Three methods present themselves whereby to overcome the difficulty. First, we may make the projection loose, the vertical line, A, being the joint; it is held in position by vertical dovetails or by horizontal wires, as shown in Fig. 78. In the latter case, the molder, when ramming the sand, withdraws the wires; and when the pattern is withdrawn from the mold, the two different projecting pieces are left in the mold, and are subsequently retracted horizontally, and then lifted out. It is obvious that this can only be done when there is sufficient space to accommodate the projecting piece as it is withdrawn from its recess in the sand, and to admit of its being raised to the surface. To this method there is the objection that the recess left by the projecting piece in the mold cannot be, in many cases, either inspected or dressed, if any reparation is required. A second plan would be to make the projecting piece join the pattern at the horizontal line, B, in Fig. 78, but separable from it; but in this case a three-part flask would have to be used, entailing double work for the molder. The third method is to affix the core prints, C C, to the sides of the pattern, leaving those sides smooth and even; and the pattern will then draw easily out of the mold. If we then core away all we have added to the pattern, as shewn by the dotted lines in Fig. 78, the casting will retain the correct shape of the pattern. To effect this coring away, we make dry sand cores of the shape of the core prints, C C, and place them in the mold. Ordinary dry sand cores are composed of a mixture of sand and flour moistened with water, and they are molded to the requisite shape in the core boxes already mentioned. They are then baked, becoming sufficiently strong to handle; but previous to the baking they are so weak that they cannot be handled without being in some way supported. It is, therefore, as great a consideration to the

pattern maker how the core is to be taken from the box as
it is how a pattern shall be drawn from the mold. We
may divide cores molded in a core box into three classes:
First, those that lie as they are made; second, those that
require turning over; and third, those that not only require turning over, but require also a bed of sand made
for them to lie upon during the process of baking. Figs.

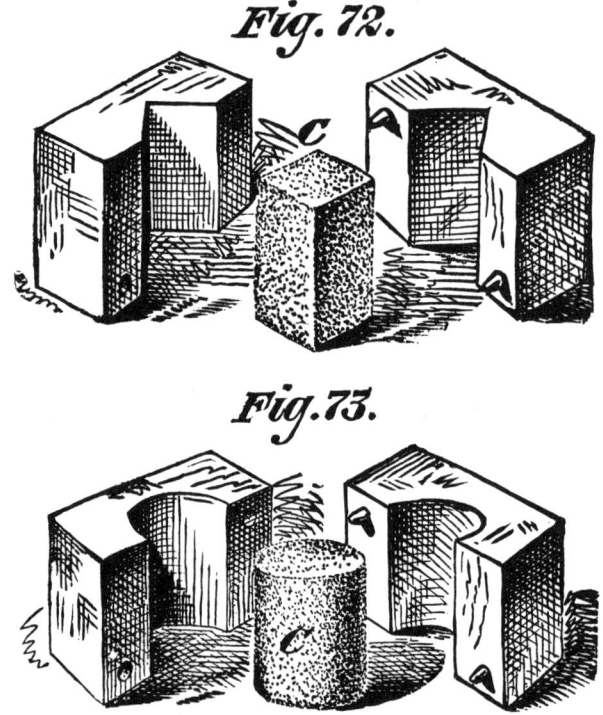

72, 73, and 74 are examples of the first, in which the cores
are represented by C. The core boxes, being made in
halves and loose at two of the opposite corners, can be
drawn away from the cores, C, leaving them standing,
just as they were made, on an iron plate ready for removal
to the oven. In a core box made as in Fig. 74, it is necessary to bore in the ends a couple of small holes for the insertion of wires to effect ventilation. In cases where suffi-

cient draft or taper can be allowed on the core, the
core box need not be made in halves, but may be made
solid, as shown in section in Fig. 75.

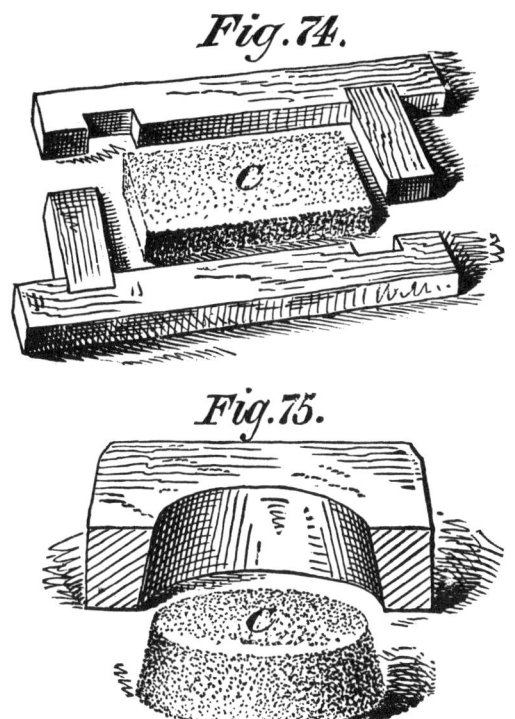

Fig. 74.

Fig. 75.

While it is the aim of the pattern maker to form his
core boxes to work in the simple manner illustrated in our
examples, there are very large classes of cores with which
such easy methods are impracticable. This, for instance,
is the case with all round cores that are of such length
that they are not able to support themselves on end, and
with those having branches, as shown in Fig. 79, which represents a core for a straight faucet. If it were attempted
to make this core in a vertical position, its overhanging
branches would fall away immediately after separating the
two halves of the box; hence it is made horizontally, and
generally in separate halves, which, after being baked, are

pasted together and again dried, thus forming the full round core. In cases, however, where great numbers of such cores are required, as in steam fitters' work, they are usually lifted from the box whole; but it is a delicate

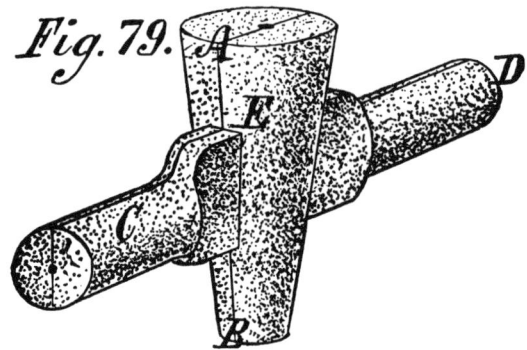

Fig. 79.

operation, involving much practice. We need not, however, go into this, the subject only being mentioned to show how a pattern maker decides whether he shall make a full core box or only half a one; for if the halves of the core are to be made separate, and one part is exactly similar to the other, then a half core box is all that is necessary. Suppose, for instance, the core of a faucet, shown in Fig. 79, to be alike at the branches, C and D; then, it being made in two halves, meeting in a point represented by the line A B, the core box may be made to mold the half, E; and two of such halves, pasted together as described, will form the whole core. In this particular example, however, there is yet another way of making the core, providing the branches, C and D, are parallel in diameter, and that is, to punch holes in the main part of the core, through holes provided in the core box, using a piece of wood for the purpose.

Fig. 80 is an illustration of a square core for a baluster; its four sides being curved, it is necessary to make it in separate halves, dividing it diagonally across the corners, as denoted by the lines A B.

We have now to give an example of the third class of core, which will not stand on end and does not present a

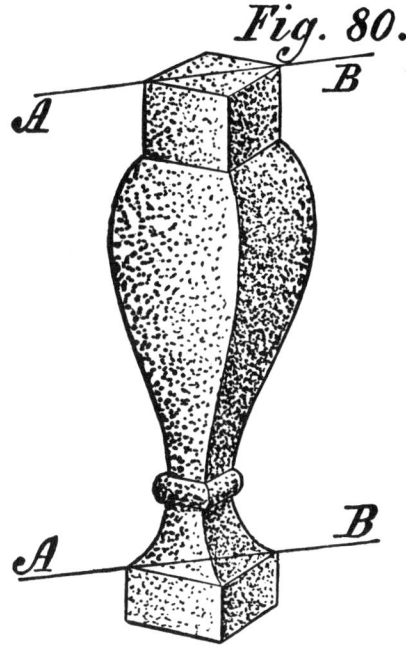

Fig. 80.

flat surface on any of its four sides, neither can it be readily divided, as in the former case. Fig. 81 is an illustration

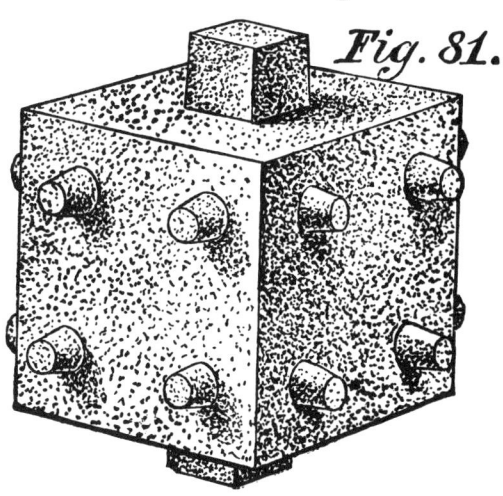

Fig. 81.

of probably the simplest kind of this class, which will require a core box that must part in all directions in order
to enable us to extract the core, which will require, in addition to this, what is called a turnover box. Fig. 82 is an
end sectional view of this

Fig. 82.

core box, having four jointed sides and a bottom, with
holes cut in them where the
projections are to be formed
on the ·core. The top, in
this case, is simply two bars
that cross the box where the
projections occur; and holes
are cut in these bars to form
the projections. The box is
retained together and kept
in position by the taper
pegs, shown at the junction
of the sides. The ends of the box are recessed to receive
the sides, but all is removable. In using this box, after
ramming up the top, the crossbars are removed, and in
their place is mounted the turnover box, shown in section
in Fig. 83, at A, which is a simple square frame, made
taper. It rests on the outer edge of the core box, so as to
give a bed of sand somewhat larger than the core itself.
Small blocks nailed to the under side, B B, keep it in position. The frame is then carefully filled with ordinary
molding sand, so as not to disturb the projecting parts of
the core, and the sand on the outside is then struck off
level. An iron plate is then placed on the top of all, and
the whole is turned upside down. The bottom of the core
box, which has now become the top, is first removed, and
then the sides and ends. Thus the turnover box affords a
bedding of sand, on which the core may rest without suf-
fering injury from its own weight.

It would be a costly matter to make core boxes for long cylindrical cores, such as are used for pipe and similar castings; hence, for such purposes, a core is made as shown in Fig. 84, in which C represents a core for a pipe, having a

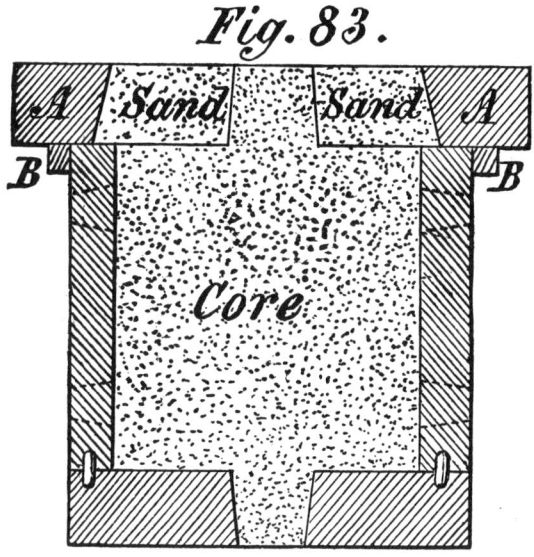

Fig. 83.

socket at one end. It is prepared as follows: Upon the two tressels, A A, is mounted the long tube, D D, which is perforated throughout its entire length with numerous small holes, and which is provided at one end with a crank handle, by means of which it may be revolved as it rests in the two rude V bearings, provided in the top of the tressels, as shown. Upon this tube a layer of rudely twisted straw rope, sufficient to make its diameter assume, from end to end, nearly the required diameter of the core, is coiled. Outside the straw rope there is then applied a coating composed of a mixture of loam and other material sufficient to increase the diameter from end to end, somewhat above finished size. To round up the core even, and make it of the necessary size, the core or loam board, B B, is employed. It is simply a board ranging in thickness

4**

from seven eighths inch upwards, according to its length. One of the edges is cut to the conformation of the required core; and all but about three sixteenths of an inch of the thickness of this edge is beveled off at an angle of about 30°. This board is laid upon the tressels with the beveled edge uppermost, and is held in position by weights placed upon it over the tressels. The core is then revolved by the

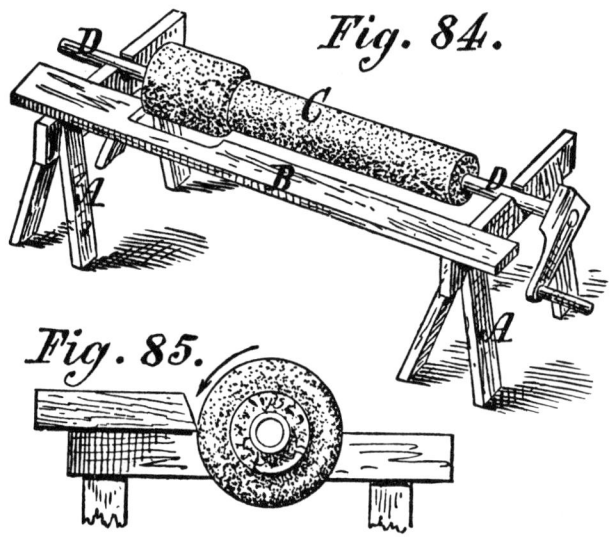

Fig. 84.

Fig. 85.

handle in the direction of the arrow, as shown in Fig. 85, in which A represents the tube, B the straw rope, C the loam coating, and D the board. It follows that, as the loam is added, the board will level it off, leaving the surface round and true, and to whatever shape the edge of the board may be made. It is customary to mix with the coating of loam, horse dung, or a substitute therefor, the object of which is as follows: It will be readily perceived that it is a difficult matter in a long casting to give vent to and permit the escape of the air and the gases formed in the mold by the molten metal; but by mixing in with the loam a combustible material, the latter becomes consumed during the baking of the core, leaving the latter porous, so that the air and gases can pass from the mold through the loam coating and thence through the straw rope, and find exit through the hollow tube upon which the latter is wound.

CHAPTER V.

EXAMPLES OF SIMPLE LATHE WORK.

WE may now commence a series of examples, accompanying each example with the explanations and considerations necessary to, and governing the method of, the construction chosen. Fig. 86 represents a drawing of a gland for which a pattern is required. Now this is a very simple pattern, and yet there are at least six different methods of making it, any of which may be followed, as will appear more clearly to the reader by his glancing over Figs. 87, 89, 90, 92, 93, and 94. The first question is how to determine which method is the most suitable. Let us suppose the pattern maker to be uninformed of the purpose the casting is to serve, or how it is to be treated: in such a case he is guided partly by his knowledge of the use of such patterns, and a consideration of being on the safe side. The form shown in Fig. 87 would suggest itself as being a very ready method of making the pattern; by coring out the hole it can be made parallel, which the **drawing seems to require.** The advantage of leaving the

Fig. 86.

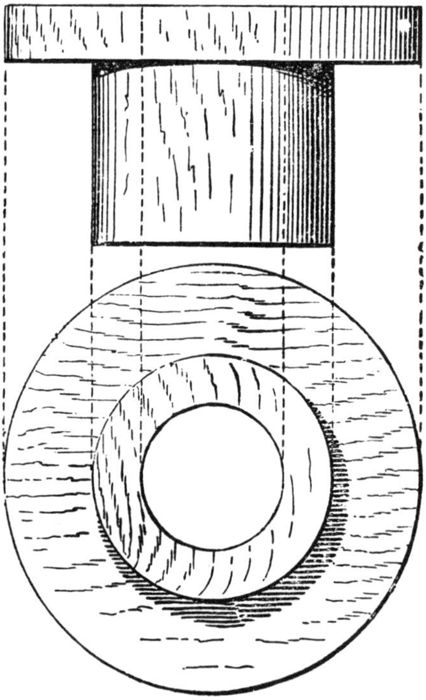

hole parallel is that less metal will require to be left for boring, in case it should be necessary; because, if the hole is made taper, the largest end of the bore will require to have the proper amount of allowance to leave metal sufficient to allow the hole to be bored out true, and the smaller end would, therefore, have more than the necessary amount: while just the least taper given to the exterior would enable the molder to withdraw the pattern from the mold. Made in this way, it would be molded as shown in Fig. 88, with the flange uppermost, because almost the whole of the pattern would be imbedded in the lower part of the flask, the top core print being all that would be contained in the

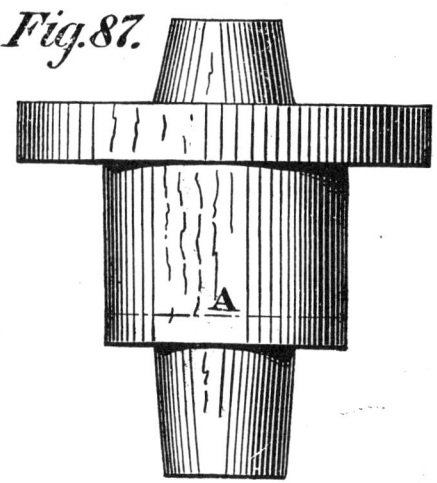

Fig. 87.

cope; and even this many be omitted if the hole requires to be bored, since the lower core print will hold the core sufficiently secure in small work, unless the core is required to be very true. The parting of the mold (at C D, in Fig. 88) being level with the top face of the flange, much taper should be given to the top print (as shown in Fig. 87), so that the cope may be lifted off easily. Were this however the only reason, we might make the top print like the bottom one, providing we left it on loose, or made it part from the pattern and adjust to its place on the pattern by a taper pin; but another advantage is gained by well tapering the top print, in that it necessitates the tapering of the core print at that end; so that, when the two parts of the mold are being put together — that is to say, when the cope is being put in place — if the core has not been placed quite upright, its tapered end may still arrive and adjust itself in the conical impression, and thus correct any slight error of position of the core. The size of the core print should be, at the part next the pattern,

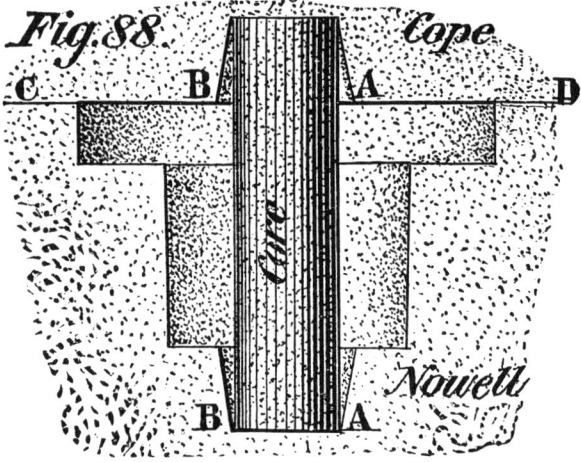

the size of the core required; for if the extremities are made of the size of the core, and the taper or draft is in excess, there will be left a useless space around the core print, as shown in A B in Fig. 88, into which space the metal will flow, producing on the casting around the hole and projecting from the end face a useless web, which is called a fin, which will of course require to be dressed off the casting.

We will now suppose that our piece, when cast, is to be turned under the flange and along the outside of the hub or body, and that the hole also is to be bored. In this case the pattern made as above would still be good, but could be much more easily made and molded if it has to leave its own core—its shape being as shown in Fig. 89— because the trouble of making a core is obviated, and the core is sure to be in the center of the casting, which it seldom is when a core is used. We must, however, allow more taper or draft to a hole in a pattern than is necessary on the outside; about one sixteenth inch on the diameter **for** every inch of hight on work of moderate size is sufficient. The allowance for boring should be one sixteenth inch at the large end of the hole, providing the diameter of the hole is not more than five or six inches, slightly exceeding this amount as the diameter increases; whereas, if the pattern had been made with core prints,

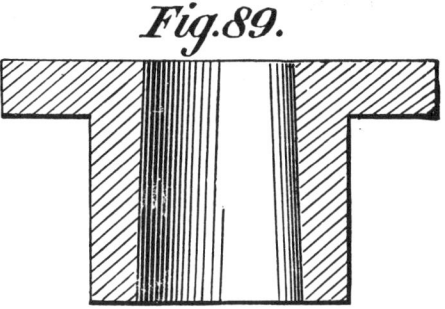

Fig. 89.

an allowance of one eighth inch for small, and three six-teenths inch for larger work would be required. These are the advantages due to making the pattern leave its own core. We have still to bear in mind, however, that, if the casting require a parallel hole, a core must be used; and furthermore, if the hole is a long one, we have the following considerations: The separate dry sand core is stronger, and therefore better adapted to cases where the length of the hole greatly exceeds the diameter. Then again, if the hole require to be bored parallel, it can be more readily done if the hole is cast parallel, because there will be less metal to cut out. The casting also will be lighter, entailing less cost, pro-viding it has to be paid for by the pound, as is usually the case. The molder is given more work by making the core; but the saving in metal and in turning more than compensates for this, provided the length of the hole is greater than the diameter of the bore.

Let it now be required that the casting is to be finished all over, such as for a gland for a piston rod. It would in that case be preferred that, if the casting should contain any blow or air holes, they should not be on the outside **face of** the flange; and this will necessitate that the piece be molded the reverse way to that shown in Fig. 88 — that is to say, it must be molded as shown in Fig. 90 — with the flange downwards; for it may be here noted that the soundest part of a casting is always that at the bottom of the mold; and furthermore, the metal there

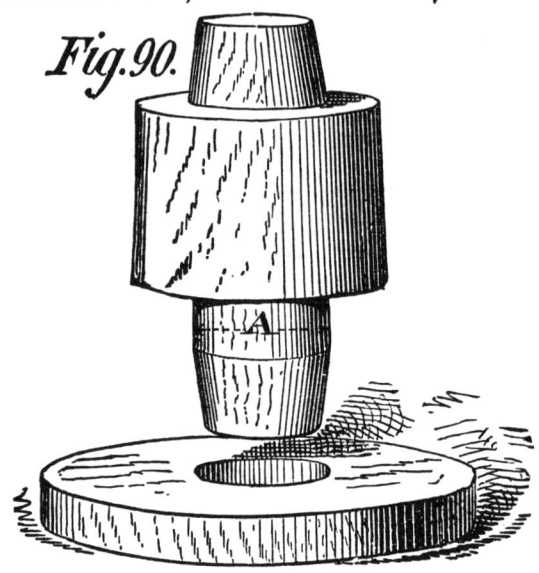

Fig.90.

is more dense, heavier, and stronger than it is at the top, for the reason that the air or gas, which does not escape from the mold, leaves holes in the top of the casting, or as near to the top as it can — by reason of the shape of the casting — rise. The bottom metal also has the weight of the metal above it, compressing it, and making an appreciable difference in its density. It must therefore be remembered, that faces requiring to be particularly sound, should be cast downwards — or at least as near the bottom of the mold as they conveniently can. Following this principle, our gland will require to be molded as shown in Fig. 91, P P representing the line of the parting of the mold; so that, when the cope is lifted off, the loose hub, A, will rise with it, leaving the flange imbedded in the lower half of the mold. It is evident that in this case the pattern must be made as shown in Fig 90, the body and core prints being in one piece and the flange in another, fitting to an easy fit on to a parallel part on one end, and adjoining the core print, as shown at A.

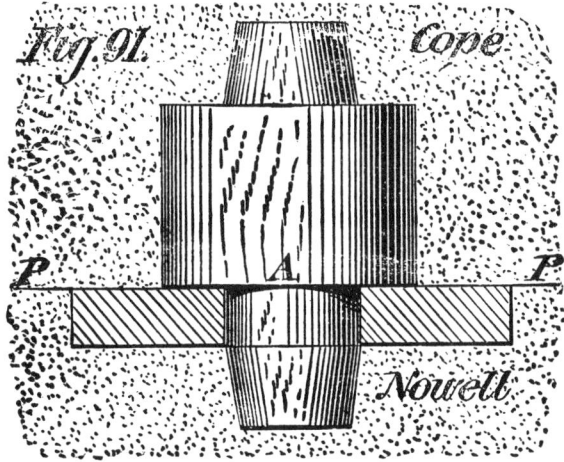

For glands of moderate size, this method is usually adopted, and it answers very well for short pieces; but in cases where the length of the body approaches say three dia-

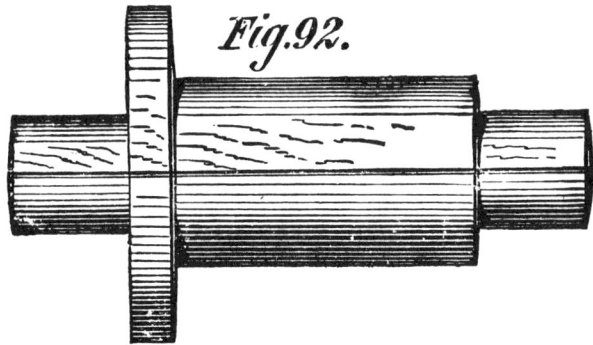

meters, the horizontal position is the best, and the pattern should be made as shown in Figs. 92, 93, or 94. Even in short pieces, when the internal diameter approaches that of the external, this plan is the best, because it is difficult for the molder to tell when his core is accurately set in position. **5**

For a pattern to be molded horizontally, Fig. 93 shows the best style in which it can be made. Its diameters are

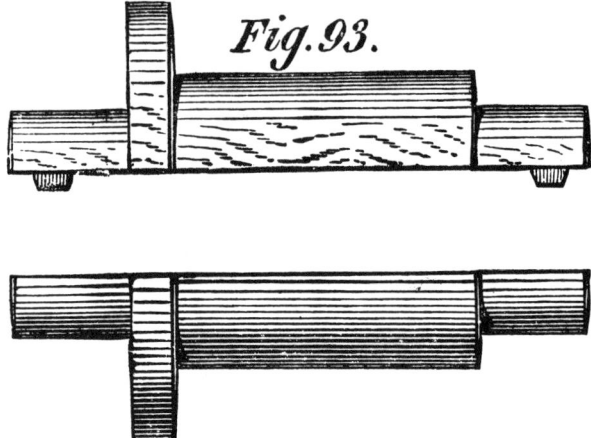

Fig.93.

turned parallel; the required draft is given by making the rim of the flange a little thinner than at the hub, and by making the end faces of the hub and the core prints slightly rounding. If the hub is very small — as, say, a half inch or less, and the flange does not much exceed it —

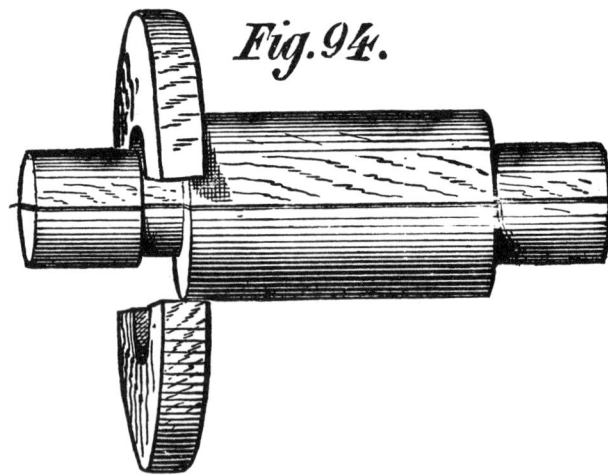

Fig.94.

the pattern may be made solid, as shown in Fig. 92; but if the hub be small and the flange large, it should be made as shown in Fig. 94.

To construct the pattern shown in Fig. 87 we proceed as follows: From a piece of plank we saw off a piece of wood a little larger and thicker than the required flange, measuring with a contraction rule — that is to say, a rule specially made for the pattern maker, and having its measurements larger than the actual standard ones, in the proportion of one eighth inch per foot: so that a foot on a contraction rule is $12\frac{1}{8}$ standard inches, and an inch is $1\frac{1}{96}$ standard inches. The reason for this is, that when the metal is poured into the mold it is expanded by heat, and as it cools it contracts; and a casting is therefore, when cold, always smaller than the size of the mold in which it was made. Brass castings are generally said to be smaller than the patterns, in the proportion of one eighth inch per foot, and cast iron castings one tenth inch per foot; and so, to avoid frequent calculations and possible errors, the contraction rule has the necessary allowance in every division of the foot and of the inch. It is not however to be supposed that the possession of such a rule renders it possible for the pattern maker to discard all further considerations upon the contraction of the casting; because there are others continually occurring. Such, for example, is the fact that the contraction will not be equal all over, but will be the greatest in those parts where the casting contains the greatest body of metal. If we are required to make a pattern for a brass, such as

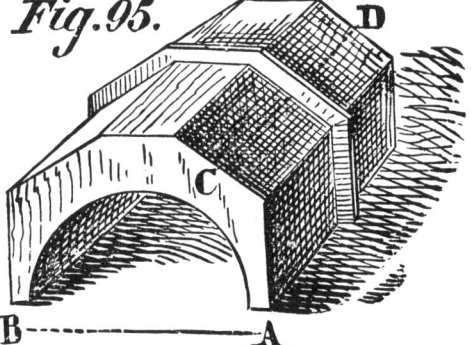

Fig. 95.

shown in Fig. 95, its bore being six inches in diameter and its length ten inches, we shall find that the diameter of the casting will be less at A B than can be accounted for on the basis of a contraction of one eighth inch **per** foot; and furthermore, the projection in the middle of the brass, which is sometimes provided instead of flanges to prevent the brass from moving endwise in the box, will cause the sides of the hexagon to cast hollow in their lengths; so that a straight edge, placed along the bevel from C to D, would touch the brass at each end, and not in the middle.

In the smaller sizes of patterns, however, such as those of 6 and less inches in diameter, there is another and a more important matter requiring attention, which is, that after a molder has imbedded the pattern in the sand, and has rammed the sand closely around it, it is held firmly by the sand and must be loosened before it can be extracted from the mold. To loosen it, the molder drives into the exposed surface of the pattern a pointed piece of steel wire, which he then strikes on all sides, causing the pattern to compress the sand away from the sides of the pattern in all directions; and as a result, the mold is larger than the pattern. In many kinds of work, this fact may be and is disregarded; but where accuracy is concerned, it is of great importance, especially in the matter of our example (brasses for journals), for they can be chipped and filed to fit their places much more rapidly than they can be planed, and it is necessary to have the castings as nearly of the correct conformation as possible. In cases where it is necessary to have the castings of the correct size without any work done to them, the shake of the pattern in the sand is of the utmost importance. If he is required to cast a piece of iron 3 inches long and 1 inch square, supposing the pattern were made to correct measure by the contraction rule, the molder, by rapping the pattern (as the loosening it in the mold is termed), would, by increasing the size of the mold above that of the pattern, cause the casting to be larger than the pattern: that is to say, it would

be longer and broader, and therefore, in those two directions, considerably above the proper size, since even the
pattern was too large to the amount allowed for contraction.
The depth, however, would be of correct size, because the
loosening process, or rapping, does not drive the pattern
any deeper in the mold. It follows that, to obtain a casting of as nearly the correct size as possible, the pattern
must be made less in width and in length than the proper
size, to the amount of the rapping; and to insure that the
molders shall always put the pattern in the sand with the
same side uppermost, the word "top" should be printed on
the face intended to lie uppermost in the mold. The
amount to be allowed for the rapping depends upon the
size of the pattern, and somewhat upon the molder, since
some molders rap the patterns more than others: hence,
where a great number of castings of accurate size are required, it is best to have two or three castings made, and
alter the pattern as the average casting indicates. For
castings of about 1 inch in size, the patterns may be made
$\frac{1}{32}$ inch too narrow and the same amount too short; but
for sizes above 6 inches, allowance for rapping may be disregarded.

In patterns for small cast gears, the rapping is of the
utmost consequence. Suppose, for instance, we have 6
rollers of 2 inches diameter, requiring to be connected
together by pinions, and to have contact one with the other
all along the rollers: if we disregarded the allowance for
rapping, the pinions will be too thick, and we shall require
to file them down, entailing a great deal of labor and
time, besides the rapid destruction of files.

To resume, then: having sawn out our piece of wood for
the flange, we plane up one side, and set a pair of compasses to the radius of the required flange, and mark a
circle upon the piece of wood, and then saw off the corners
nearly to the circle. We then true up a facing chuck in

the lathe, and fix the flange to it by screws passing through the chuck from the back, placing them far enough from the center to avoid their coming into contact with the hole which we shall require to bore in the flange. We then dress off the face of the flange to nearly the required thickness, using the gouge to rough it out with, and the scraping chisel to finish. It is not necessary to finish right down to the center, but merely down to a diameter somewhat smaller than the hole in the flange will be. Our next procedure is to mark the size of the hole, which is done by setting the compasses to the required diameter, and then holding them with one leg resting upon the hand rest; and by bringing the point into contact with the face of the work, we may describe upon the latter a true circle, somewhat smaller in diameter than that required. This circle will serve as a guide to us while we hold both compass points against the work to describe a circle of the correct diameter, which will be done by keeping the compass points at equal distances, one on each side of the circle first described. We must, in the last operation, hold the compass points lightly against the work until we can see that the line described by one point falls in the same line as that described by the other, and then we may make a deep mark. This method is quite as easy an operation as setting the compasses to the radius of the hole, and, putting one leg in the center of the work, describing a circle with the other; and this process is also more exact when the wood is rough. We next take a chisel of about $\frac{1}{8}$ inch wide, and cut out the hole at one cut, by forcing the chisel lightly through the thickness of the flange, taking care to cut the hole nearly $\frac{1}{32}$ inch too small, so as to allow finishing with the diamond point or side tool. The hole being finished, we may turn the outside diameter of the flange with a very sharp gouge, leaving about $\frac{1}{32}$ inch for finishing, which may be done with the scraper. When the scraping chisel — as indeed all scraping tools — is in proper order, a slight burr can be felt on the top face of the tool, which is caused by oilstoning the beveled face of the chisel last.

To form the body of the pattern, we take a piece of timber of sufficient size to make the hub and core prints in one piece, and, with an ax, we hack off the corners, so as to save lathe work. We then place it in the lathe between the centers, using the fork shown in Fig. 48 as the running center and to drive the piece of wood, and screwing up the back center sufficiently firm to hold the wood tightly. The large diameter is turned to its size with the gouge and scraper, using the latter to finish with, and bearing in mind that the wood is apt to become loose between the lathe centers, by reason of the latter becoming imbedded in the wood; and it is necessary, therefore, during the earlier portion of the turning, to try the back center and screw it

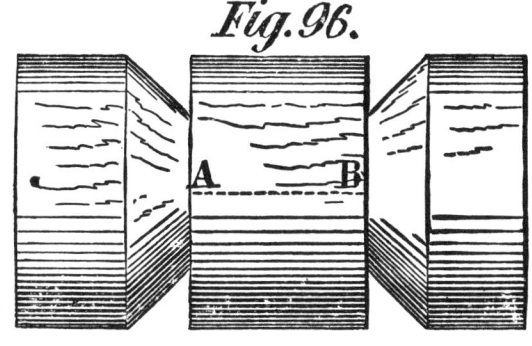

Fig. 96.

up into the work, if necessary. Then, with the skew chisel, we cut two recesses, as shown in Fig. 96, the distance from A to B being the length of the body or hub of

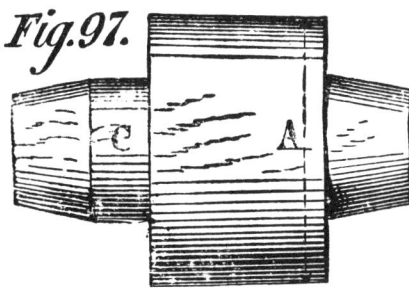

Fig. 97.

the pattern, and the small diameter of the recess being a little above the required diameter of the core prints. We next turn down the core prints to the required sizes, and turn the part shown at C, in Fig. 97, to fit the hole tight to the flange; and it will be perceived that, by leaving a longer end outside of the recess or nick at one end than at the other, we have left room for the flange, and so kept the core prints of equal length at each end, as shown in Fig. 97. The part that protrudes through the flange will in this case be for the top print, and it is therefore given an excess of taper, for reasons before explained. The hub or body of the pattern is also made taper, being a little the smallest at the end farthest from the flange (A, in Figs. 87 and 96), because this hub, being cast endwise, requires draft to permit it to be extracted easily from the mold.

Having brought our pattern, as nearly as possible, to the requisite size and form with the cutting tools, it is necessary to consider those final processes which so much add to the appearance and smoothness of pattern work. The first of these processes is termed sand-papering or glass-papering. Sand-paper is a sort of Will-o'-the-wisp to the beginner, luring him on to scamp his work, under the impression that sand-paper will hide the defects, and bring it all right, while the fact is nearer the reverse; for, let a pattern be ever so truly shaped and turned, if the sand-papering be injudiciously performed, the sharpness of its outline will be destroyed, and very likely its size and shape be seriously interfered with. It is true that it is scarcely possible to do much damage to large surfaces; but that is merely because of the great disproportion that would exist between an error engendered by sand-papering and the whole size of the pattern itself. If we have an inch cube to sand-paper, and should take $\frac{1}{64}$ inch more off one side than off another, our error would amount to the $\frac{1}{64}$ of the length of the pattern; but had the same thing been done upon a 12-inch cube, the error arising therefrom would only amount to $\frac{1}{768}$ of the length of the pattern. Again, to remove $\frac{1}{64}$ inch from one side of each of these respective cubes, we should have 144 times as much wood to abrade away in the one case as in the other; so that it will be readily perceived that the difficulties attending the sand-papering of a pattern, so as to preserve its true form and size, increase in a two-fold ratio as the size of pattern diminishes, until at last it becomes impracticable. Exactly where this point is reached, it is not possible to state; it will, however, vary with the capabilities of the workman, the steadiness of his eye and hand, and the nature and material of the work. It must have happened to many that they have made patterns so small that they dared not attempt to sand-paper them, and that they have turned intricate details upon a piece of work which could not be preserved in its sharpness under the abrasion of sand-paper. While, therefore, we respect sand-paper, let us respect our tools more, and let the pattern or core box, as the case may be, be brought as nearly to the form required as practicable with the cutting instrument, and then let the sand-paper be applied, not by folding it together and rubbing it upon the work, but by considering the shape we intend to finish, and preparing a piece of wood to correspond to the shape. Such a piece of wood is called a rubber. A flat surface requires a flat rubber, a convex surface a concave rubber, and *vice versa*. Rubbers are made of a size suitable to hold in the hand, and in length range up to 12 inches. Longer

Fig.98.

than this would be useless for one sheet of sand-paper, and that is all that is generally used at a time. Turned cylinders make good rubbers for core boxes that are semicircular, up to about 3 inches in diameter; above that size, the turned rubber becomes clumsy, and a piece flat on one side and planed to suit the curve is used. Such a piece is shown in Fig. 98.

To use it, place one fold of sand-paper only around the rubber; and applying it to the work, move it over the surface of the work, and across the grain of the timber, if it is possible. If the size of the work is smaller than the rubber, we must take short strokes, so as to be able to move the latter steadily, and not round off the work at and toward the edges. A very good plan, where extra care is required, is to either glue the sand-paper to the rubber, or else fasten it with a few tacks. Sand-paper glued to a flat board is very useful for small surfaces; but in this case, we rub the work upon the paper, and not the paper upon the work. The grades of sand-paper used upon pattern work range from No. $\frac{1}{2}$ up to No. 2, Nos. 1 and $1\frac{1}{2}$ being most commonly employed.

The surfaces of the hub or body of our gland pattern being straight in their outlines, we sand-paper them in the lathe, with the paper wrapped once around a flat rubber, applying the paper lightly to the work, and moving it very slowly over the work, in the manner in which a file is used. We next fasten the flange to the body by gluing it, by using finishing nails, or by both. If finishing nails are used, care must be taken to use a bradawl before inserting the nails, for fear of splitting the wood.

To make the pattern in the manner shown in Fig. 90, the method of procedure is the same as the above, with the exception that the tapering of the core prints must be *vice versa*, as in this case the core print the farthest from the flange will be the top one in the mold, and must therefore be given the most taper. And since the body of the pattern will lift with the cope, while the flange will remain in the nowel of the flask when the mold is taken apart (as shown in Fig. 91), the flange of the pattern must be made an easy fit to its place on the body or hub, and must not be left of a tight fit, as in the former case. A pattern of the form shown in Fig. 92 may be turned, flange and all, out of a solid piece of wood; or, if too large for this, we may plane up a piece for the flange, and glue a hub to it; and when the glue is dry, turn up the whole pattern at one chucking in the lathe.

The construction shown in Figs. 92, 93, and 94 is so nearly the same, and the slight difference is so obvious, that an explanation of Fig. 94 will cover the ground. For Fig. 94 we plane up a piece over twice as long and more than half the size of the required flange, and out of this piece cut the two half flanges. If, however, the flange is of sufficient size to make it necessary to study economy, the two half flanges may be set out on the plank, lapping each other, as shown in Fig. 99. We next, with a flat scriber, draw a line on the chuck exactly through its cen-

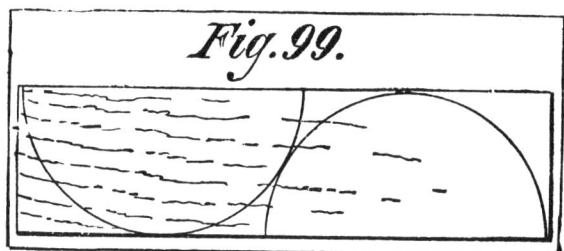

ter, and set the half flanges to this line, and then screw them to the chuck, and turn them as if they were solid. By setting the halves exactly true to the line, it is insured that the flange shall part exactly at the center.

To make the pattern shown in Fig. 93, we take two pieces of wood long enough to make the two halves, and allow about half an inch or an inch to turn off each end, so that the impressions of the fork and center may not appear on and disfigure the finished work, and for other reasons hereafter to be mentioned. We plane these pieces on one edge and on one face, making them of equal thickness. We make the flat surfaces which come together, true, trying them with the winding strips shown in Fig. 37, to detect any twist. Our next operation is to insert the pegs,

and we may, for this purpose, adopt either of the two following methods, the more ready of which we will take first :
Clamping the two jointed faces together, as shown in Fig.
100, we bore two holes right through the top piece and into

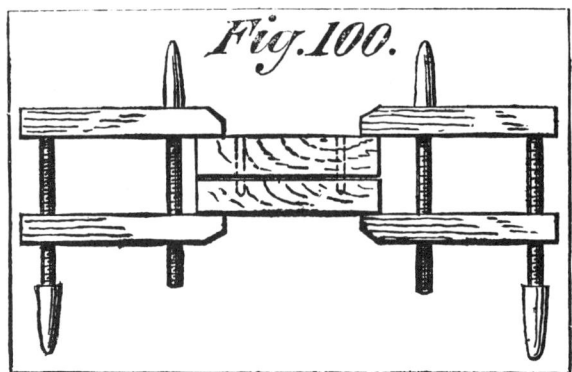

Fig. 100.

the bottom, one to a little greater depth than the hight to
which the pin is intended to project, as shown by the dotted lines.   We then plane up a piece of hard wood, about
two and a half feet long, to fit the holes tightly.   It is just
as easy to plane a long piece as a short one, and what is

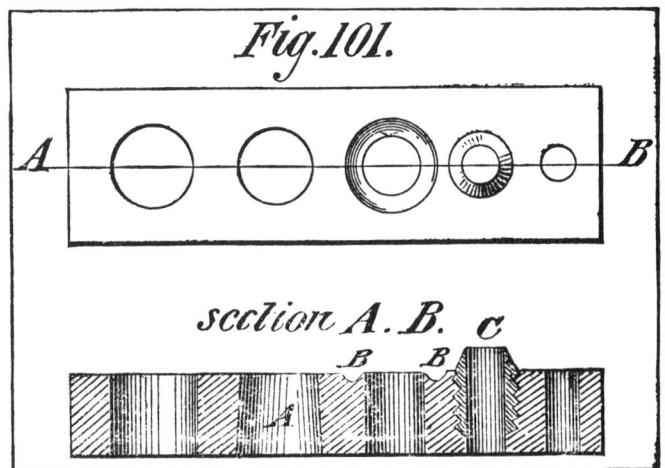

Fig. 101.

A   B

section A. B. c

left over will serve for a future occasion.   A useful tool for
preparing pin stuff is illustrated in Fig. 101, which repre-

sents a hardened plate of steel, pierced with holes of the sizes of the pins usually required. The wood for the pins having been planed up to the required size, is driven with a mallet through the plate, saving a great deal of time, and making the pins more nearly round than is possible by hand work. In some of these plates the holes are made taper, as shown at A, in Fig. 101; this, however, is detrimental, and the parallel hole is the best, because it guides and supports the stick, while it does not impede the cutting action of the tool. A hollow formed around the edge of the hole, as shown in the sectional view, at B B, would improve that action; or it might be still further improved by inserting bushes in the plate, with a portion left projecting above the plate and beveled off to resemble a chisel, as shown at C.

The pin stuff being prepared and inserted into one half of the pattern, the projecting end is then tapered off, as shown in Fig. 102. The formation of this projecting pin may seem a very simple matter; but if sufficient consideration is not given to it, a great deal of annoyance is caused to the molder, and the castings will

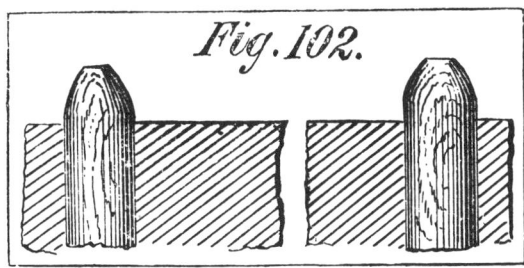

Fig. 102.

be imperfect. If we reflect for what purpose these pins are inserted, we shall find the proper shape. First, with regard to the projecting length, some workmen seem to be guided by the diameter of the pin, making it project to a distance equal to its diameter; but it is obvious that a short peg or pin will govern the position as well as a long one, and will be less liable to stick in the loose half of the pattern: hence it is better to let the protruding end stand out from three sixteenths to one half inch, and let from one sixteenth to one eighth inch of the large part fit the hole, the nut being tapered off so as to be sure that the pin can be released easily. These conditions inevitably bring us to the parabolic form shown in Fig. 102. Another point to be observed is to make the pin of as large a diameter as is consistent with the work; for the larger the pin, the longer it will remain free from shake. Above all, it is essential that the pin be perfectly round at the part that fits the hole; and if these elements are neglected, castings will be produced of which the halves will not match, which is always very unsightly. Nothing is gained by making the pins to a tight fit in the loose half of the pattern, as they will not work that way; and the molder will enlarge the holes with a red hot rod, and then, after a little while, the charred part around the hole falls out, and the pin becomes too slack.

After inserting our pins, the two halves of our patterns are to be fastened firmly together; and this may be readily done by brushing the end faces with hot glue for a breadth of one half or one inch, according to the amount we have allowed our pieces to be larger than the finished work. Then we hold them firmly together with a screw clamp, leaving them until they are perfectly dry. If there is not time for the gluing, the two halves may be screwed

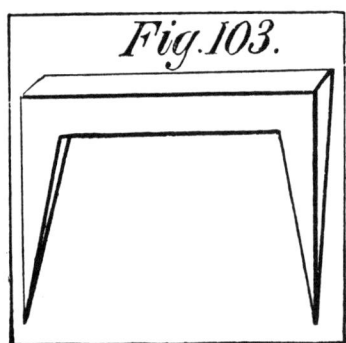

Fig. 103.

together; and indeed, if the job be a heavy one, it will not be safe to trust entirely to glue, but to use screws or dogs. Dogs are a kind of square staple, made of steel, and of the form shown in Fig. 103; and two of them driven in each end of a pattern will hold its loose halves very firmly together. While very handy, however, on large or small work, they are cumbrous; and the gluing or screwing is preferable. The work can now be mounted in the lathe, and turned as though it were solid. Care must be taken that the center points are exactly in the joint, and it was to ascertain if this was the case that our two halves were planed of equal thickness; for if, in the process of turning, one flat is seen to be narrower than the other, as shown in Fig. 104, at A B, it is proof that the centers are not in the joint; and unless the error is corrected, one half of the finish-ed pattern would be thicker than the other. To remedy this error,

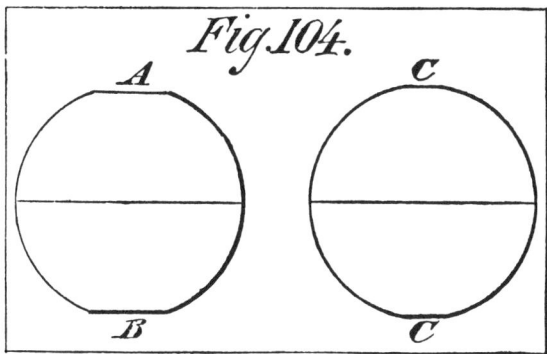

Fig. 104.

we tap at the pattern lightly with a hammer in the requir-ed direction, and then screw up the lathe centers a little more, continuing the process until the flat sides upon the pattern, when very nearly trued up—as shown in Fig. 104, at C C—are equal, and finally disappear simultaneously.

Our pattern being then turned and sand-papered, as already directed, the next proceeding is to stop up all holes or cracks that are not desired to appear, with either bees-wax or putty. This is a simple process, but it may have been noticed that some workmen take a much longer time over it than others, at least when beeswax is the stopping material. One who is expert at this work guesses just the proper amount necessary for each hole or crack; then he forms the wax into a worm-like shape, and with a warm chisel (that is not hot enough to make the wax run but only to cut it easily) he presses the wax into the hole, and seldom leaves any surplus to remove. The same knack is necessary in filleting, that is, in filling in an internal square sharp corner, when it is thought too small to be filled in with wood; for if the worm or string of wax of the right size be laid along the corner, the pressure of a warmed gouge will cause it to expand to the required fillet; while if too much wax is inserted, much time will be occupied in trimming off the surplus.

The third and last of the finishing processes is the application of two or more coats of spirit varnish, which adds to the appearance of the pattern, and increases its durability by giving it a surface impervious to water, and by producing that smoothness so necessary for its easy extraction from the sand. A varnished pattern escapes much of the rough usage commonly bestowed upon patterns, because the molder does not rap it so much as he otherwise would do. Several thin coats of varnish give a much finer appearance than fewer and thicker ones. The first coat fills up the pores of the wood and fixes the fibrous projections left by the sand-paper; and after the first coat is dry, fine sand-paper is again applied to remove the fibers so fixed. The second and succeeding coats give the gloss.

The pattern maker invariably mixes his own varnish, which he does in the following manner: The varnish pot should be of stone, and not of iron, which would discolor the varnish. The cover should be of thick leather, having through the middle a hole of such size that the brush handle, forced through it, will be suspended, and will not pass through to the bottom of the pot. The object of making the cover of leather is that the varnish collects around the lid and sticks the cover down, requiring sometimes so much force to remove it that wood would be liable to split. In the pot is placed so much shellac, and there is added just sufficient alcohol to cover the shellac, the whole being occasionally stirred with a piece of stick, and not with the brush. The consistence should be that of raw linseed oil; and to hasten the mixing, a little warmth may be applied.

The color of the varnish used is, strictly speaking, optional. The usual plan, however, is to use clear varnish for the pattern, and black for core prints and the insides of core boxes, which thus distinguishes them. The black is made by adding the best dry ivory black to the clear varnish. A very durable varnish may be made by adding powdered oxide of iron to the clear varnish, which gives a hard varnish with a reddish brown color. In mixing colored varnishes, however, we must remember, that the lighter the pigment, the easier they work. Ivory black is the lightest pigment, and so always pervades the varnish, and does not readily settle to the bottom; hence it does not often require stirring. Oxide of iron requires frequent stirring, even in the course of varnishing one pattern, if it be a large one; because it settles so rapidly that a perceptible difference in the coat is apparent, unless the varnish is stirred previously to each insertion of the brush. The brush should never go to the bottom of the pot, and the pot should always be kept covered when not in actual use. Varnishing lathe work cannot be done while running the lathe; but after the work is varnished, running the lathe hastens the drying. Work should always, if possible, be varnished on a dry day; for if the air is damp, the varnish becomes what is technically termed chilled — that is, it assumes a soapy or milky appearance, as though it had absorbed water — and hence is spotty when dry.

Having thus finished our example, we may now explain the process of putting pins in patterns, which we omitted to do when speaking upon that subject, to avoid digression. There are many cases in which it is not suitable for the pin hole to show on the outside of the pattern; and again, in large work, the holes would require to be bored so deep, and the pins made so long, that it would be too elaborate an affair altogether. In such circumstances, lines are resorted to, being drawn in the following manner: Place the

5**

pieces side by side, with the planed edges touching **and**
the ends fair, as shown in Fig. 105, the line, G, representing
the edges; and make two fine notches at A B.   Then separate the pieces, **and square the very fine lines, C C, D D,**

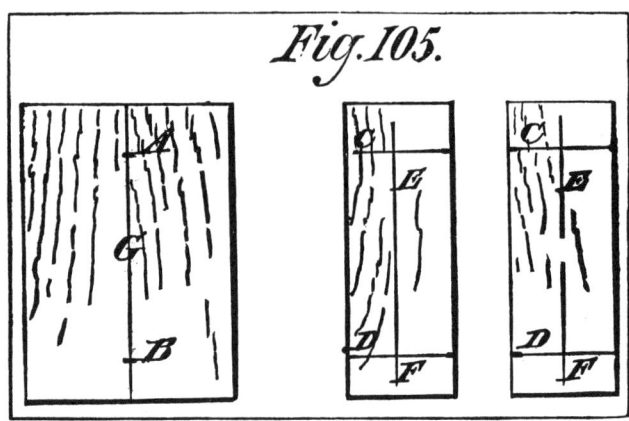

Fig. 105.

across with a knife.   Then set **a gage to half the width of**
the pieces, and mark the intersecting lines, E F; and the
centers for the respective pin holes will be the intersection
of the lines, C E and D F.   If, however, we have no planed
edge to work from, and the job is of such size as to in-
volve so much labor as not to admit of planing, we may take
two small brads or finishing nails (or as many as we desire
to have pins), and drive them almost entirely into one piece
of the wood, in the spots where the pins are ultimately to
be, and then file the projecting part of each to a point. By
then resting the other half in its proper relative position
upon the filed points, and, when adjusted, applying a little
pressure to it, the nail points will enter the top piece and
mark the corresponding centers for the holes to receive the
pins.   We may then extract the brads or nails, and proceed to bore the holes and insert the pins.

Another method of marking the pin holes, is to provide
some ordinary lead shot, and make shallow holes with **a**
brad-awl, slightly less in diameter than the shot.   **Where**

pins are to be inserted, place the shot in the hole, so that they project beyond the surface, and then proceed as described for the brad points—the latter being the more expeditious method of the two.

Our second example, Fig. 106, is a design for another kind of gland, such as is often fitted to glands for pump rods and spindles. For the small sizes, the glands are usually cast solid, and the hole is drilled out in the lathe;

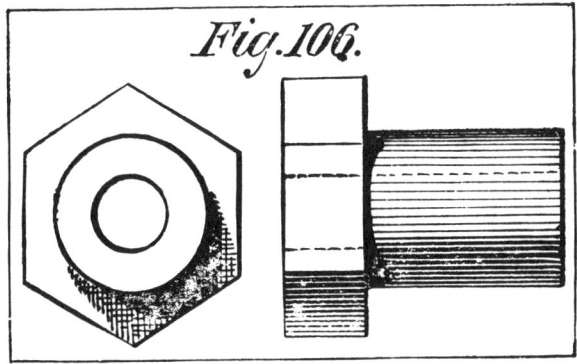

Fig. 106.

in which case, providing the gland is not very deep, it would be molded vertically, with the head in the nowel, and would be turned out of the solid piece of wood in the style of our previous example, treating for the moment the hexagonal part as a flange, whose diameter must be turned to the size of the hexagon across the corners. After the turning is done, we mark the hexagon as follows. We set a pair of compasses as nearly as possible to the radius of the turned piece that is to form the hexagon, and divide that piece off into six divisions, in the manner shown in Fig. 107—for the radius of a circle will divide its circumference into six equal parts—so that, if the compasses are correctly set, one trial will be sufficient; but if not, we must readjust the compasses, and go around again. Then, from these points, we square lines, as shown in Fig. 107, at 1, 2, 3, 4, 5, 6; and then, with the paring chisel, we pare off the sides to the lines. It is not necessary to actually draw the hexagon on the circumference, by joining the lines of division on the top of the flange; for a straight edge being applied as the paring proceeds, will be all that is necessary to produce a true hexagon. Nevertheless it is possible

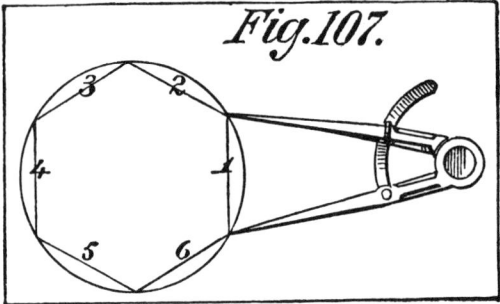

that error may have crept in, though we have performed the above operation with the greatest of care; it is therefore imperative upon us to apply correcting tests to our work, such as a pair of calipers, to try if each pair of the opposite sides are parallel; also the bevel, to verify if each angle of the figure contains 120°. Hexagon shapes are so common that a special hexagon gage is very useful; and such a gage, of the most approved form, is shown in Fig.

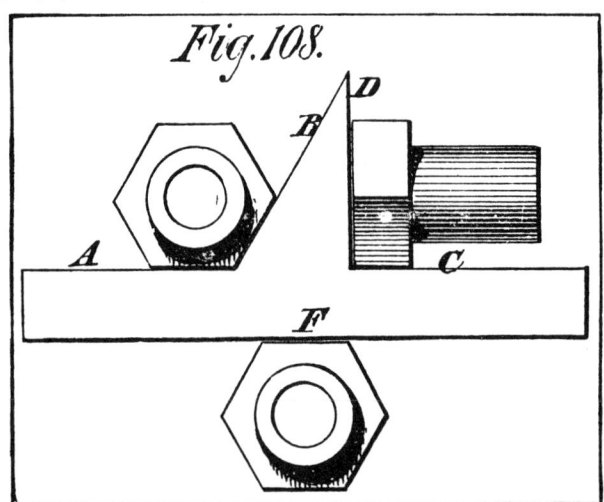

108, together with its method of application, the edges, A B, being to try the hexagon, and C D to square the edge to the face, and the edge, F, being used as a straight edge. If, however, we have not such a gage, we may set the bevel square, shown in Fig. 23, in the following manner: Take a piece of board, planed on one side and on one edge, and let A B, in Fig. 109, represent the planed edge, from which we mark with the gage the line, C D. Then taking any point, such as I, in the line C D, as a center, at a convenient distance, we describe with a pair of compasses the arc, F G. We then take the compasses, and, without shifting their points at all, we rest one point on the intersection of the lines, C D and F G, and then mark the arc, H. If then we draw a line from the intersection of the arc, F G, and the arc, H, to the center, I, upon which the arc, F G, has struck, the lines, H I, I C, form the angle required; and we may apply the stock of the bevel square to the planed edge, A B, and set the blade to the line, I H, as denoted by the dotted lines. The bevel being set, we test the work as it proceeds, first cutting down one hexagonal side, and then applying the bevel to gage the angle of the others; and as the diametrically opposite sides are finished, we apply the calipers. The lines of division upon all good pattern work are made very fine, in fact, merely distinguishable; and the instrument by which they are

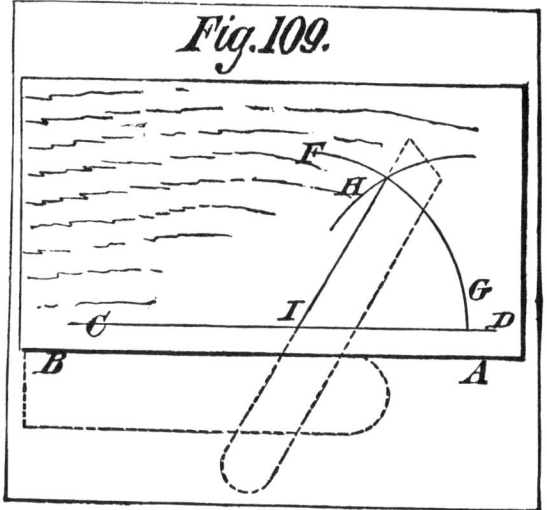

Fig. 109.

drawn is shown in Fig. 110. It is called a cutting scriber, and the end at A is beveled off at both sides, like a skew chisel, forming a knife edge. The end, B, is ground to a point, and both ends are finished on an oilstone. The point end is for drawing lines along the grain, while the cutting edge, A, is for drawing lines across the grain of the wood. The wooden handle in the center is to enable the operator

Fig. 110.

to hold it more firmly. It sometimes happens that the size of the hexagon is given across the flat sides instead of over the angle; and when that is so, we proceed as follows: We describe upon a piece of board, as in Fig. 111, a circle of a diameter equal to the given distance between the flat sides. We then take a hexagon gage, or else set the bevel square to an angle of 120°; and applying it to the planed edge of the board, we draw the line, C D, in Fig. 111, in which figure A is the circle of the size of the flat sides of

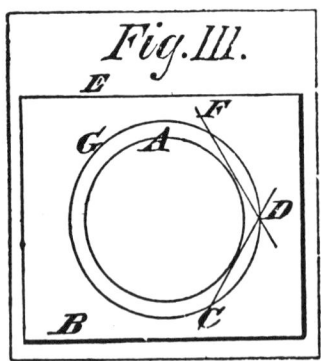

Fig. 111.

Fig. 112.

the hexagon, and B E are the planed edges of the board. We next reverse the bevel; and from the opposite edge of the board we strike the line, F D, cutting C D at the point D, where both the lines cut the circumference of the circle, A. Then from the center of the circle A, we draw the circle G, intersecting the point D. The diameter of G will be the size of the hexagon across the corners.

If the gland is a long one, it will be better to make it in halves, letting it part across two corners, as shown in Fig. 112. When a gland of this kind is made in halves, the corners at the parting are liable, from their weakness, to chip off, and it is therefore proper to make it **of hard wood.**

CHAPTER VI.

Our next example is what is called a T, a drawing for which is shown in Fig. 113. It is shown with flanges on the main body, and a hexagon on the branch. Sometimes a flange is employed instead of the hexagon, but this de-

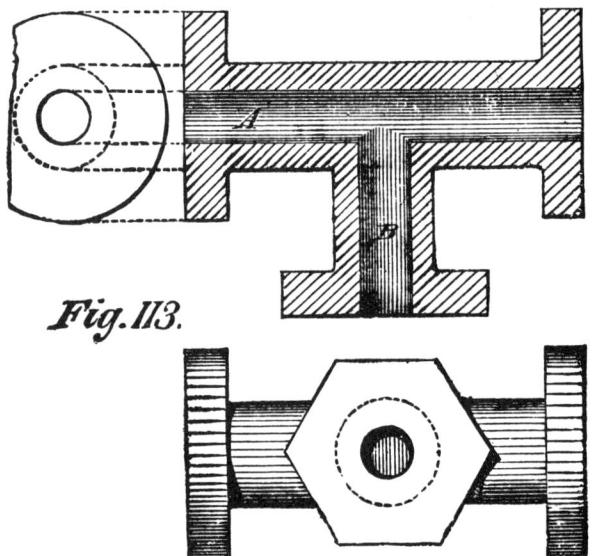

Fig. 113.

pends upon the connections to which it is to be attached. Patterns of this class are often made so that either round flanges or hexagonal connections may be put on at will; and it is in that style that we propose to make our example. It is apparent that the pattern will be the most easily molded with its body and branch both lying horizontally in the mold; so that, if we suppose the surface of this paper to represent the surface of the mold, the engraving shows just how the pattern will lie in it. It will be advisable, there-fore, to make the pattern in halves.

We first prepare the body and flanges, in the same manner as described for the body of our gland; the only difference being that we have, in this case, to fit a flange on each end. The same method is pursued in making the branch, with the exception that we only require a core print on one end, the other end abutting against the body. The first question that arises is, How long shall we make the branch? and this depends upon how far the branch follows the curvature of the body. In our example, the branch and body are of the same diameter, and therefore the branch will follow exactly half way around the body. We turn up the branch piece, then, to its requisite diameter, and make its length equal to the diameter to which it should stand out from the body, added to half the diameter of the body. The pieces we have made, then, are those shown in Fig. 114, in which A represents the piece for the body, and B, the piece for the branch. Our next proceeding is to cut

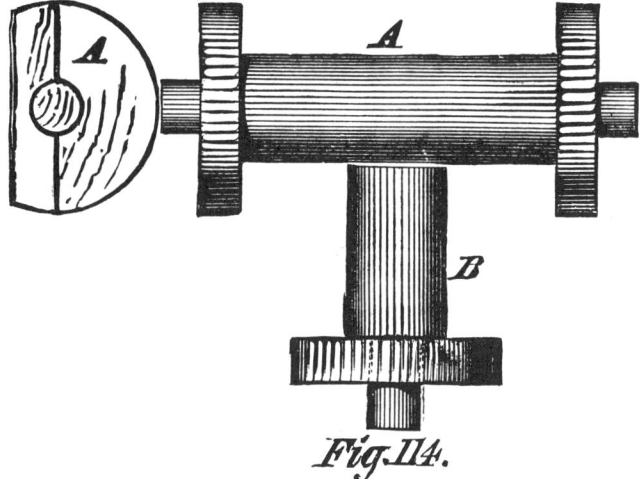

Fig. 114.

out the abutting end of the branch to fit to the curvature of the body, and this we perform as follows: We first set the bevel square to an angle of 45°, by the process shown in Fig. 109, and then, taking the branch halves apart, and

6

placing the bevel square with its back across the end **face** of the branch (the blade lying on the joint face of the half branch), we mark the two lines, A B, in Fig. 115, which

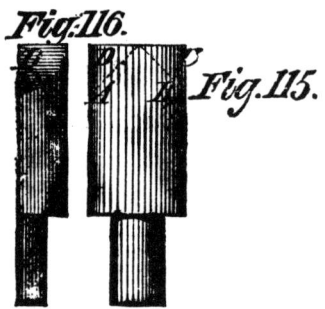

Fig. 116.

Fig. 115.

must meet exactly in the center of the branch and at the extreme end, as shown in Fig. 116. We then pare off the angular piece, C D, down to the lines, A B. If, before we do the paring, however, we give our half branch a quarter turn around, it will appear as shown in Fig. 116; the curve formed by the intersection of the plane surface (just made) with the round surface of the piece, is the true curve of the body of the T.

Turning to the other half of the branch, we perform upon it the same operation ; and we may then cut away with the gouge the intervening timber from between the curve lines. Our two halves will be of the proper curve at the end, to fit exactly to the body of the T, as shown in Fig. 117, in

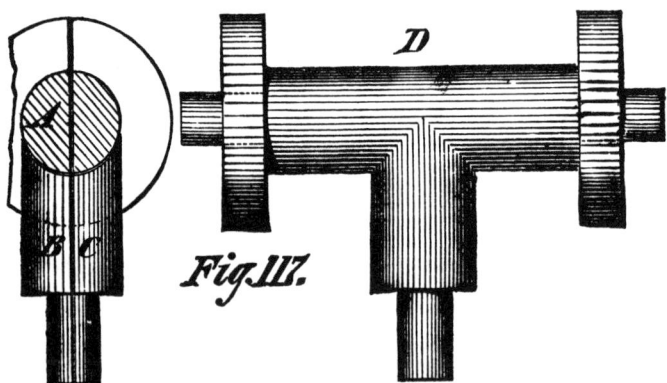

Fig. 117.

which A represents a sectional view of the body of the T, and B C are the two halves of the branch ; while the view D shows the body of the T lying horizontally, with the branch attached.

We have now to fasten the branch to the body of the **T**; and here we must pause to consider whether the pattern is required to serve simply for the production of a few castings; whether it is to be cast aside after the first casting, never to be used again (which is often the case), or whether it is intended for standard or continuous use. For a temporary purpose, a few screws will be sufficient; but for a permanent pattern, a much stronger joint may be made as follows: Brush with hot glue the ends of the branch piece, and let them stand until the glue has been absorbed into the pores of the wood. This is called sizing, and is always necessary in gluing end wood, as it is called—meaning the end grain of wood. The reason that sizing is in that case necessary is, that the pores of the wood all meet the surface in the end grain, and the sizing is necessary to fill them. We then take a truly planed piece of board, and lay one half of the body down upon it, placing a piece of thin paper between the body and the board, so that any glue that may run out may not touch the board : otherwise it may glue the work so fast to the board that, in parting them, some of the fibers of the wood may get torn out. Then we fasten temporarily the half body to the board, and lay one half of the branch with its flat surface on the same board, and glue it to its place, drawing it well up to the body piece with dogs or clamps, at the same time observing that it is

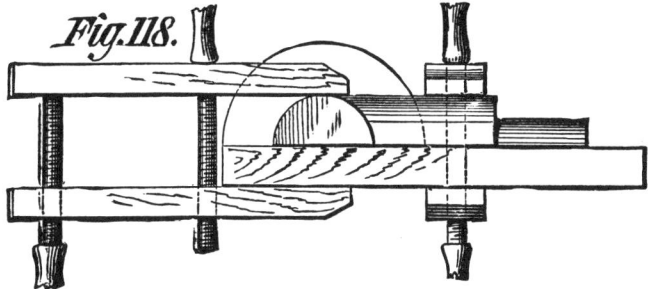

Fig. 118.

close down to the board, and fixing it temporarily there, as shown in Fig. 118, and allowing it to remain until the glue is dry. In putting on the second half of the branch, **the** board need not be used, since the first half, already in position, will serve as a guide. A piece of paper must, however, be placed between the two halves of the branch, to prevent them from adhering together. When all is dry, put a strong screw in the position denoted at A, in Fig. 119, cut out a recess on the flat face of each half, and let in a

Fig. 119.

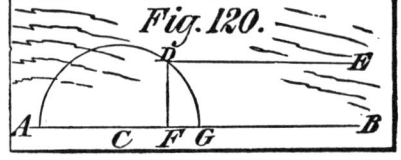

piece of hard wood, as shown by the dotted lines in the same figure.

Let us now suppose that, in our example, the diameter of the branch had been smaller than that of the body of the T. In that case we must first ascertain its proper length by the process illustrated in Fig. 120, which represents a piece of board, upon which we strike the line A B ; and from the point C, we make the semicircle D, which must be of the same radius as the body of the pattern. Then, parallel with the line A B, we draw the line D E—the distance between these two lines being equal to half the

Fig. 120.

diameter of the branch of the pattern. Then from the junction of the line D E with the semicircle D, we strike the line D F, at a right angle to A B ; and then from F to G, added to the distance which the branch requires to stand out from the edge of the body, is the length we require to make the branch.

To draw the curve on this branch so as to cut it out to fit the body, we proceed as follows : Fig. 121 represents the application of a peculiar trammel, designed for this and similar purposes. It enables the operator to strike a true circle upon a round or uneven surface. It is composed of the turned bar or rod of metal, A, of about half an inch diameter, and upon it slides the piece of brass tube, B, upon which is contrived a support for the sliding arm, C, as well as a set screw for fastening the arm, C, in any desired position. At the end of the arm, C, is placed an arrangement for fastening the scriber, D, so that we may set the scriber at any requisite distance from the rod,

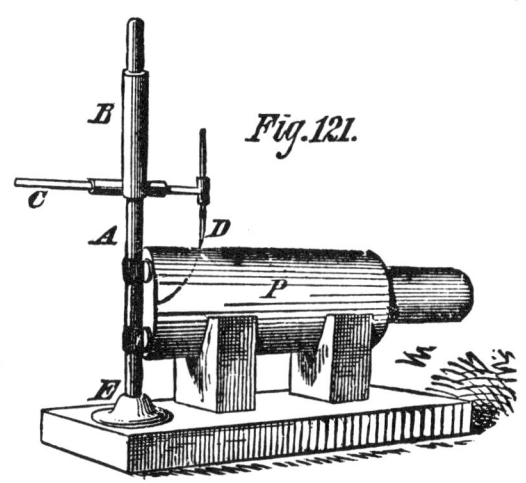

A, by adjusting and fastening the arm, C, and revolve it about while lifting or lowering it upon the rod, A. When properly made, this is a most useful tool; and if not in use, it may be taken apart in an instant, and it occupies but very little room in a tool box. If the stand, E, pierced with holes for screwing down, is provided, it will be a very useful addition, but it may be dispensed with; whereas the tool proper, or some improvised substitute for it, is absolutely necessary, for the curve must be struck somehow. If the pipe or branch is large—say even six inches in diameter—to attempt to fit it by guessing and trying, is the work of a novice and not of a workman. To apply this tool to our branch, we proceed as follows: Taking a planed board, we gage a line upon it, and at a point on this line we describe

a circle upon it of the size of the foot of the instrument. We then make two V blocks, such as shown in Fig. 122, to carry the branch. We then place these V blocks with the apex of the V exactly over the gaged line, and place the branch in the V's. We then set the point of the scriber at a distance from the rod of the trammel equal to the diameter of the branch, which may be readily done if the size of the rod be known. We next mark upon the top of the branch, as it lays in the V's (with the joint of the two halves standing vertically), the distance it requires to be cut out to form the curve, which distance will correspond to the distance of F G, in Fig. 120. We then draw the branch forward, until this mark falls exactly under the scriber, keeping the joint faces vertical; and this adjustment being made, we fix temporarily the branch to the piece of board whereon it and the V's rest. Then we move the arm, C, in Fig. 121, a half circle; and letting the point of the scriber contact with the branch, we draw the necessary line. It will be found, however, that it is requisite to mark the lines while lifting the arm, to prevent the scriber from digging into the wood. Thus one side of the branch will be marked, and we must then turn it upside down on the V's, set the joint vertically again, adjust the mark to the scriber point, and proceed as before to mark the other side of the branch. We may then cut out the corners to the lines, which may be most rapidly performed by a band saw, sawing exactly to the line—the branch being held on a board, as it was when being marked. In fact, a piece of wood should be fitted underneath, where the saw cut will come, so as to

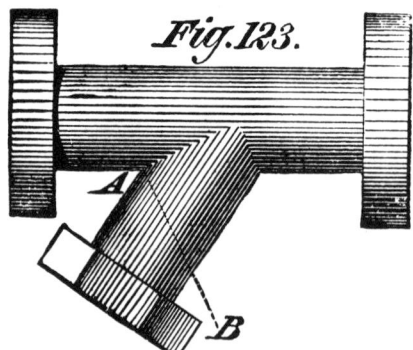

Fig. 123.

prevent the fibers of the wood from being torn out at the edge, showing a ragged cut—as it is very apt to do, especially if the band saw is not in first-class order.

Should the branch be required to stand obliquely to the body of the pattern, as shown in Fig. 123, it may be struck out in the same manner; but instead of being set square with the rod of the trammel, as in the former case, it must be set at the bevel at which it is to be fixed upon the body of the pattern. When marking one side, the branch must make an angle with the upright equal to the angle at A, in Fig. 123; while, when marking the other side, it must form an angle equal to that at B, in the same figure. It will pay, where two or three pattern makers are employed, to have this marking apparatus always standing ready for use upon a board, with the degrees of angles marked thereon; so that a workman could mark off his job in five minutes, and cut it out with a band saw. Cutting out with a gouge, and trying to its place, may take four or five hours. It must be borne in mind that too much care cannot be given to striking out the piece accurately, and to sawing them true to the lines. The saw must be sharp, and of a width suitable to the curve, and not tremble, or " dither," as band sawers say. By attending to these matters, a fit may be obtained with a minimum of labor to the workman ; and this is desirable in itself, and is an item of profit in the cost of the pattern.

We need not dwell upon the half core box, which is necessary for this pattern if the branch stands at a right angle to the body ; or the full one, necessary if it is required to stand obliquely. When the body of the T is much larger in diameter than is the branch, we may joint the two in a simpler way, which, so long as it does not entail a great weakening of the body, will be found more advantageous than the method described. This simpler method is : Having found the amount of the length of the branch necessary to allow for curvature of the body (by the process shown

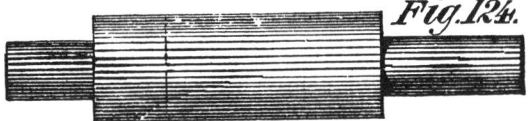

Fig.124.

in Fig. 116), we turn upon the branch end an additional projection or stem, as shown in Fig. 124, somewhat smaller in diameter than the branch itself; and we then cut in the body a recess to receive the branch and turned stem or projection, which recess may be either cut out with a gouge or turned out in the lathe, the latter being, for obvious reasons, the best method. For this latter operation, we take a chuck, similar to that described in Fig. 58, as a

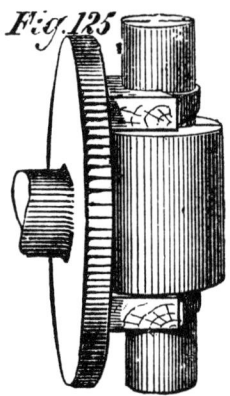

Fig. 125.

cement chuck; and having verified that the point and the face of the chuck run quite true, we draw a center line across it, set the apexes of the two V blocks exactly over this line, and then fasten them. Having marked upon the body the center of the branch, we find a point diametrically opposite to it upon the body, and place the body so that the steel center point enters the point so found, at the same time as the body rests in the V's.

We then fix it in this position by thin straps of hoop-iron, or any other contrivance that will not project so as to prevent the lathe rest (or tool rest, as it may be more properly termed) from being brought close to the work. The work must be securely screwed to the chuck, on account of the high velocity of the lathe in turning. To cut out the recess, we commence by placing a center bit in the back lathe center, and boring a hole, as large as convenient and very nearly to the required depth. A screw bit is not available for this purpose, for it would in many cases be right through the work before there was time to stop the lathe, which is not usually sufficiently under control. We may next take a turning tool, and turn out the recess to fit the end of the branch; and after taking the job from the lathe, we fasten each half of the branch by gluing and screws. In connection with this method, there is yet another advantage: it is, that by cutting away the body instead of the branch, it renders us indifferent as to whether the shape of the body be spherical, as in a globe valve, or elliptical, or even vase-shaped : because, in this case, the shape adds nothing to the difficulty of the job. Should it occur that one end of the T is larger than the other, we may find the height necessary for each of the V pieces (whereon the body rests during the turning process) as follows : Draw upon a piece of board the line A D, in Fig. 126, which will represent the plane of the chuck ; and let the point C represent the center point of the lathe. Then, from C, we square up the line D ; and we set the compasses to the radius of the body of the pattern at the center of the place where the branch is to be. We take a radius

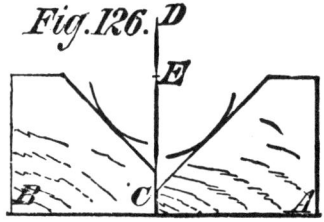

from C, and about $\frac{1}{16}$ inch up from the line A B, and with this radius we mark on the line D, the point E. From this point, as a center, we strike the axes, E and F, whose radii correspond to the unequal sizes of the pattern, where the V's are required to be. Then we draw tangents to each of these arcs, and complete the forms of the V blocks, as shown in Fig. 127, in which half of each V block is shown.

We have now to make a core box for our T; and for clearness of illustration we will make the drawing somewhat larger than those for the T itself. Fig. 127 represents three views of the core box; that portion which projects below the line, at B, may be made separately, and need not, therefore, be given any consideration. Having drawn the plan of the box, as shown in Fig. 127 at 1, we draw the end and side views, as shown at 2 and 3, and divide these latter into courses of a thickness to suit the stuff at hand, from which the core box is to be made. The courses may be made of equal or unequal depth. Courses 1 and 2 are got out of the full size of the box, while courses

6*

3 and 4 must be of the length of the box, but **their width** will differ according to the curvature of the half circle of the core, as shown in Fig. 127, at 2 and 3; 5 and 6 will be similar to 3 and 4, and may be marked from them. All

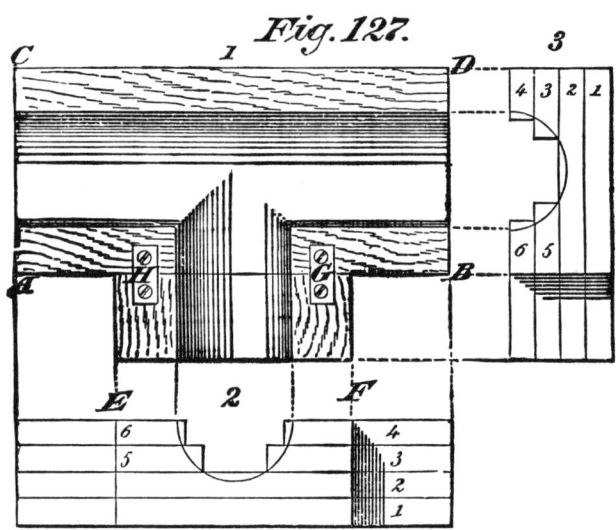

Fig. 127.

these pieces must be planed to a true surface and glued together, each course being allowed to dry before the next one is put on; but for greater expedition, nails, in addition to the glue, may be used, in which case care must be taken that they do not come so close as to interfere with the cutting out of the half circle. The part A B, if very short, say under 3 inches, may be made in one piece; but if over 3 inches and not over 6 inches, we take two pieces of the required length and width, and of half the thickness, and chuck them in the manner previously explained for making flanges in halves; then we place the work in the lathe, and bore a hole for the core, then take them from the chuck and glue them, first together and next to the body of the core box. We next turn the body part of the core to a semicircle of the required size, and all that will then remain to be cut is that part of the branch that is above the line A B. If, however, the part below A B, in Fig. 127, should be required still longer, then it had better be built up in the same manner as the other part. The lengths of the pieces forming the courses will be the same, and may be measured on Fig. 127., from A B outwards. The widths will differ, and may be measured from E or F, inwards. This separate portion, from the grain of the wood being enduric, cannot be firmly fixed to the main body of the box with glue; we must, therefore, in addition, place battens below the box, and let in pieces of hard wood or metal above, as represented in Fig. 127, at **G and H.**

CHAPTER VII.

WHEEL AND PULLEY WORK.

Our fourth example is a double flanged pulley, shown in section in Fig. 128; and our first consideration is, how it shall be molded. It evidently should lie in the sand in

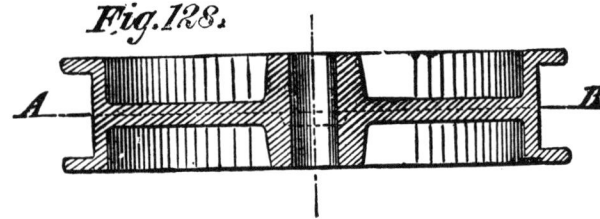

the position shown in Fig. 129; but it will be observed that the sand is confined between two flanges, rendering it practically impossible to retract the pattern from the

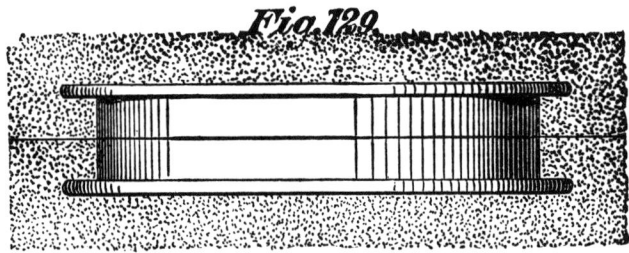

mold, if it is made in one piece. We say practically impossible, meaning that it cannot be done economically; for strictly speaking, an expert molder with every requisite appliance, can mold almost anything, as any one will conclude who examines the various works of art in bronze which appear in art exhibitions and elsewhere. Our pattern must, for ease of molding, be made in two parts. If the disk (or spokes, if it be a spoke-wheel) be sufficiently thick to allow it, the division may be made at the center, that is to say, on the line A P, in Fig. 128. The operation of the molder may be understood from Fig. 129, three distinct beds of sand being necessary. It may be that a part of a flask is used for each bed, or it may be arranged as shown in Fig. 129, it being a matter of indifference to the pattern maker. In either case, however, draught should be allowed both inside and outside, that is to say, both the interior and exterior diameters of the pattern should be made smallest at the line of parting, the diameters increasing slightly as they approach the flanges. The hubs also should, in like manner, be slightly tapered. Inside sharp corners should be avoided; they should, in fact, always be rounded by cutting them out with a round-nosed tool. To construct this pattern, we proceed as follows: For a small pattern, we take two pieces, somewhat thicker than half the thickness of the finished pattern, and large enough to allow for turning. We then chuck them, as shown in **Fig.** 130, and turn them up. The recesses, shown at the

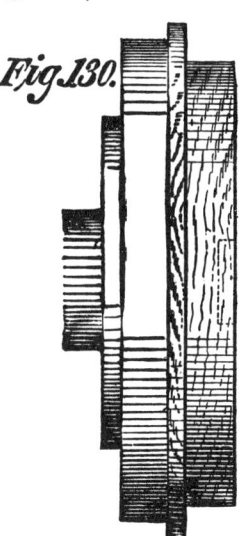

Fig. 130.

center by the dotted lines, must be made of equal size in the halves of the pattern; and we prepare a chuck with a projection across the center to fit into the recess, and thus rechuck the pieces, and turn out the opposite sides, cutting the hubs out of the solid. We may then fit a plug into the recess in one half of the pattern, and glue it fast, allowing it to project so as to fit into the recess in the other half; and the pattern is complete, unless the hole in the hub is to be cored, in which case it will be necessary to fix core prints on the top and bottom, in the manner described in our first example.

A useful hint may here be given to the effect that **when** it is decided to fix prints in the center of a piece of turned work, a slight recess may be made to receive the print, which is then sure to stand true; and should it at any time get accidentally knocked off, as prints often do, another may be immediately affixed without the trouble of finding the center.   The pattern now supposed to be made, though good enough for many purposes, has one great defect which will be readily perceived when we bear in mind our remarks on the properties of timber.   It is, that it will gradually be-**come** oval; and to avoid this, we must have **recourse to**

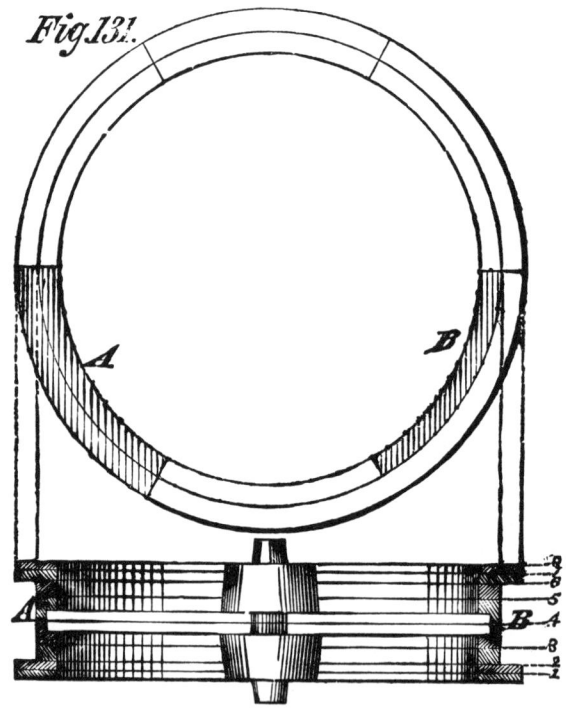

Fig.131.

what is termed building up, a process which must in any event be used, if the pattern is a large one.   To build up such a pattern, we proceed as follows : After drawing the pulley in section and in plan, as shown in Fig. 131, we divide the whole height of the section into courses, the number of courses being regulated so as to have each of a convenient thickness. It is advisable, however, to have at least two courses in the flange, which will greatly increase its strength. After dividing one of the circles in the plan view into six parts, we draw lines from the points of division to the center, as shown; and then we make a template of one division, as shown at A, which must be made a little larger than the division, and this forms a template whereby to cut out the segments forming the courses which make up the flanges. A similar template, cut out somewhat larger than the space devoted to B, in Fig. 131, will serve to cut out the sections to be used in forming the body of the pattern. The flanges being made in two courses each, and there being six sections in each course, we shall require 26 pieces of the size of the large template; and allowing each half of the body likewise to consist of two courses, we shall require the same number, to form the body of the pattern, of the size of the small template.

Our templates being made, we plane up some pieces of board a trifle thicker than the courses are intended to be. It is easier to plane up the pieces of the board while yet square, than to plane up the segments separately. From the template, with a black lead pencil, we mark off on the planed pieces of board the requisite number of segments, and cut them out with a band or jig saw. We now proceed to building up, for which purpose we employ a chuck as a base whereon to build. It will save time, however, to have two chucks, building one half of the pattern on each, and both halves simultaneously, which will give sufficient time for each course to dry, without requiring nails or pegs to assist the glue in holding them together. The two chucks having been prepared, we glue to them strips of paper at intervals where the points of the segments will come, as shown in Fig. 132; and if the segments are very long, we glue another strip between each of these strips, so that the segment may lie level on the chuck. As the building proceeds, the end of each segment must be planed; and for this purpose, we require what is called a shooting board, which is a simple

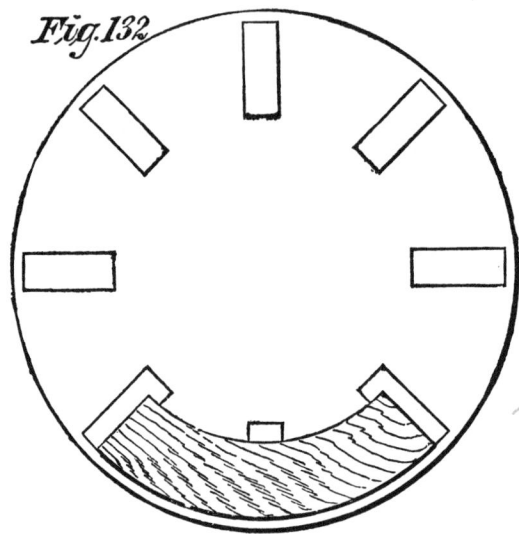

Fig. 132.

contrivance, made in the following manner: We take a piece of board about 2 feet long, 8 or 9 inches wide, and nearly 1 inch thick, and also a piece of the same length, but 6 inches wide, and $\frac{5}{8}$ inch thick; and after planing them up straight, we screw one to the other, as shown in Fig. 133, at A B. S is a raised piece called a stop, and it should be recessed about $\frac{3}{8}$ inch into B, and dovetailed. It should not be glued, as the shooting board is useful for other purposes besides dressing segments: and it may be necessary to change the stop for one of a different height. In Fig. 133, the segment is shown in position for being dressed; while in Fig. 132 *a*, the truing plane is shown lying upon its side, in which position it works along the board, guided by the piece B.

The shooting board, made as above, when in use, lies upon the bench, butting against the bench stop, B G.

In cases, however, where the space is confined, the work bench being small, the shooting board may be worked lying across the bench, providing the stop, C, be affixed to it. The use of the shooting board, then, is to plane the end of each segment to its necessary length and angle; and having so dressed one segment, we glue it to the pieces of paper on the chuck, upon which a circle of the necessary diameter has been marked, as a guide whereby to set the first course of segments. We must not forget, while gluing the segment to the pieces of paper on the chuck, to give the ends of the segment a coat of glue for sizing, as explained in a previous example. Our next segment we treat in a

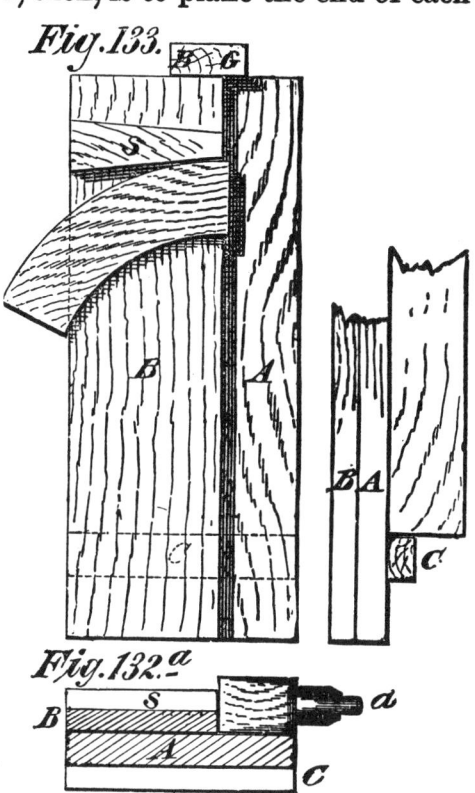

Fig.133.

Fig.132.

precisely similar manner, save that, while gluing it to the chuck, we also glue it on the ends, so that it shall be sized at one end, and glued at the other to the segment already glued to the chuck, the object of the end gluing being to strengthen the building, and at the same time to prevent the corners of the segments from breaking out during the process of turning them in the lathe. As each segment is glued to its place, it should be clamped or weighted down, so as to expel the excess of glue, and also to prevent it from shifting while its neighbor is being butted against it.

6**

Having completed one course (which will, of course, be one of those intended for the flange), and allowed sufficient time for the glue to dry, we put the chuck in the lathe, and true up by facing off this layer of segments to its proper thickness, making the face straight, and testing the same by using a chalked straight-edge to make the high places more plainly visible. We then true the diameter of the course.

Our work is at present fastened to the chuck by the glue only; and for small work, only two or three courses high, this will suffice. But if the work is large, one screw should be inserted through the chuck into each segment, about half way between the points; and even then, if we build far out from the chuck, it will be necessary, after a few more courses have been added, to replace these screws by longer ones, which may be done (without disturbing the work) by replacing them one by one. If screws are inadmissible by reason of the danger of splitting the segments (as is sometimes the case), we must adopt another method; and that is, to discard the paper, and glue an extra course of segments firmly to the chuck, this extra course being afterwards turned away, until cut through.

The second and consecutive courses of segments are built up in the same manner as the first, the planed faces of the segments being glued to the respective faced courses on the chuck, until we arrive at the last course in the half pattern; and into this the half spokes or disc, whichever it may be, must be recessed, as shown in Fig. 131. The hubs are to be turned in the lathe separately, with a short plug on the under side, to fit a slight recess turned in the disk. If it is preferred, the disk or spokes may be made solid, and fixed to one half of the pattern, the other half and its half hub being left loose.

As we have stated that this may be a spoke wheel, it will be as well to explain the operation of making and fit-

ting the spokes or arms. If the spokes are four in number, the process is very simple. We take two pieces of
timber long enough to reach across the wheel, and plane
them to the required thickness of arm, and have them
sufficiently wide to shape the hollows about the hub and
towards the rim. Then we make a mark with a pencil on
one side of each, which we call the face. We then set a
gage to half the thickness of the spoke, and with it mark
lines on both edges of each piece, always gaging from
the face side. We meet at the center of the length, cut a
recess out of each sufficiently wide and deep to admit the
other, so that the pieces, when put together, form a cross,
which we let into the wheel and fix temporarily with
brads. We now place the work in the lathe, and start
the lathe so as to find the center of the wheel, from which
center we draw out the arms, and then turn out the recess
to receive the hub. We mark the arms to their respective places in the rim, so as to be able to correctly replace
them, and then we take them out of the rim, and shape them
to their proper conformation. This being done, we glue
them to their places in the rim. In the case of six arms
being required, all these operations are similar, with the
exception that there are three pieces to be framed together for the spokes instead of two; and we proceed in
the following manner: We divide the thickness of any
one piece into three equal parts, and mark lines to these
equal divisions on the edges of all the pieces. These
gage lines need not extend the full length of the pieces,
but only for some distance, about the center of the length,
where it is expected the recess will be cut out. We next
gage center lines on the flat sides, and find the centers of
the length approximately. A, B, and C, in Fig. 134, represent our three pieces, which, when put together, are to
form the six arms. Setting the compasses to a radius of
one half the width of the pieces, we mark (from the centers

already found) circles on one side of the pieces A and C, and also on both sides of B. We next set a bevel square to an angle of 60°; and with this, set to touch the edge of the circle, we draw, on A and C, tangents crossing each other; and on the piece B, four such tangents, two on each side, must be marked. The piece A must now be recessed between one pair of tangents to a depth of two thirds of its thickness, and between the other pair to a depth of one third. B must be recessed on each side to a depth of one third its thickness; while on the piece C, the whole of the space included between the tangents must be cut away to the depth of two thirds. The recesses must be cut true to the lines, and level, a rabbet plane being useful for the purpose, unless the work is small; and if the job has been carefully executed, the pieces will fit

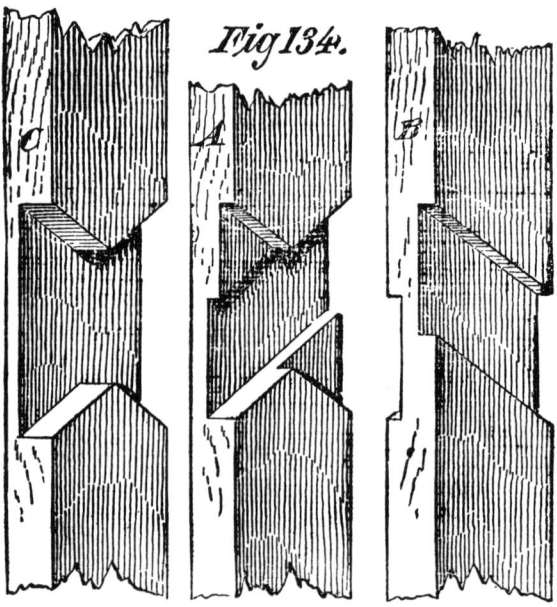

Fig 134.

right together, and may be glued without further labor. For an odd number of arms, such as 3, 5, or 7, the method of putting together is different, and is not so strong as the

foregoing. It is as follows: Upon a flat piece of board, fasten a piece of paper, and describe upon the latter a circle; then divide the circumference of the latter into as many equal parts as it is required to have arms, and draw lines from this center of the circle to the circumferential points of division, as shown in Fig. 135. Then bevel the

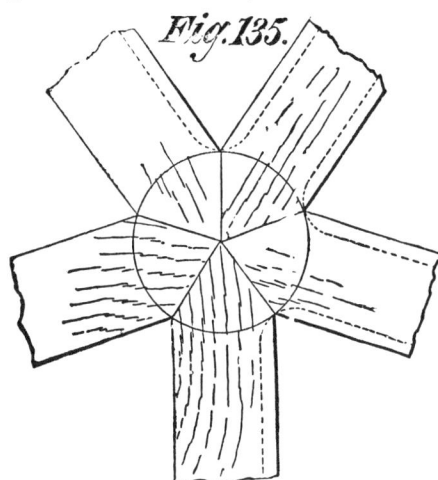

ends of the pieces equally on each side, so that each shall exactly cover its own division of the circle; and as each is fitted, fasten it temporarily down, and when all are fitted, verify the work as follows: Observe if the pieces are equidistant from one another, at an equal distance from the center of the circle, and at or near the extremities, when any error will be easily detected and rectified. Then glue the pointed ends all together, fastening each piece temporarily to the board, as before, and set the whole away, until it is quite dry, when the piece may be taken from the board, and the required form given to the arms, ready for finally fixing to the rim of the pattern.

In almost all cases it is necessary that wheels of this kind be provided with hubs; and by the attachment of the latter, the joints of the spokes at the center, when made as shown in Fig. 135, are very much strengthened. But in the rare event of having to put together such a combination of arms without hubs, it will be advisable to turn out a recess at the center, making it as large as practicable, and fitting into it a disk of hard wood. Before cutting out the spaces in the rim to receive the extremities of the arms, it is necessary to turn out that part of the rim to the finished size, as it will be inaccessible to the turning tool, when the arms are glued in. The arms being fitted to their places, and made fast to the rim, we proceed to turn all that can be got at—that is to say, the exterior diameter of the body of the half of the half-pattern, and also the flange. It is needless to add that each half of the pattern must be similarly treated.

The work is now to be reversed on the chuck, and the inside turned out, together with a recess at the center, to receive the hub. To maintain the two halves of the pattern in coincidence, two, and sometimes three or more, pegs are inserted in the arms of one half, which pegs fit into holes bored to correspond in the arms of the other half of the pattern. In some cases, the flanges of the pattern are required to be so thin as not to admit of two layers or courses of segments in their composition, in which event—especially if the flanges extend far from the body of the pattern—it is well to strengthen the joints of the segments. Perhaps the neatest way of accomplishing this, is to make a saw cut in the ends of each segment, and, at the time of gluing, to insert a tongue or thin strip of wood, nicely filling the saw cut, the grain of the tongue being at right angles to the line of the joint of the segments. Care should, however, be taken to have the saw cut in each at a similar distance from the face of the segment. It will be perceived that the flanges might be omitted without making any difference in the method of construction; nor does the method to be pursued vary to any great extent for all kinds of rope or chain pulleys.

CHAPTER VIII.

PIPE BENDS, AND LAGGING.

Our next example will be a pipe bend, such as is shown in section in Fig. 136. It will be seen upon examination that the bend proper is included in that portion contained within the dotted lines, C C and D D, which meet at the center from which the arcs, forming the bend, are struck. Those parts exterior to the dotted lines are made separately from the bend proper, and are subjects in plain turning,

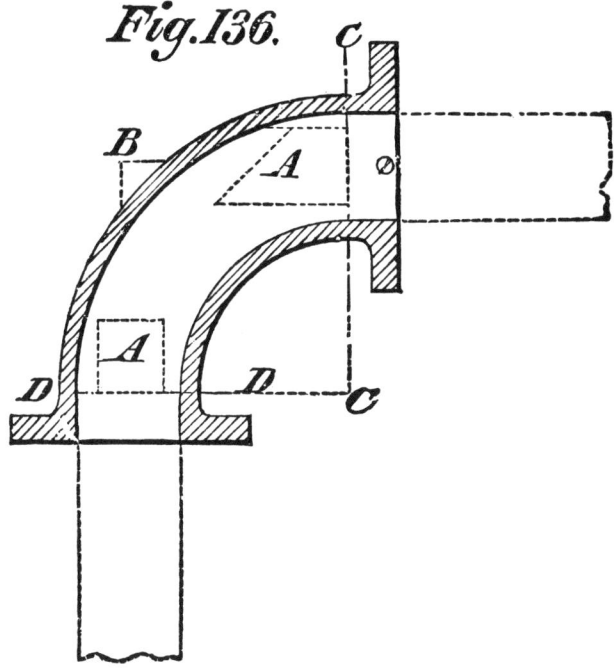

Fig. 136.

similar to those already treated upon. It will be noted, however, that in this kind of pattern the core is not so well supported as in our previous examples; and it has, therefore, a tendency to sag or droop towards the center of the arc, and also to rise above its proper level when the metal is poured into the mold. To obviate this, we must make the core, and hence the core prints, extra long, as shown by the dotted lines in Fig. 136. It is usual also to make a provision for fastening these external pieces to the bend proper, as follows: The flange is one piece, the bend proper another, and the core print yet another. The core print fits into the flange, and has a projecting piece extending into a recess or hole, provided in the bend proper to receive it, as shown, and thus is the pattern strengthened. If the core prints are made so short that the core overbalances itself when placed in the mold, the molder inserts into the mold, stays or supports to keep the print in position; and these supports are called chaplets. They consist of pieces of thin sheet iron, bent to about the curvature of the core, and riveted to a piece of wire, the device being pressed like a flat-headed nail into the sand. The piece of sheet iron represents the nail head upon which the core rests, and it is inserted into the cope and nowel, so that they pro-ject the proper distance. They act to prevent the core from either sagging or lifting, by floating upon the molten metal. Then, when the casting is taken from the mold, the projecting wires are chipped off, and that remaining in the casting is riveted. This trouble can be, in many cases, saved, by simply making the core prints a few inches longer; besides, wherever there is a chaplet, there is an excrescence left upon the casting. In the case of large work, however, the matter is different, on account of the expense of making very long prints, and their awkward-ness in being handled.

The bend part of our pattern may be either turned in the lathe or pared by hand; and sometimes it is a difficult matter to decide which of the two will best answer the purpose. To turn up a bend, it is necessary to turn up a

ring semicircular in section, as shown in Fig. 137, and of a radius corresponding to that of the required bend. This ring is then cut up into portions of the length of arc required, and about one half is in most cases left over. The

Fig. 137.

advantage of this method is the direct and ready manner in which the required form is obtained; whereas, in paring and shaping, the bending by hand, though the operation be ever so skillfully performed, will not be so true as if turned. And when we consider that castings only three thirty-seconds of an inch in thickness are sometimes required, we perceive that the slightest error or deviation from the true shape will be perceptible, and will often result in the loss of a large proportion of the castings. For all small work, then, the turning is of decided advantage; but since such is not always the case with large work, and since the line must be drawn somewhere, a correct decision will always be largely influenced by the facilities afforded

Fig. 138.

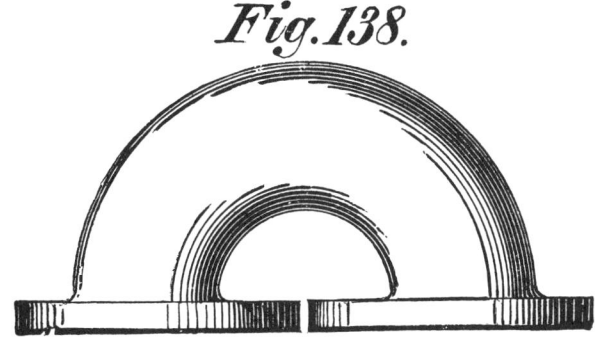

by the tools, etc., in the shop. In the example shown in Fig. 138, which is what is called a return bend, the whole of a ring, turned as above described, would be appropri-

7

ated : therefore, there being no loss of material, the method by turning will in this instance always be preferable.

In fixing the half flanges for work of this kind, not exceeding six or seven inches in size, one screw passing through the center of the pattern into the flange will be sufficient. Care must, however, be taken to hold the flange firmly in its exact position, while boring for and during the insertion of the screw. It should not be forgotten to add the small projecting piece, B, shown in Fig. 136, which lies in the center line of each arm of the bend, which is provided to enable the casting to be conveniently swung in the lathe.

Before quitting examples of this kind, it will be well to once more direct the reader's attention to the core boxes, so as to impress upon him the important fact that, where equal thickness of metal is required, the core box should be as the pattern is. A round pattern demands a round core box; the one is of equal importance with the other. For example, in the designing of a bend, the required thickness is determined by the amount of internal strain to which the casting will be subjected. If, then, we give a round bend and an oval core box, we either make the bend too weak, or we cause the manufacturer to pay for so many pounds of metal which he does not require. In the case of castings so thin as to require care to make the metal flow throughout the mold, an unduly thin place or spot will prevent the flow (at that part) of the metal, and thus spoil a large proportion of the castings.

A half core box for either a bend or a T may be made by preparing a block sufficiently large to cut out the whole recess, as shown by the full lines in Fig. 139. In this case, after the block has been surfaced truly on one side and edge—the grain of the wood being in the direction denoted by the arrow—the center lines are marked upon it, and also upon the pattern. We then lay one half of the pattern

upon the block, and make the center lines upon them come
exactly fair and even; and then we mark upon the face
of the block the outline of the pattern, core prints and all.
The core prints will, of course, be the right size of the core;
but the outline marks thus produced form a guide to work
by, and the distance between these outline marks and the
edge of the core will represent the thickness of metal in
the finished casting. A margin of stuff in the block is

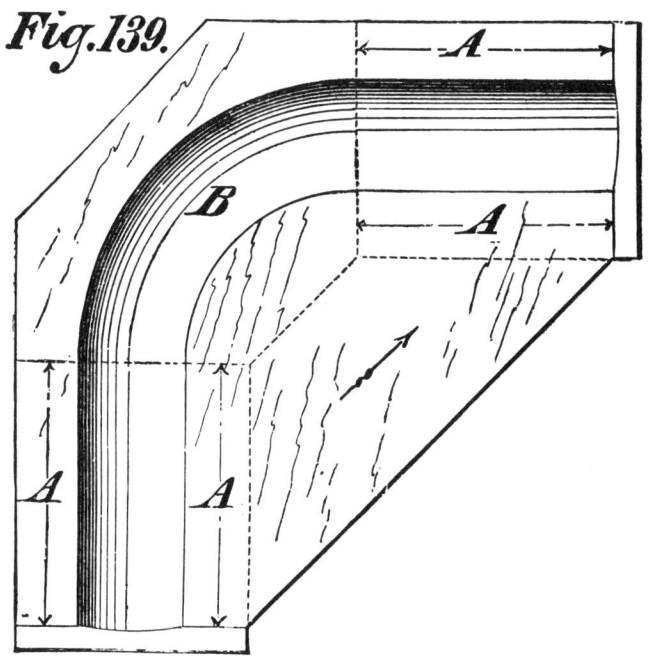

Fig. 139.

required outside of the outline marks, so as to give the core
box sufficient strength. We next trace out a plan of the
core, and then, upon the ends or sides of the block, we describe semicircles representing the exits of the recess to be
cut out, the block being left so deep as to leave stuff enough
below the depth of the recess to afford ample strength.
We may now proceed to cut out the core by our hand
tools, finishing it with the plane shown in Fig. 14, and

smoothing it with sand-paper wrapped around a **piece of** wood of a sweep or curve a little less in radius than that of the core box recess.

Another method of getting out a core box for a bend is shown by the dotted lines in Fig. 139; and in this instance we make the core box in three pieces—the object being to turn up the end pieces, A A, in the lathe—the manner of procedure being as follows : We get out the two pieces marked A A, and square up the faces truly, and chuck them, with the planed faces placed together in the chuck shown in Figs. 56 and 57, taking care that they are chucked so that, when the hole is bored in them, it will be half in each piece, or, in other words, chucking them truly, with the joint between the two. We then pare out the curved part in the middle section, and then glue on the end pieces, A A, A A, and strengthen the whole by placing battens on the bottom and sides.

Fig. 140 represents a half core box for T. In half core boxes it is necessary to close the openings in the ends or

Fig. 140.

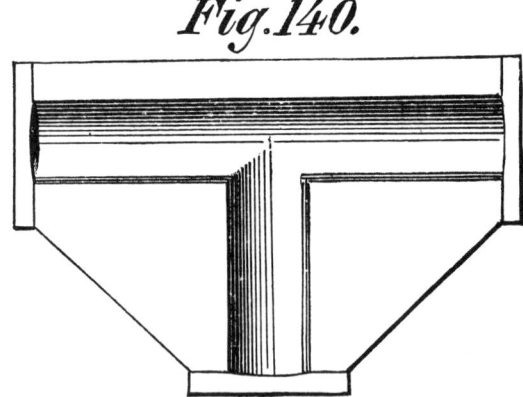

sides by bradding on pieces of light board, taking care to give draught by paring them slightly. concave at the top, and thus making the ends of the core similar to the slight-ly rounded ends of the pattern. When these pieces are omitted, the core maker has to extemporize them. When a full core box is required, as in the case of the oblique T, it is sufficient to mark the shape of the core upon one half only of the box; and when this is cut out, we may place the two half boxes together, and trace the second half from the finished one, using a large bent scriber for the purpose of marking.

Economy in timber and in the cutting must be studied as much in the core box as in the pattern; hence, when the pattern is of such a size as to render it economical to build it in pieces, it will be equally desirable to build the core box in like manner. For the bend itself, however, it is scarcely necessary to speak, for the core can be made with a simple contrivance; whereas the building of a half box, though not offering any elements of difficulty, demands so much labor in the cutting out, compared with the extra labor devolving upon the core maker employing the contrivance referred to, that such boxes are for large work seldom or ever constructed. We proceed, therefore, to describe the contrivance with which the core maker is usually supplied. It is applicable to all sizes where loam cores are used; but the core box is preferable when its construction involves no great outlay.

Having determined upon the size of the core from end to end of the prints, we proceed to make a pattern from which one or two iron plates may be cast. Upon these plates the core, in separate halves, is made and dried. The plates are generally about $\frac{3}{8}$ inch thick, and of such a width as to leave a small margin around the core, to support what is called the strike. In Fig. 141, P represents the plate, C the core, and S the strike; this latter is cut from a piece of board from $\frac{3}{8}$ to 1 inch thick, the semicircular hole cut in it being the size of the required core. The grain of the wood may run in the direction of the **arrow**. It is strengthened, if necessary, by the two battens, shown in Fig. 141 *a*, at B B. The edges of the semicircle are beveled off, which causes the strike to work more smoothly and correctly over the composition forming the core.

A few flat-headed tacks should be driven into the surfaces of the strike that come into contact with the iron plate, so as to prevent the wood from wearing rapidly away, and thus altering the shape of the core, and causing it to be oval. The core maker places upon the iron plate enough

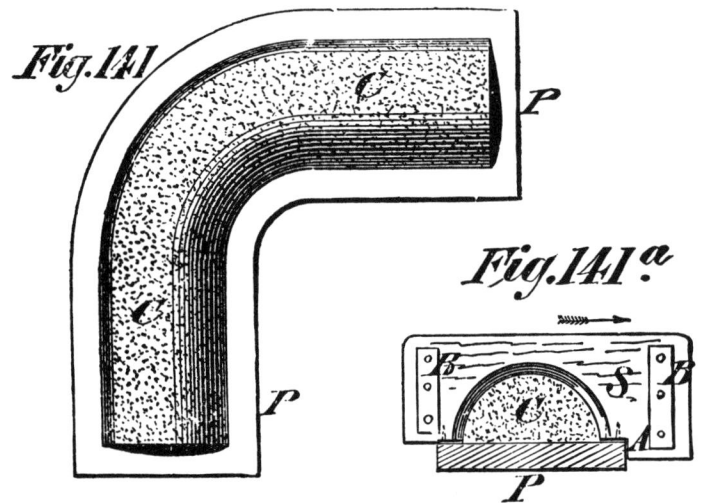

material to make the core, and, taking the strike, places it so that the edge or shoulder, A, in Fig. 141 *a*, contacts with the edge of the plate. He then sweeps the strike over the material; the semicircle leaves the core upon the plate, and sweeps off the surplus material, the sweeping process being completed until the perfect half core is formed. In Fig. 141 *a*, P represents the plate, S the sweep, and C the material or core, the figure being an end view, and the tacks referred to being shown, so as to mark their location.

We have hitherto treated of building patterns of such size that they could be made out of the solid; it often

happens, however, that the pattern maker is required to
build up a pattern by what is called staving or lagging.
As an example of this kind of work, let it be required to
stave up a pipe, 18 inches diameter inside, with 1 inch
thickness of metal. We proceed by taking a clean board,
and drawing on it the line, A O, in Fig. 142; and then we
describe upon it the semicircle, A B O (for we will suppose
the pattern to be made in halves), of the required finished
size of the pattern, the shrinkage being allowed for. This
semicircle we divide off into as many equal parts as it is
intended to have staves; and we next draw radii from the
points of division to the center of the semicircle. We then

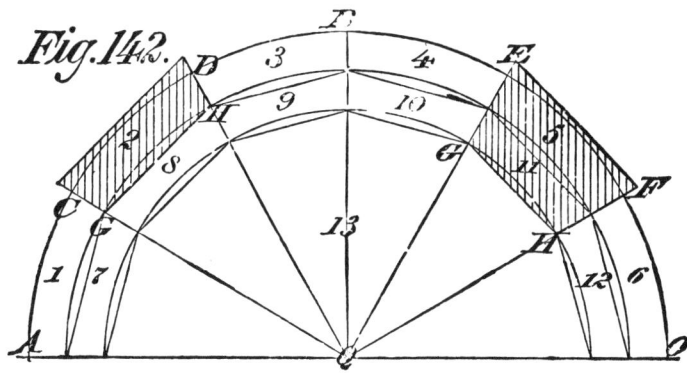

Fig. 142.

take any one of these divisions — of which there are six
shown in Fig. 142 — and draw the line, E F, parallel to an
imaginary line joining the points of division, C D. The
distance of the line, E F, from the arc is the amount allowed for the lathe turning — say in this case, $\frac{1}{8}$ inch. We
next draw the line, G H, parallel to E F, and the figure, E
F G H, is the exact size and form required for each stave.
From the center, Q, we then describe a semicircle passing
through the points, G H, and cutting each of the radii;
and by joining all these points, we form the half polygon,
shown by the whole figure. This shows the exact size

and shape of the disk to which the staves are to be fixed. In Fig. 142, this whole process is drawn twice, showing thick staves and thin ones; from 1 to 6 representing the thick, and from 7 to 12 the thin staves, while 13 repre-sents the disk of wood. The thin staves are to form the body of the pipe; but when it is desired to have the points solid with the body, we must use the thick staves. The first procedure is to prepare the requisite number of disks, making them of the form shown; and some pattern makers do this by turning the disks, and then flattening them off to form the sides of the polygon. But when a band saw is accessible, the turning is unnecessary; and we may simply draw them out and saw almost to the line, allowing say $\frac{1}{16}$ inch for finishing. Each half disk should be pegged to its mate, and a template, like the figure E F G H, is useful in preparing the staves and verifying their sizes. To prepare the staves, we cut out with the rip saw the required number of pieces, a little wider than E F, in Fig. 142; or if there is a circular saw at hand, we use it in preference, and it will save time to resaw the pieces, to give them the required bevel, which may be done by canting the saw table. In the absence of any provision for canting, we may fix a packing piece to the table, so as to elevate one edge of the stave. After sawing, we plane the bevel edges to correspond to the template, leaving just a shade of stuff to allow for joint-ing the staves at a close fit together.

Having prepared the staves, we set up the pattern, as follows: On a planed board, the requisite number of half disks are placed, perfectly in line with each other; and the outer ones must be at such a distance apart as to allow for turning up the ends of the staves. The inter-mediate disks, if any (and they should occur about every 2 or $2\frac{1}{2}$ feet), are to be distributed at equal distances in the space that intervenes. These disks we then fix temporarily to the board, paper being laid at the ends of the disks to catch the surplus glue.

The staves are glued, and each screwed with one screw to the disk. The boring of the stave to receive the screw should be performed before applying the glue, and the head of the screw should be well sunk beneath the surface, so as to admit of a wood plug being glued in on top of it. First, a hole is bored in the stave, a little larger in size than the head of the screw, and nearly as deep as the screw head is to be sunk; for, in tightening the screw, the head will be sure to be driven $\frac{1}{8}$ or $\frac{1}{4}$ inch deeper than the hole is bored—that is, providing the material is a soft wood, as is usually the case. The stave is now to be completely pierced with a hole just fitting the plain part of the screw. If it is larger, the head of the screw will sink deeper; while, if it is smaller, a thread will be cut in it by the screw, and it may prevent the stave from being drawn to its place. The glue should be applied and the screw inserted while the glue is hot. It is best to join on a stave back and front; that is, at each end first, and to then put in the middle or connecting stave, thus completing one length of the staves, the top one being, preferably, the first erected. In putting on the succeeding staves, each one should be properly jointed to its fixed neighbor; a little chalk being rubbed on the fixed stave will show if its fellow bears or joints properly. When one half of the pattern is finished, we may dispense with the board, using the finished half in its stead, and taking care to insert paper between the two, to prevent the glue from sticking them together.

In lagging up a branch for a T, the disk at one end should be set back sufficiently far to allow for the part to be cut away in fitting the branch to the body of the T, as explained when treating that subject. This method of staving is that regularly employed for cylinders, pipes,

7*

rollers, and similar jobs; and though sufficiently simple for straight pieces, it becomes very complicated when applied to a bend. It is not, therefore, usual to stave up a bend, but to build it in the manner illustrated in Fig. 143.

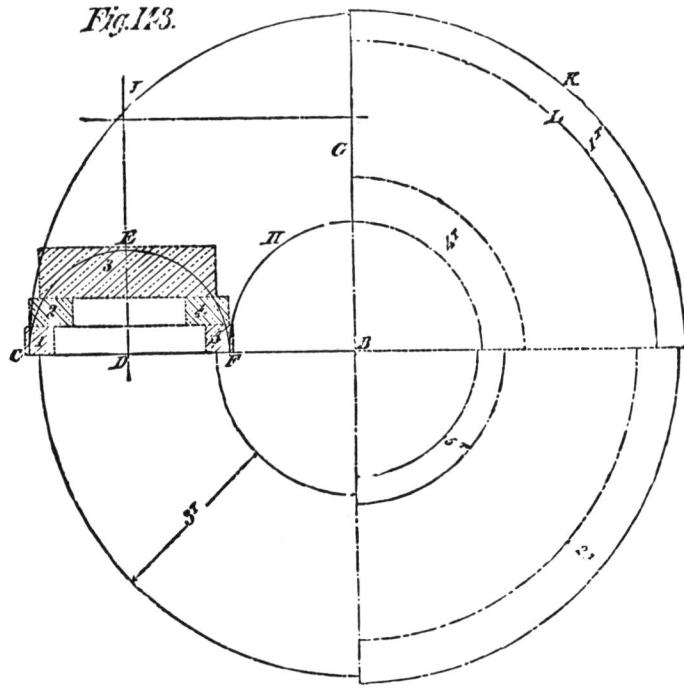

Fig.143.

The operation is, to first draw the bend in plan, of the full size, upon a board. Let B, in Fig. 143, represent the center from which it is struck, the plan in this case being a quarter circle bend, denoted in Fig. 143 by the line C D F, the line G, and the sections of a circle, H and J. We have decided to build up our pattern with five pieces, an end view of the half pattern being denoted by the circle C E F, and five pieces or layers being denoted by dotted lines, so that by adopting this method we show the plan and end view of the bend in one drawing. It would be well now to cut out forms, in card or in very thin wood,

as templates, one for each of the pieces, marked from 1 to
5 respectively. To obtain these templates, we draw the
line C B; and from the center, D, we describe the semicircle C E F, representing the diameter of the half bend. We
then lay off the tires from 1 to 3, as shown by the dotted
lines; and to find the bends necessary for each respective
piece, we proceed as follows: Setting our compasses at a
distance equal to that between the center from which our
bend is struck (B in Fig. 143) and the extreme outside of
the piece marked 1, we draw the quarter circle denoted by
the dotted line, K. Then setting our compasses from D to
the inside of piece 1, we draw from the center, D, the
quarter circle denoted by the dotted line, L. The space
included between those quarter circles, and denoted by
I T, is the sweep for the piece 1; and we may cut it out for
use as a template wherefrom to mark out piece 1. By setting the compasses in like manner for each respective piece,
2, 3, 4, and 5, we obtain the templates, 2 T to 5 T, respectively, for use in marking out the pieces upon the board
from which they are to be sawn. In building the pieces
up, we lay those forming the lower tier on the plan previously drawn out on the piece of board, putting them a
little outside the lines, to allow for finishing. We then
temporarily fix them in that position — the faces being, of
course, planed up. We now glue on the next tier. It is
well, however, to have a semicircle made of a piece of thin
wood, and of the size of that shown in Fig. 143, by C E F,
which we may place upright against the ends of the first
tier, as a guide in adjusting the position of the second and
succeeding tiers. The number of tires is discretionary;
but it is well to have the top piece comparatively thick, so
that it shall not be liable to curl, as it would be apt to do
if the turning left it thin. If the joints of the tiers are
well surfaced and well glued, neither nails nor screws will
be needed. It is not compulsory to make each layer a

continuous piece, and it will save stuff to make every alternate layer of two pieces; but the bottom and the top layers are better, if each be made in one piece.

It will be observed that this staving up a bend is both laborious and wasteful; yet there are cases in which it becomes imperatively necessary to make it in this manner. A very common job of this kind is lagging up a steam pipe, such as shown in Fig. 144. The pipe is usually covered with felt or some other non-conducting material, and

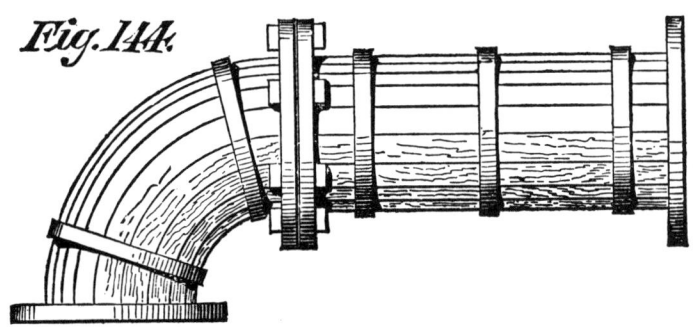

Fig. 144.

covered round with mahogany or walnut. Now, it would be very unsightly to have the joints in the bend out of line with those on the straight part of the pipes. A hollow bend of wood has, therefore, to be constructed, having in it the same number of staves as there are for the straight pipe. To get out the pieces for such a bend, we proceed as illustrated in Fig. 145, in which there are shown 6 sections or staves, the semicircle G H representing the required inside diameter of the bend; while the semicircle A E represents the required outer diameter. We then divide off one of the semicircles into the required number of divisions; and we draw radii, and then form rectangles around each division or space representing a stave, as shown by dotted lines in Fig. 145 at 2, 3, and 5. The method pursued in getting out these staves is precisely similar to that pursued in building up in our last example. In this case, however, as each stave is fitted to its fellow, it should be held to its place by dowels—that is, small pins of wire placed at frequent intervals—which will serve instead of glue, which would not answer, by reason of the heat from the steam pipe. The disks upon which the bend is built, and of which there should be at least three, are merely temporary; and therefore the staves are not to be fastened to them,

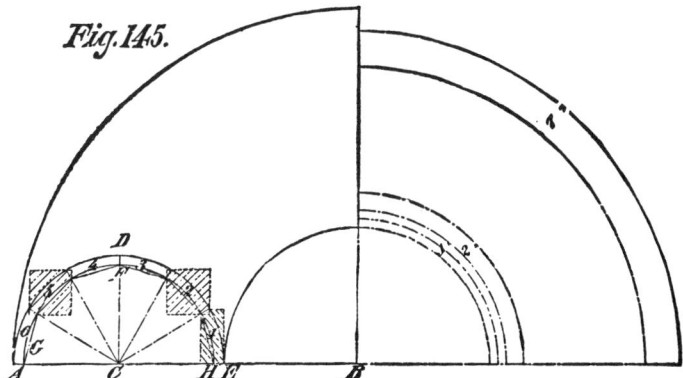

except for convenience, so as to keep them in position. For this purpose, a piece of paper, with a little hot glue on each side, should be placed between the stave and the disk; it will make a fastening sufficiently strong, if a little pressure be applied during the drying. Neither nails, screws, nor staples, are admissible on this kind of job, as they would mar the appearance of the work when finished and polished. The two halves of the bend being completed, they are made to go together with loose pegs—that is to say, pegs that do not fit the holes tightly, as the dowels do. The halves should be held together by polished brass or plated bands; and the neatness of the finished appearance will amply repay the cost and the trouble, for the polished wood forms a pleasing contrast to the contents of an engine room, where almost everything the eye can rest on is iron.

CHAPTER IX.

EXAMPLES IN GLOBE VALVES.

In Fig. 146, we have for an example a common globe valve, shown partly in section and with a gas thread cut

Fig. 146.

in the openings. The flanges vary in shape; but, as a rule, small valves are provided with hexagons, and large ones with round flanges suitable for bolting to similar flanges to make joints. For small valves, say up to 2 inches, the

Fig. 147.

pattern is usually made with the hexagons cut out of the solid, but for sizes above that, they should be made in separate pieces, as shown in Fig. 147, and screwed to the pattern, so that in case of necessity they may be removed, and flanges substituted in their stead. In Fig. 148 we have a perspective view of the finished pattern; and Fig. 149 represents the pattern as prepared, ready to receive a flange or hexagon as may be required. A globe valve pattern should be made in halves, as shown in Fig. 150, the parting line of the two halves being denoted by A B. To make this pattern, we first prepare two pieces of wood so large that, when

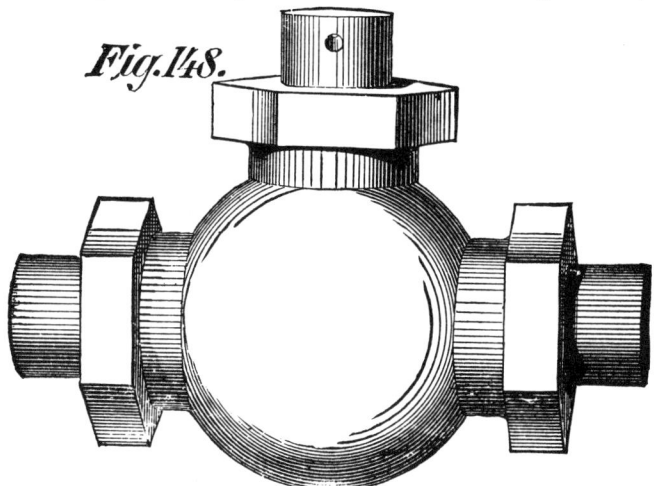

Fig. 148.

pegged together, the ball or body of the pattern can be turned out of them, and long enough not only to reach from P to P, in Fig. 149, but also to allow an excess by means of which the two pieces may be glued or otherwise fixed together. These two pieces we plane to an equal thickness, and then peg them to retain them in a fixed position, taking care, however, that the pegs do not occur where the screws to hold the flanges will require to be. We also place two pegs within a short distance of what will be the ends of the pattern when the excess in length referred to is turned off. We next prepare, in the same way, two more pieces, to form the two halves of the branch, shown at B, in Fig. 150, for which, however, one peg only will be necessary. These pieces must be somewhat wider than the size of the required hexagon across the corners—that is, supposing the hexagon is to be solid with the branch—otherwise we must make them a little wider than the diameter of the hub of the flange or of the round part of the hexagonal pieces. Their lengths must be such as to afford a good portion to be let into the ball or body of the pattern (as shown by the dotted lines in Fig. 149), which is necessary to give sufficient strength. The two pieces

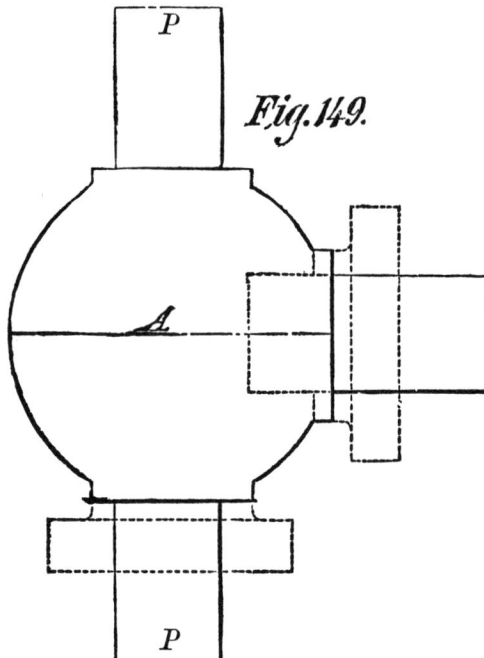

Fig. 149.

must be firmly fixed together, and then turned in the lathe.

During the early stages of the turning, or, in other words, during the roughing out, we must occasionally stop the lathe and examine the flat places on the body; for unless these places disappear evenly, the work is not true, and one half will be thicker than the other, so that the joint of the pattern will not be in the middle. It was to insure this, that the pieces were directed to be planed of equal thickness, since, if such

is the case, and the flat sides disappear equally and simultaneously during the turning, the joint or parting of the pattern is sure to be central. If the lathe centers are

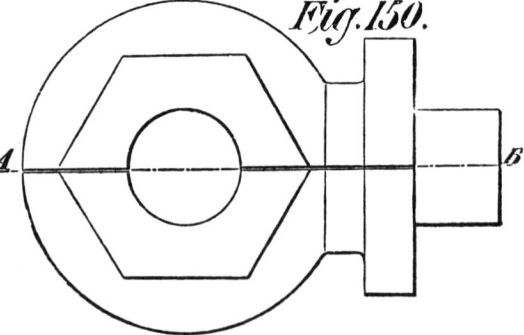

Fig. 150.

not exactly true in the joint of the two pieces, they may be made so by tapping the work on the side having the narrowest flat place, the process being continued, and the work being trued with the turning tool at each trial, until the flat places become equal. By this means we insure, without much trouble, two exact halves in the pattern, which is very important in a globe valve pattern, on account of the branches and other parts, not to mention the molding. Having turned the body of the pattern to the requisite outline, and made while in the lathe a fine line around the center of the ball where the center of the branch is to come, as shown in Fig. 149, by the line A, we make a prick point (with a scriber) at each crossing of the line A and the joint or parting of the pattern. We then mount the body upon a lathe chuck, in the manner shown in Fig 151.

A point center should be placed in the lathe, and should come exactly even with the line A. In Fig. 151, V V are two V blocks made to receive the core prints. These V's are screwed to the lathe chuck, and the pattern is held to them by two thin straps of iron placed over the core prints and fastened to the V's by screws. If the chuck and center point run true, the V blocks are of equal height, and the core

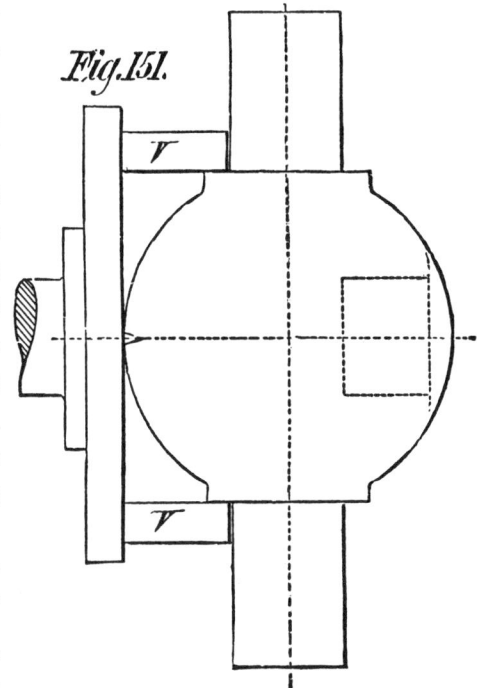

Fig.151.

prints are equal in diameter, the prick point opposite to the one placed to the center point will run quite true; and we may face off the ball or body to the required diameter of branch, and bore the recess to receive the same. We make the holes in the flanges of the same size as the core prints; but we should not check in the print, because, if a flange with a different length of hub were substituted, it would be a disadvantage. To obtain the half flanges, we take a chuck and face it off true in the lathe; then, with a fine scriber point, we mark the center while the chuck is revolving. We then stop the lathe, and placing a straight-edge to intersect the chuck center, we draw a straight line across the chuck face. We then take two pieces suitable for the half flanges, and plane up one flat side and one edge of each piece. If the flanges are not large ones, they may be planed all at once in a long strip. We place the pieces in pairs, and mark on each pair a circle a little larger than the required finished size of flange. We then fix each pair to the chuck, with the planed faces against the chuck, and the planed edges placed in contact, their joint coming exactly even with the straight line marked on the chuck face, and we may then turn them as though they were made in one piece and to the requisite size.

In Fig. 152, we have a representation of one half of a

suitable core box, the other half being exactly the same, with the exception that the position of the internal partition is reversed. To get out this core box, we plane up two pieces of exactly the same size and length as the pattern, and of such width and thickness as will give sufficient strength around the sphere, allowing space for the third opening. After pegging these two pieces together, we gage, on the joint face of each, lines representing the centers of the openings and the center of the sphere. We then chuck them (separately) in the lathe, and turn out the half sphere. We next place the two halves together, and chuck the block so formed in the three positions necessary to bore out the openings; or, if preferred, we may pare them out. The partition (A, in Fig. 152) follows the roundness of the center hole, and is on that account more difficult to extract from the core, than if it were straight and vertical. When, however, the partitions are of this curved form, the pieces of which they are formed are composed of metal, brass being generally preferred. Patterns have in this case to be made, wherefrom to cast these pieces, and they may be made as follows: First, two half pieces, such as shown in Fig. 153, are turned; each is then

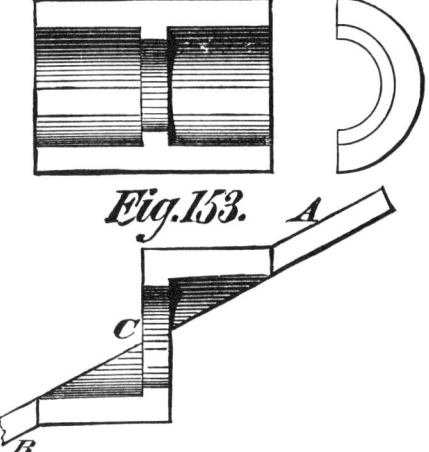

cut away so as to leave the shape as shown at C, in the same figure, and is then fitted into the spherical recess in the core box, letting each down until both are nearly but not quite level. The two pieces, A and B, in Fig. 153, are then fastened on, and this pattern is complete. When the pieces are cast, they must be filed to fit the core box, and finished off level with its joint face, a small hole being drilled in the center, and a pin being driven through the piece and into the box, to steady the corners. We then saw the pieces in halves with a very fine saw.

If the partition, instead of following the roundness of the valve seat, is made straight, the construction of the core box is much more simple. In this case, a zigzag mortise is made clear through each half of the box, its size and shape being that of the required partition. Fig. 154 repre-

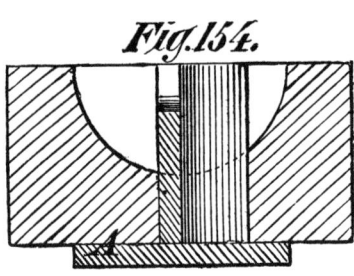

Fig.154.

sents a half core box of this kind. A piece of wood, A, is fixed as shown to the partition, to enable the core maker to draw it out before removing the core from the box. The mortise for the partition should be turned out before the half spherical recess—the mortise being temporarily plugged with wood, to render easy the operation of turning.

In very large valves (say 10 or 12 inches) a half core box is generally made to serve, by fitting the two half partitions, shown at C, in Fig. 153, to a half core box, and keeping them in position by means of pegs; a half core being made first with one, and then one with the other in the core box.

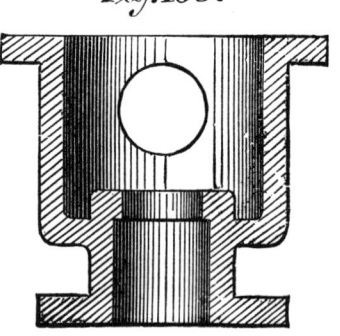

Fig.155.

It is often necessary to form a raised seat in the body of an angle valve, such as shown in Fig. 155, which represents a section of such a body. It is shown with flanged openings, though in small valves hexagons, to receive a wrench, would be substituted.

Fig. 156 is a plan of half the core box necessary for forming the raised seat. From this construction it will be seen that the large core, though solid with the branch core, is not solid with that forming the hole in the seat and the part below it; therefore the core prints on the body pattern must be left extra long, to give sufficient support in the mold for the overhanging cores. The loose round plug, P, is made of the size of the outside of the seat, and fitted to the box. The part outside the box is a roughly shaped handle to draw it out by. The diminished part, D, is a print, and into the impression left by it is inserted the core made in box, shown in Fig. 157.

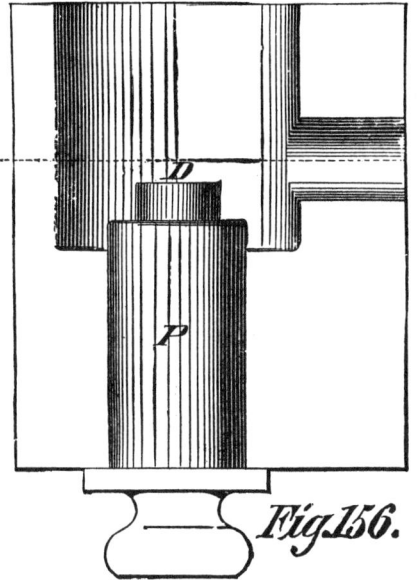

Fig. 156.

The print, D, is of the same diameter as the hole in the

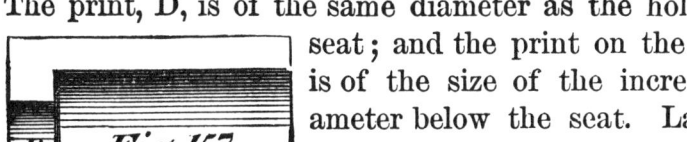

Fig. 157.

seat; and the print on the pattern is of the size of the increased diameter below the seat. Large angle valves are made with half a core box, by making a branch opening in the box right and left, a semicircular plug being provided. Two half cores are made with the plug, first in one and then in the other branch opening. The plug, P, should be in this case only half round.

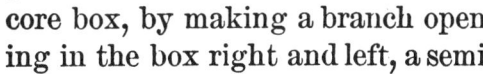

CHAPTER X.

JOINTS, AND EXAMPLES IN BENCH WORK.

Turning now for a space from examples requiring so much lathe work, we come to deal more particularly with the bench, and the devices and operations connected with it.

A good bench is a great assistance to a pattern maker. It should be perfectly true on its upper surface, which is best made of hard wood, and covered with a coat of varnish to prevent dust or drippings of glue from adhering to it, so that it is always cleanly in appearance. The vise, when screwed close to the bench, should come level with its top, and the butt or stop for work to press against, should be so constructed that its height may be readily altered, as this will have to be done perhaps fifty times a day. In the absence of a well contrived mechanical stop, which always admits of re-adjustment without stooping, I should recommend a stop of wood made by placing two wedges

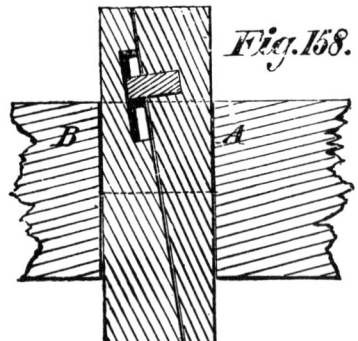

together, as shown at A and B, Fig. 158. A pin is fixed tightly in the wedge A, which slides in a groove, in B, for a short distance; this prevents the wedges from falling apart when loosened. A light tap on B loosens, and one on A tightens the stop. The ordinary contrivances used at the bench, in addition to the workman's tools, are the shooting board (already described), the mitre box, and the bench hook. The mitre box is a contrivance to enable a workman to saw moldings, pipe patterns, etc., to an angle of 45°. It is simply a trough with saw cuts made at the required angle. The stuff to be cut is laid in the trough and pressed to one of its sides, the saw being guided by the saw cut. The bench hook is a piece of wood sawn to the shape shown in Fig. 159,

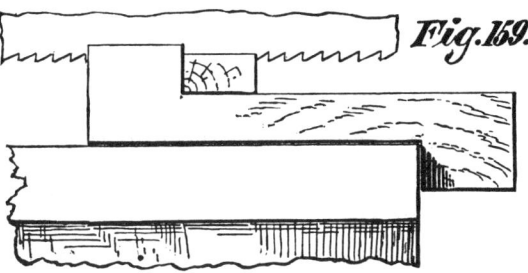

Fig.159.

and is used as a butt; for timber, in cross-cutting work, should not be sawn directly on the bench.

Figs. 160, 161, and 162, are illustrations of different methods of jointing pieces of wood together so as to form a square or any angle. Fig. 160 represents a tenon and mortise joint, made as follows: The two pieces, A and B, having been planed or otherwise made to size as required, are marked for the position and length of the mortise in one case, and for the length of the tenon in the other; both pieces are now gaged with a mortise gage, both being marked alike; and then from the face side

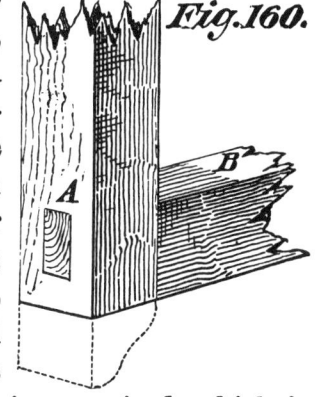

Fig.160.

we mark a tenon or mortise of the size required, which is generally a third of the thickness of the stuff. Where the mortise approaches the end of the piece, a provision has to be made to insure strength, by adding the extension denoted in Fig. 160 by the dotted lines. This practice, however, though often adopted in carpentry, is rarely admissible in pattern work; and in its stead, the tenon, or the piece B, is diminished in width, as shown in Fig. 163, the mortise being made to correspond. In order to avoid breakage during the cutting of the mortise, the

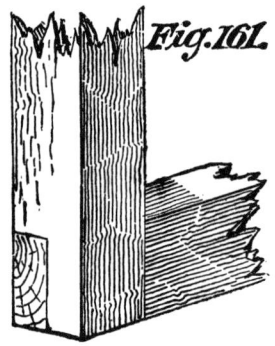

piece A, Fig. 160, is got out an inch or two longer, which excess is sawn off after the glue is dry. An excess of the tenon, as it is necessary to chamfer off the corners of the tenon, so that in driving it may not damage the mortise. To prevent the tenon from, in time, working out, the mortise is slightly tapered— that is, made wider on the side remote from the piece carrying the tenon. Then the tenon is provided with two saw cuts, one on each side, near the edge; and after being driven home, wedges are driven into these cuts, thus locking the joint. A joint, more commonly in use among pattern makers, is the half lap, shown in Fig. 161, which has been already described. When this joint occurs away from the end of the pieces, the

mortise need not, and should not, extend through the piece. This joint, besides being glued, may be fastened with screws, or if very thin, riveted with short pieces of lead wire.

A very superior method of jointing is the dovetail, shown in Fig. 164, which is serviceable for connecting the ends and sides of a box, or any article in that form. The strength of the corner formed in this way is only limited by that of the material itself; therefore, it should be preferred, when available, in making standard patterns, or for work too thin to admit nails or screws. The corner formed by this joint is not limited to 90° or square, so called, but may form any angle. Nor is it imperative that the sides or ends of the box or other article be parallel. They may incline towards one another like a pyramid ; a mill hopper is a familiar example of this. If it be required to dove-tail a box together, get out four pieces for the sides and ends, to be of the full length and width of the box outside, respectively. They are to be planed all over, not omitting the ends. The gage, that is already set to the thickness of the stuff, must now be run along the ends, marking a line on both sides of each piece. Then mark and cut out the pins as on the piece A ; the dovetail openings, in B, are traced from the pins in A. The pieces, having been tried and found to go together, are finally brought into contact and held in their places with glue.

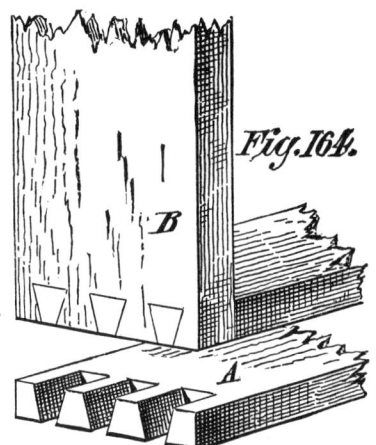

Fig. 162 is a mitre joint—the only one serviceable to moldings, pipes, and other curved pieces. It is not a strong form of joint, and is only used where the preceding kinds are inapplicable. It is made with glue, the pieces having been previously sized ; and as an additional pre-caution, if the work will admit, nails, brads, or screws, are inserted at right angles to one another.

In Fig. H is shown a mitre box exceedingly useful as a shop fixture, but of course, being made of iron, it is not intended to form a part of a journeyman pattern maker's kit of tools, but rather from its superiority to dispense with the necessity for the same. The saw blade is guided

by the rolls shown upon the upright spindles, and leaden
rolls below regulate the depth to which the saw will cut,

Fig. II

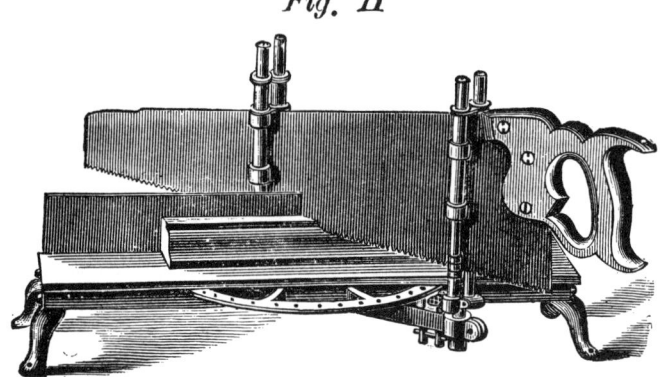

and thus preserve the saw teeth from contact with the
iron frame.

This mitre box can be used with a back saw or a
panel saw equally well. If a back saw is used, both
links which connect the rollers, or guides, are left in the
upper grooves, and the back of the saw is passed through
under the links. If a panel saw is used, the link which
connects the rollers on the back spindle is changed to the
lower groove; and then the blade of the saw will be stiffly
supported by both sets of rollers, and be made to serve as
well as a back saw.

As an example, to make the pattern for a pillow block,
as shown in Fig. 165. This pattern will be more easily
molded with the base up; that is to say, it will lie in the
sand in the reverse position to what it is drawn in Fig. 165.
Prints will be required for the bolt holes, square prints for
the recesses in the block intended to be cored out to receive
the heads of the cap bolts, round prints on the tops of
the cheeks, and oval prints on the base. We first plane
a piece for the base, B B, to the correct size, allowing
$\frac{1}{10}$ inch to the foot for the contraction of the casting in
cooling. We next draw center lines upon it on both sides.

It must now be observed that a hollow or filleted corner appears where the cheeks of the block meet the base; and

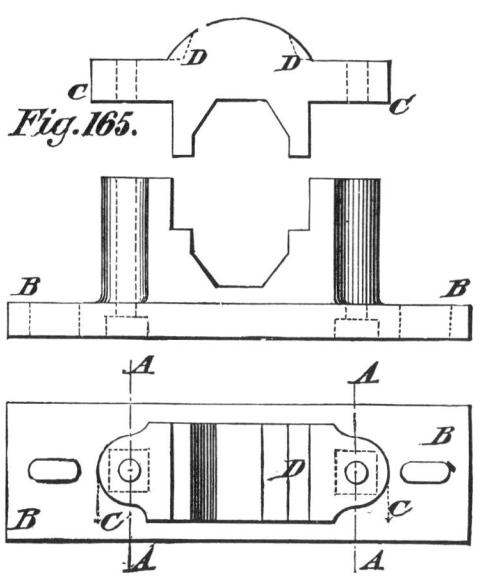

Fig.165.

further, that the recess in the block to receive the brasses is drawn to a depth coinciding with the height of the hollow or fillet. It will be advisable, therefore, to prepare a piece of the length from C to C, and to shape the ends to the outline of the cheeks, and, forming in this piece all the fillet, the cheeks may next be prepared of a thickness from the line A to D. These must be strongly fastened, and are best mortised clear through the base, and glued fast. Two semicircular pieces must be turned for the portions outside the lines A A, and three-cornered pieces must be fitted in the square recess, to make it octagonal as required. Nothing now remains but to attach the core prints, and make a suitable core box. A half box will suffice for the cap bolt-holes, and a whole one for the holes in the base, as the cores for these latter will stand on end. To make the cap, we take a piece of timber large enough to make that portion of the cap that is above the line C C; and we line or mark out the form of the cap on both sides (using a center line to make the two sides correspond), and pare away the surplus wood down to the lines. The pieces below the line C C are to be afterwards glued and nailed on. It is advisable to cut out a recess in the top of the cap, as shown in Fig. 166, at A B, to afford

convenience to the machinist in using the wrench upon
the nuts.   Fig. 167 is a sectional view of a pattern for the
brasses; and this pattern requires great care in its making,
for the following reasons: Brasses of this kind, and of a
size not larger than is required for a journal about ten
inches in diameter, can be fitted in much quicker by chip-
ping and filing than by any other method; and in any
event, a great deal of labor and metal can be saved by
constructing the pattern of the necessary shape.   Since,
however, to give the required shape without the reasons
therefor, would not convince the reader of the correctness

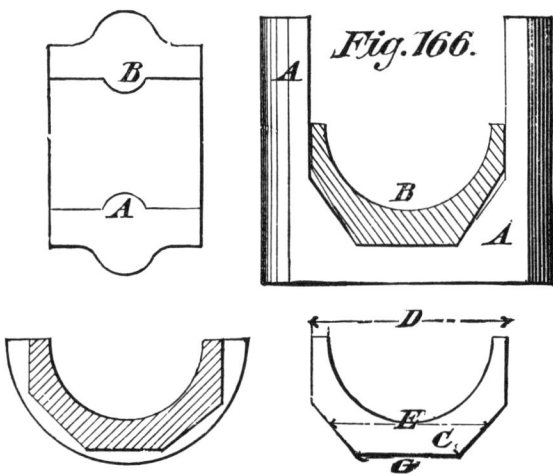

Fig. 166.

of the method, I will fully explain the two.   It has been
stated in former remarks that brass castings are smaller
than the patterns from which they are cast, by an amount
of $\frac{1}{8}$ inch per foot, which is due to the contraction of the
metal in cooling.   Now, in addition to this contraction,
the casting of a brass also contracts across the bore.   Suppose, for example, that, in Fig. 166, A A represents a locomotive axle box, and that B represents the brass for the
same, the two being shown in section, while C represents
the casting for the brass.   Beginning, then, with the casting, C, we have the following considerations: The diameter

of the brass across D will be less than it should be, because such castings always close in that direction more than is due to the contraction in cooling. As a consequence of this, the top of the bevels, as denoted by the dotted line, E, becomes less than it should be; and when the brass is fitted on the sides, and let down in the box ready to fit on the crown and on the bevels, the bottom of the brass will bed, and the bevels will not, as shown in the illustration. Now supposing the angles to be at the top $\frac{1}{16}$ of an inch from the bevels of the box, then it will require about $\frac{1}{8}$ of an inch to be taken off the bottom of the brass to let the sides come to a fit; whereas if, when the bevels of the brass contact with the bevels of the box, the bottom of the brass were $\frac{1}{8}$ inch from the bottom of the box, $\frac{1}{16}$ inch taken off the bevels would let the bottom come home. It is then easy to see that the pattern maker should make the pattern so as to allow for the shrinkage across D, and at the same time insure that the bevels of the brass shall contact with the box before the bottom does. Then, by the time that the machinist has taken sufficient off the bevels of the brass to fit them to the bevels of the box, the crown will come home; and the best way to insure this is to make the bevels of the brass of the same shape as those in the box, and then take a certain amount off the crown face of the brass (G, in Fig. 166). What this amount should be, depends upon the angle of the bevels. For bevels of 45° the proportions should be, for brasses of two and less inches bore, a full $\frac{1}{32}$ inch; for brasses having a bore of from two to four inches, $\frac{1}{16}$ inch will answer; while, if the bore is from four to seven inches diameter, $\frac{1}{8}$ inch will be a good proportion. If, however, the bevel is greater, these proportions may be increased. This is an important matter, and should never be overlooked or neglected, since it reduces the labor of fitting the brasses by at least one half.

The method to be pursued to make the pattern for the brass, is as follows: Take a piece of wood of sufficient size to form the body of the brass, and make it of the necessary size and form, observing the direction above given as to the bevels; and make the flanges by turning the two halves in one, as explained in a previous example, omitting to turn out the inside, as this would effect no saving, and such boring would weaken the flange, and render it liable to split in attaching it to the body of the pattern. To fasten the flanges, glue them on; and when dry insert brads, setting the flanges by lines. Then pare out the flange even with the bore of the brass. In many cases brasses are dispensed with, and Babbitt metal is employed in their stead. The requisite form of casting for this purpose is shown in Fig. 167, the Babbitt metal being con-

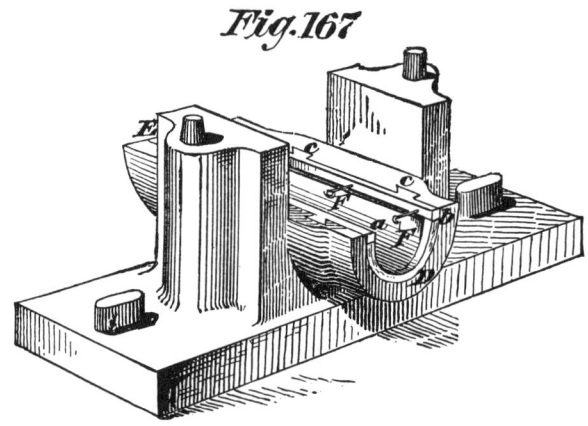

Fig.167

tained within the thin ridges which extend all around the edges of the half circular bearing. In addition to this, however, the machinist sometimes drills small holes in the cavity for the Babbitt metal. The ridges are cast solid with the box, and the two at the end (D and E, in Fig. 167) make no difference to the molding, since they will leave the sand readily and easily. But the ridges or strips that extend lengthwise of the bearing, must be made detachable from the pattern, the strips referred to being held in position by the dovetails shown at C. The recesses to receive the dovetails are first cut out, and the dovetails are made to a neat fit therein. Then we take the strips required to form the ridges, and having just spotted the faces of the dovetails with glue, while they are in their places, we press the strips against them for a moment, and adjust the strips and leave them in position for the glue to dry. By this means the dovetails are fastened to the strips exactly in the required position. When dry, the strips with the attached dovetails may be withdrawn from the pattern, and should then be more securely fastened together by the addition of screws or nails. In many cases, wires are employed in place of the dovetails; they being inserted, as shown in Fig. 167, at F; and when they are used, it becomes a consideration whether the molder can conveniently extract them. If he can, they are preferable to the dovetails, as these latter are sometimes apt to stick.

Bearings of this class (Babbitt metal) are often formed in the framework of a machine, or in other patterns that do not permit of being molded in the direction suitable for the above example. Fig. 168 represents such an example,

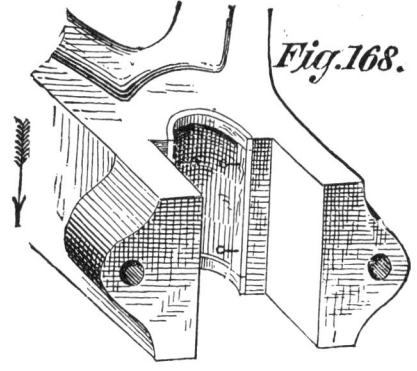

Fig. 168.

which requires to be molded in the direction denoted by the arrow. It will be advisable to core out the whole space for the cap and bearing, the core box in this case being fitted with the strips in a manner similar to that above described for the Babbitted pillow block. The pattern in this case is made as shown in Fig. 169, the space for the bearing being blocked up, and the block extending through, as shown

at A, to form a core print. The core box shown **beneath**
may be, in the smaller sizes, cut out of the solid wood, the

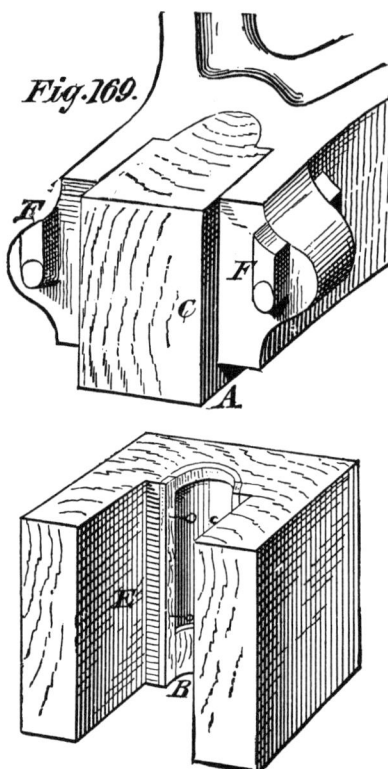

Fig.169.

part B being made thick,
because it includes the thickness of the ridge on that end,
and also the depth of the
print, as shown at A. The
reason that the block or core
print protrudes at C, is, that
a ridge may be formed in
the mold to steady the core
while inserting it in the
mold; and the depth of the
core box, at E, must be made
to suit it. It will be noted
that the core prints, at F F,
are carried to the top of the
pattern; and it will be readily
perceived that they must be
so made in order that the
pattern may lift from the
sand. Then, after the mold
is made, the core for the hole
is first inserted, and then a small core is fitted into the

recess in the mold; and thus
is the top part of the recess
(above the core print) stopped
off. The circles marked on
the faces of the prints, F, are
to be painted on the pattern
in black varnish, and their
purpose is to denote that the
core proper is round. If these
black circles were not made,
the pattern maker would

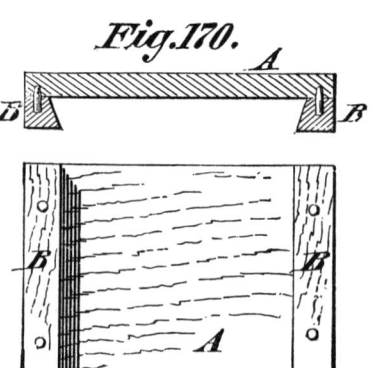

Fig.170.

require to make a similar circle and cross marks with chalk or pencil, that the molder may know how the core is to be left.

Fig. 170 is a representation of a pattern for a slide; it has the projections simply set on with pegs, to prevent the pattern being locked in the sand. In molding this piece, a false core is laid between these projections. After the cope is lifted, the plate A may be taken out; and after removing the false core, the pieces B B can be withdrawn.

8*

CHAPTER XI.

Our next example shall be for a square or rectangular column, which, though very simple in construction, yet necessitates a departure from the ordinary method pursued in pattern making—the object being to save the making of an entirely new pattern for every required column. In view of the thousands of columns of this kind that have been cast, it is not to be wondered at that measures have been taken to cheapen the cost of the pattern, and lessen the labor in preparing the mold; but it is to be remarked that no one has been able to invent a permanent mold for this class of work. In cast iron columns, the strict rules of architecture are not rigidly followed. The slight but graceful curve prescribed for every column and pilaster is frequently neglected, and various parts of the column are modified in their contour— to their detriment, as may be easily seen by comparing the details of a stone building with those of an iron one.

Square iron columns are usually made parallel throughout their lengths; while, on the end view, two of the sides incline towards one another, on account of the draft or taper given to the pattern. Round column patterns are not made parallel, but are smaller at the cap than at the base. The curve above mentioned is given to the shaft; but as the pattern is made to serve for all lengths of columns of that diameter, the curve can only, in most cases, be an approximation. In foundries that make a specialty of this class of work, numbers of blocks of various sizes and lengths are kept, and they simply require the addition of such ornaments as the design comprises, which ornaments—such as moldings, flutings, and the like—are often ready to hand, to complete the column pattern. These blocks are, for small columns, made solid; but for large columns they are constructed like boxes or troughs, with pieces filled in at short distances to give strength. (See Fig. 172.) Fig. 171 is a perspective view of a block, mounted with moldings and other ornamentation, so as to form a column pattern ready to go into the sand. The base, B, and its moldings, *a* and *b*, are to be cast solid with the shaft of the column; this, however — as may be inferred from what has been said — is not compulsory. It will be seen that the base forms a guide for the stopping-off blocks, A A, at that end; at the other end of the column the guides, C C, are attached. The distance between the stopping-off blocks, A A, is of course the length of the column, *plus* shrinkage and *plus* the amount left for cutting off to square up the ends of the cast column. The wires shown are for the purpose of holding the ornaments in position upon the block. The ornaments on the face

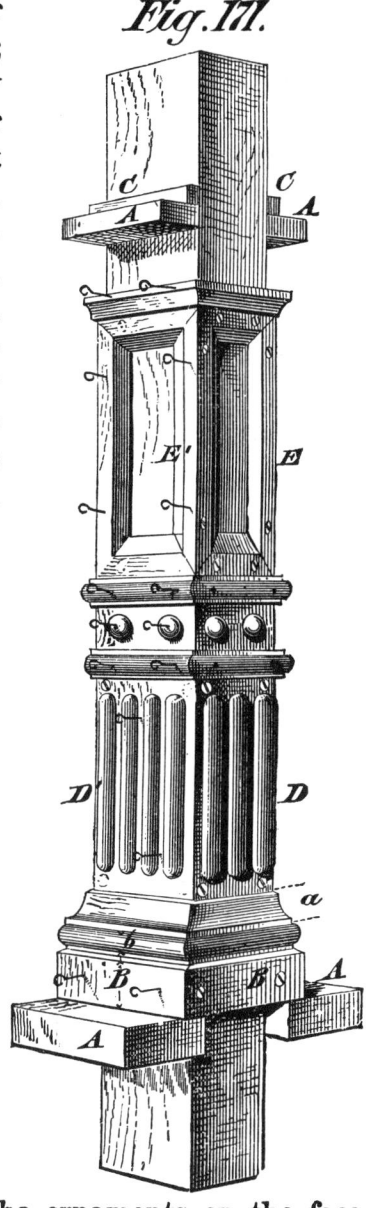

Fig. 171.

are held by loose pegs, except the cabling, D, and the paneling, E, which are made fast on the face by nails or screws.

Let it be required to prepare a pattern for a column 12 feet long, of 12 inches face, and 14 inches deep, to be of the style shown in Fig. 171. Select a block similar to that shown in Fig. 172, in which the top piece is shown removed, so that the distance pieces may be seen.

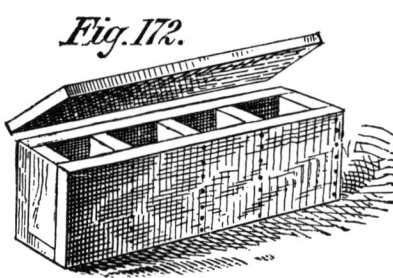

Fig. 172.

We will suppose our column to require mounting on the face and one side; then $\frac{1}{2}$ inch or $\frac{5}{8}$ inch will be taken up on the face and side by the margins, E, which form, with their moldings, the paneling: therefore, if $\frac{1}{2}$ inch margins are used, the block should measure $11\frac{1}{2}$ by $13\frac{1}{2}$ inches, and $\frac{1}{8}$ less if $\frac{5}{8}$ margins are employed. The length of the block is immaterial, so that it be not less than 20 inches longer than the column. This excess is for core prints at the ends of the pattern. Lay off upon the block the length of the column pattern; this will be 12 feet $+ \frac{12}{10}$ inch for shrinkage $+ \frac{1}{8}$ or $\frac{3}{16}$ inch at each end for squaring up. Space off upon the block the position of the various members, and apply them as directed. It must be noted that the moldings and base pieces on the face overrun those upon the side, and also extend according to their contour over the side that is not mounted (see Figs. 171 and 173). The reason of this is that by removing these face moldings and base pieces, except the cabling and paneling (which are fast), the molder can make a bevel parting. When the parting

Fig. 173.

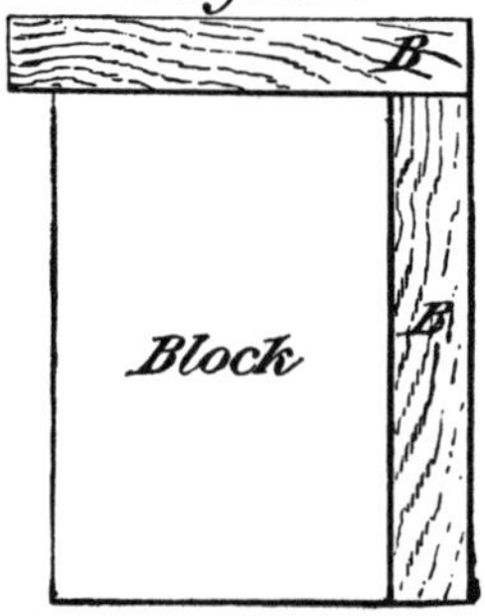

Block

is made, the pieces are then replaced, and will be taken up again by the cope. A rectangular column is invariably molded with the face up, because of the facility such a position gives for supporting the main core by means of the cores which make the openings always formed at the back of these columns.

For stopping off the column to the right length, we simply prepare four pieces, as shown at A, Fig. 171, of a length equal to the depth of the column at the ends, not including the base piece, as that will be stopped off in the cope. In ramming up the column, when in the sand, these pieces are bedded in, in the position shown. Some provision is necessary to prevent them from being rammed out of the perpendicular. This is provided in this case by the base pieces, B ; but at the other end of the column temporary strips are bradded to the block, as shown at C. To find the place for these guiding strips, add to the length of the column pattern the thickness of the stopping-off piece, square a line at this point down each side of the block, and nail on the guides outside this line, but with one edge touching it. Columns are often cast without bases or caps—these latter being cast thin, and attached by screws after the columns are set up.

The ornamentation of columns is varied constantly, depending upon the taste of individuals; therefore, it is impossible to lay down precise directions in this matter. It is thought, however, that the above remarks will be of service; and I may add that, in place of cabling, fluting is often employed. This is never to be cut out of the block, but formed in extra pieces. The cabling on the side is made by fastening the strips to a piece of board, and this is attached to the block by wires. Fig. 174 shows this arrangement. Baked or dry sand is not used for the main core of square columns, and we proceed to describe

Fig. 174.

the method of making the green sand core now invariably adopted. Fig. 175 shows a sort of universal core bore, employed for making these cores. A is a cast iron plate, laid upon the floor of the foundry, generally in close proximity to the mold; upon this are set up two stout boards, B, about two inches thick. These boards are adjustable, so as to take in any breadth of face, by the brackets, D, moving along slots in the plate. Nipping screws in the brackets admit of the boards being pressed together on the end pieces, which must be changed for every width of

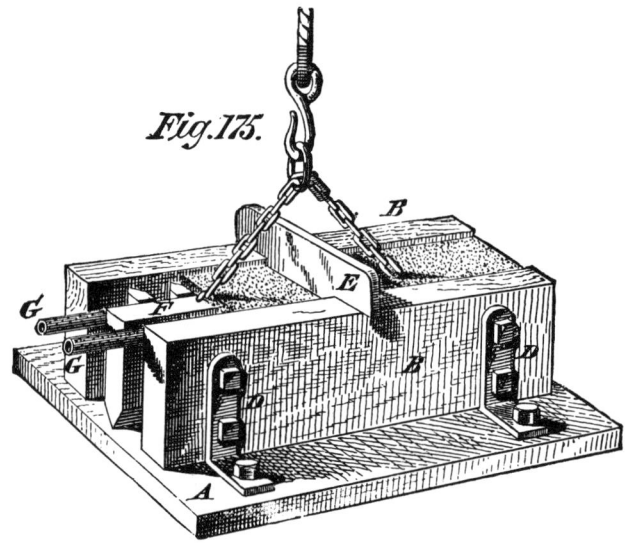

Fig. 175.

column; the height of the core is regulated by means of the strike, E. On account of the exceedingly fragile nature of a green sand core, it is necessary to imbed within it a strong bar of cast iron, called a core bar, such as is represented at F, Fig. 175. It consists of a strong center bar with pieces cast solid with it, ranged on each side, called wings; the bar itself is made to taper off to a narrow ridge towards the under part, as also are the wings which taper at the edges. The sand, being rammed between these wings, is able not only to sustain itself, but also a small portion extending beyond them — namely, to the correct outline of the core. The bar is generally from half an inch to one inch smaller than the core, as will be seen in the sectional end view, Fig. 177. A notch is cut out of

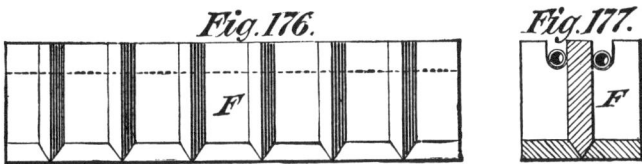

each wing, to admit of the insertion of a perforated tube on each side, for ventilation. The core bar, F, and the perforated tubes, G G, are shown in Fig. 175, imbedded in the core.

As there are not any core prints required to form the openings at the back of the column, the cores for these openings are made in a box not thicker than the intended thickness of metal in the column. Such a box is shown in Fig. 178; though for the sake of cheapness, when the columns are not more than half an inch thick, the core box is sawn out of one piece.

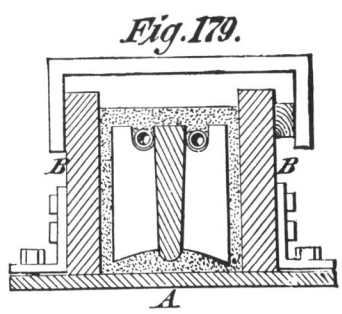

Fig. 179 is an end view of the core box, with core, shown in Fig. 175, but with the addition of the wooden binder, which serves to assist the brackets in holding the sides, B, of the core box together, which is necessary when the core box is very deep.

Round columns are either plain, fluted, or of a mixed design, to agree with the square columns in the same building. Fig. 180 represents a plain round column; but it must be remembered that, even though the shaft be plain, the design of the base and cap may be modified according to taste. In the case of so simple a one as we have illustrated, it would probably be cast solid, as represented; though if of very large size—as those in the crypts of churches, perhaps 18 inches in diameter—a great deal of metal would be saved by simply casting a plain round shaft with the moldings, N and O, upon it, and of a length measured from the lower part of the base to the top of the cap. This casting takes the weight of the building. The base, B, with its molding, B M, and the cap, C, with its molding, C M, are thin castings fixed to the column by screws. P P are the core prints. Little need be said as to the method of preparing a pattern of this description. If small, it will be turned from the solid wood; and if large, it will be lagged or staved up, as we have described in examples of lagging and staving. In any case, the pattern must be made in halves. Some foundries require a half core box; while in others, the core is struck up in the manner described on pages 89, 90.

We may now pass to the consideration of the fluted column, shown in Fig. 181. D is a plan of the peculiar cap required for this kind of column; it is neither square nor round, but of a shape which harmonizes beautifully with the carved work below, all of which, including the cap, is added afterwards, the column being cast a plain round above the member marked N, and also below that marked O. The extension, A, is the part which passes between the joists of the flooring; it is often flattened to admit of this, as shown at C, Fig. 182. B is a section of

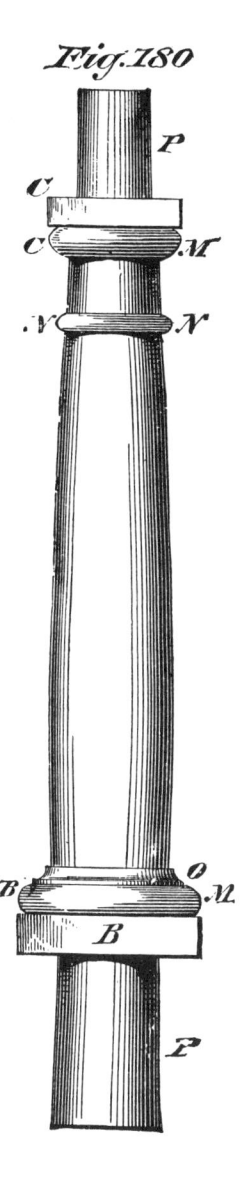

Fig.180

P

C

C. .M

.N N

B. O.M

B

P

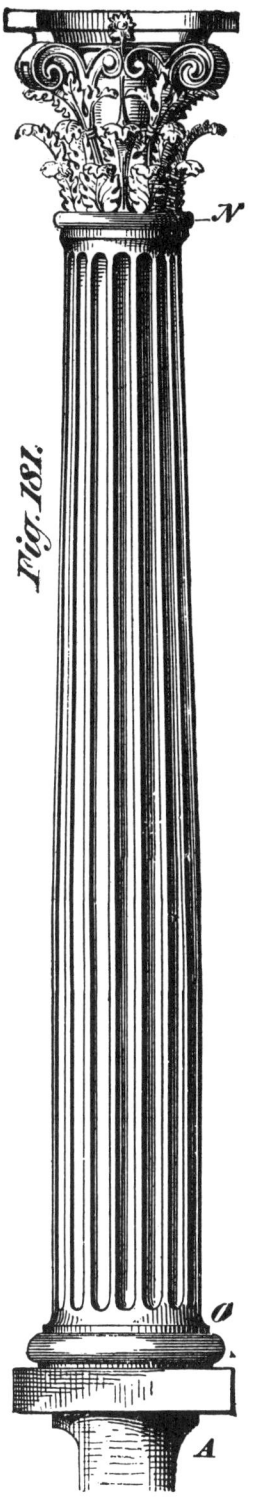

Fig.181.

N

O

A

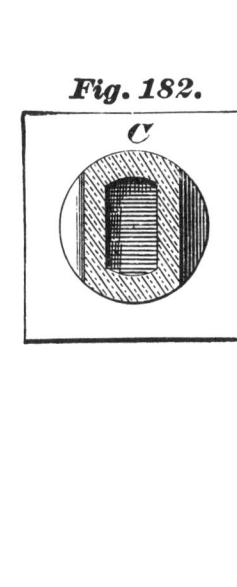

Fig. 182.

C

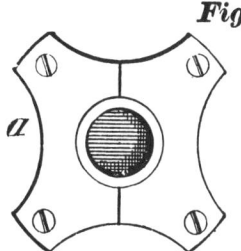

Fig. 182.

a

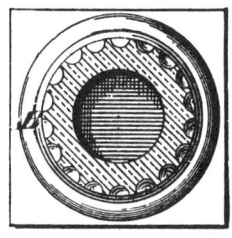

the column through the fluted part. It is not thought necessary to show the prints, as they would be similar to those shown in Fig. 180, the lower one being flattened if the extension A were required.

We have now arrived at the most important part of this branch of our subject, and that is, how to make the fluted pattern column so that it may be extracted with facility from the mold; for, by referring to Fig. 181, it will be seen that the rammed sand, by entering the flutes, would lock the pattern down, unless this difficulty were provided for. To overcome this difficulty, we refer the reader to Figs. 183, 184, 185. Fig. 183 is a sectional view of a column, turned extra large at the part intended to be fluted, so as to form a plain core print all around the column. A convenient number—divisible by 3 or 4—of flutes must be taken; we have taken 12 flutes in the half column. A suitable core box must be constructed with, say, four flutes; these cores, when packed around the mold, will core out the flutes in the column. This method is only given because there may be special cases where it would be most suitable; but it is not that generally adopted.

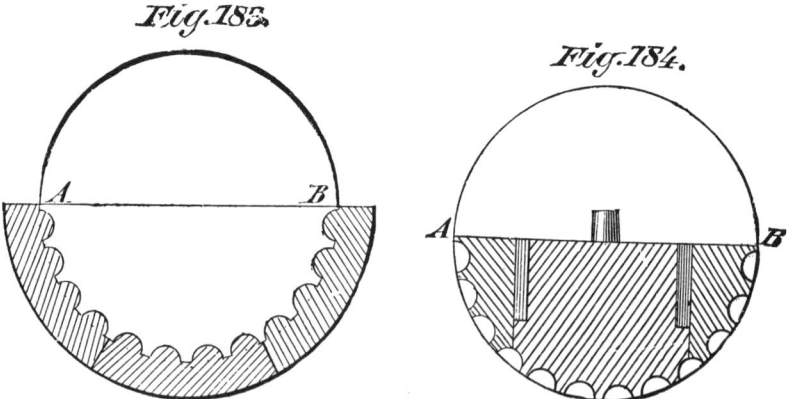

Fig. 183. Fig. 184.

In Fig. 184, each half of the column is formed of three pieces, which are held together by taper dovetails; in this case the middle piece is first drawn from the mold and then the side pieces. This method will accommodate any even number of flutes, and is quite practicable; the objection to it, however, is, that the dovetails are liable to stick, and also that, when the middle piece is drawn out, the side pieces sometimes fall into the mold, to its irretrievable injury.

Fig. 185 represents the arrangement in most general use. It is not nearly so expensive as that shown in Fig. 183, nor is it open to the objections mentioned in connection with Fig. 184. The three pieces marked S are the main staves of the column pattern, but the number is not arbitrary. We may take four or any other number, depending on the size of the column; it is advisable, however, to have as few pieces as possible. What we have to do is to notice the direction taken by the pieces as they are drawn out, and if it appears that the flutes do not escape properly, then a larger number of divisions must be made. The pieces marked f are the supplementary staves in which the flutes are cut; they are attached to the inner staves by screws, which are removed by the molder, who is then able to extract the pattern. The side pieces, f f, are then drawn out, and lastly the lower pieces, the process being, it will be noticed, the reverse of that shown in Fig. 183. In each

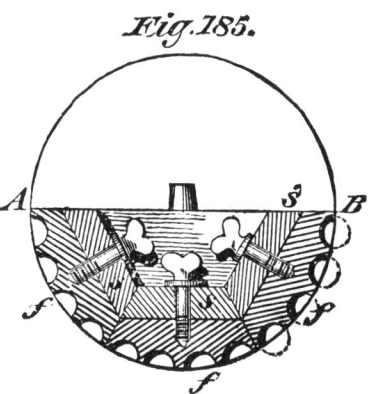

Fig.185.

case, the line A B is the parting line of the pattern, which must always occur in the middle of a ridge and not in a flute. The flutes should be cut out to a half circle, and eased off slightly towards the ridges with sand paper. They must not be in the least undercut, because of the draft in the mold. The pattern should be made as smooth as possible by alternately sand-papering and varnishing, using well worn sand-paper to insure smoothness.

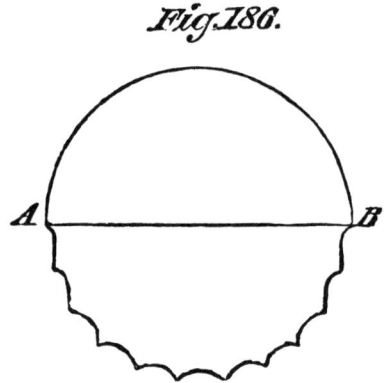

Fig. 186.

In Fig. 186 are shown what are called bastard flutes. Their use gives a cheap but not beautiful style, and they are sometimes employed on lamp posts and columns in the cheaper class of tenement houses. The flutes, it will be noted, are made shallow and of a shape to permit the whole half pattern to be removed from the sand. The flutes are cut out of the solid, the front ones being the deepest, and the side ones so shallow that many of them are scarcely distinguishable.

In columns whose designs are of a mixed character, the methods illustrated for fluting are equally suitable for cabling, as shown in Fig. 185, where the cabling is shown in dotted lines; while rosettes, rope moldings, and the like, are either attached by wires, as shown in the illustration of square columns, or they must be cast separately and afterwards affixed by screws, as are many other ornaments whose shapes preclude their being molded solid with the columns.

CHAPTER XII.

EXAMPLES IN THIN WORK.

In the examples we have hitherto presented to the reader, we have supposed the pattern to be of such substance or thickness, as to be able to bear the pressure of the sand being rammed about it in molding, without breaking or altering its form; but this is not always the case. The parts of a stove, for instance, are cast often less than $\frac{1}{8}$ inch in thickness; the same may be said of most of the ornamental ironwork used in architecture, and even

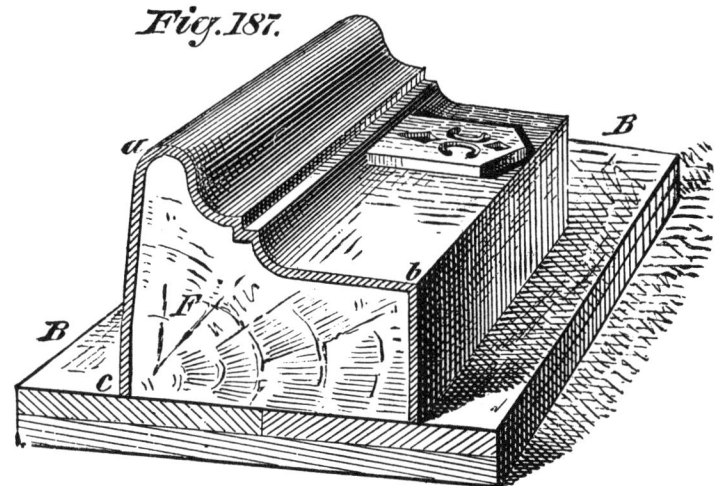

Fig. 187.

cornices and window sills range only about $\frac{3}{16}$ or $\frac{1}{4}$ inch thick. It is true that for this kind of work metal patterns are almost invariably used; but for the pattern maker this is indifferent, as wood patterns have to be made from which the metal patterns are to be cast. Take, for example, the window sill, shown in section in Fig. 187. To enable it to withstand the pressure of the sand, while ramming, we must fill the interior with a form or block, shown at F, which is to be used in conjunction with the board B.　This form and board are no less useful to the pattern maker than to the molder; for let the form be once obtained of the proper size and shape, and the construction of the pattern is so far simplified as to be merely a covering of this form with wood slightly thinner than the required thickness of metal.　Most thin work is made in this manner, especially if the patterns are of such size or shape as to need the joining together of many pieces.　It is not the pattern itself that demands our first attention, but rather the form that supports it.

Thin work demands great care and patience, on account of its fragile nature.　Scarcely any hold can be obtained for nails; and though the best glue is used, it cannot always be relied upon.　Dovetails for square corners, if they are end wood to end wood, will be found very superior to glued joints.　Furthermore, as few joints should be made as possible, and the pattern should be well protected by several coats of varnish.　In working out thin moldings— as for instance, the portion of the sill from *a* to *b*, which should be of one piece—we plane up a piece of a suitable width and thickness, and trace the outline of the molding upon each end of the piece;

Fig. 188.

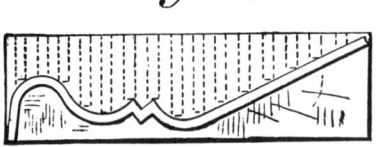

then, as it lies flat upon the bench, we work out on one side to the lines which will fit the form, as in Fig. 188, and then, by temporarily fastening the piece to the form, F, to give it proper support, we are enabled to work out the opposite side to the required shape.　In working out thin moldings, a circular saw with an adjustable table will be of great assistance, as by its means we may make a series of saw cuts so close together as practically to take out half the stuff, and form an excellent guide for cutting away the other half (see Fig. 188). The part from *a* to *c*, Fig. 187, should not be formed by gluing thin stuff together at the obtuse angle, but should be of one piece. Fig. 189 is a section of a cornice lying upon its bed or follower board, B; it may be made of one piece, as in the previous example.

Fig. 189.

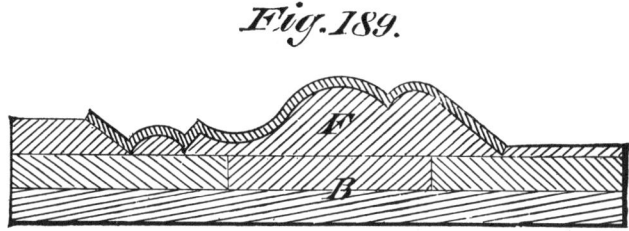

In molding work of this kind, the procedure is as follows: The board, B, with the form and pattern, is placed upon a level bed of sand, so that it may not wind or twist under the weight that is to be put upon it, which will consist of the nowel rammed full of sand. The board and nowel are fastened together by clamps, and, the ramming finished, the whole is turned over; the board and form are then removed. There is no longer any necessity for the support of the latter, as the sand, having been once rammed, does not press upon the pattern to its injury, but keeps its position, and becomes a good and sufficient support to it during the ramming up of the cope, which is now placed in position, and the molding continued in the usual manner.

Fig. 190.

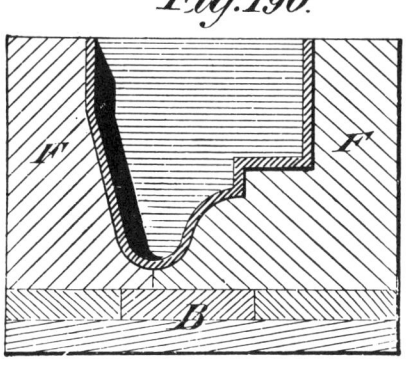

Instead of the form, F, which fills the interior of the pattern, we may provide a strong enveloping form, as shown in Fig. 190; the difference is that the reverse side of the casting will be uppermost as compared with the other case. The form must fit that side of the pattern which we wish to come next the cope. Forms of an irregular or difficult shape are often advantageously made by simply pouring plaster of Paris into the patterns for which they are intended. A great deal of thin work is formed by dry sand coring, often from necessity; but when practicable, the dry sand core is discarded, and the pattern made to leave its own core. This insures greater accuracy, is cheaper, and causes the interior surface of the casting to be the same as the exterior. When dry sand cores are employed, there is no difference between thin work and thick, and therefore the methods described in former pages are a sufficient explanation of the process.

CHAPTER XIII.

The above title applies to a class of work, generally of large size, in which boards or sweeps, fixed to a revolving spindle, serve instead of patterns to form the molds. This arrangement, of course, will only produce circular molds; patterns may, however, be used in conjunction with the sweeps, as we shall endeavor to illustrate further on. The spindle above named is a light vertical shaft, revolving in a step below and a bearing overhead; when a part of a mold has been swept up, the spindle can be raised out of the step sufficiently to enable the work to be removed and preparations for the next piece substituted.

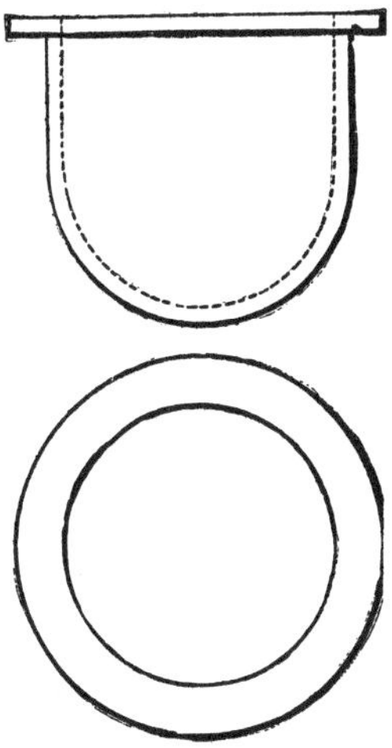

Let it be required to produce a casting, such as is shown in Fig. 191—a sort of pan or boiler, often used. Fig. 194 is a sectional view of the mold complete. It is formed of two parts, the lower being called the " seat," and the upper the " cope." Figs. 192 and 193 illustrate the method of forming each of those parts. The material used by the founder is called loam—a clayey, plastic composition, very soft. After a certain quantity of this material has been piled up, the sweep is revolved; it shears down the high places and indicates the holes or hollows. Into the latter more material is placed, and the sweep is passed round again; and so on until the job is perfected. It will be noticed in Fig. 194, that the two parts of the mold are retained in their proper position by a projection on one

Fig. 191.

9

fitting into a recess in the other; this is the seat proper, and is indicated throughout by S S. The pattern maker's

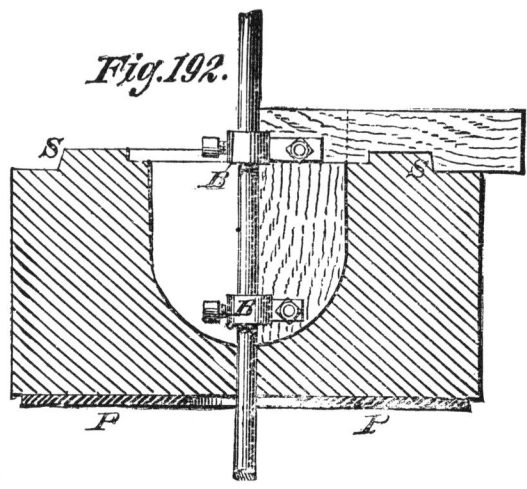

Fig.192.

part is to form the sweeps, which he does in the following manner: On a piece of board of the proper thickness for a sweep—the size of which depends on the size of the work—he draws an outline of the job, interior and exterior, from the center outwards; and beyond this he lays off his seat, as shown at Fig. 193—the dotted lines representing the interior of the piece. He has then simply to cut away to the interior line, and also the step at S, and one board is finished, unless he knows the diameter of the spindle and the position of the holes in the carrying bracket attached thereto; in which case he is supposed to cut off, parallel with the center line, a portion equal to the radius of the spindle, as a recess for the hub of the bracket, B, and to bore the holes for the bolts. The board, Fig. 192, when reversed, should fit that in Fig. 193 at the lower part, and be of a shape to coincide with the dotted line. Its length must be enough to extend to the center, *minus* the radius of the spindle, as shown in Fig. 192.

It will be seen by the lines showing the grain of the

wood that the board in Fig. 192 is formed of two pieces, lapped at the corner, to give strength; and, to avoid too

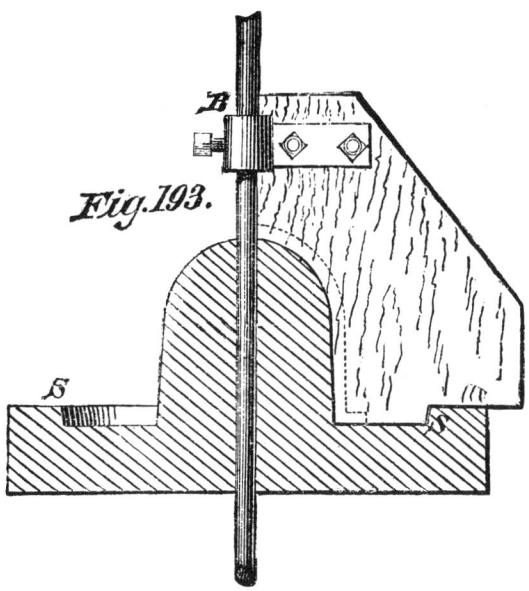

Fig. 193.

much cross grain, battens may be added when it is thought necessary. As I have already remarked, in

Fig. 194.

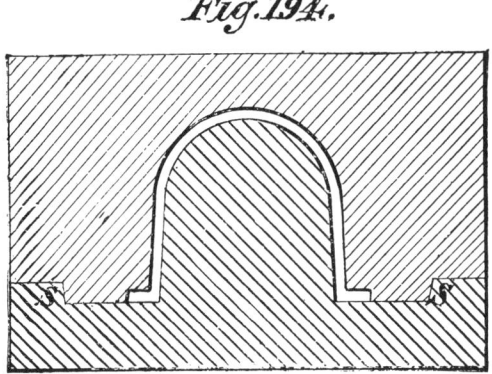

striking up cores with a horizontal spindle, the working edge of the board should be beveled; and it is hardly necessary to say that the same is applicable in this case.

P P, Fig. 192, is a circular plate of cast iron, used to support the mold while soft; it is not shown in Fig. 193. By

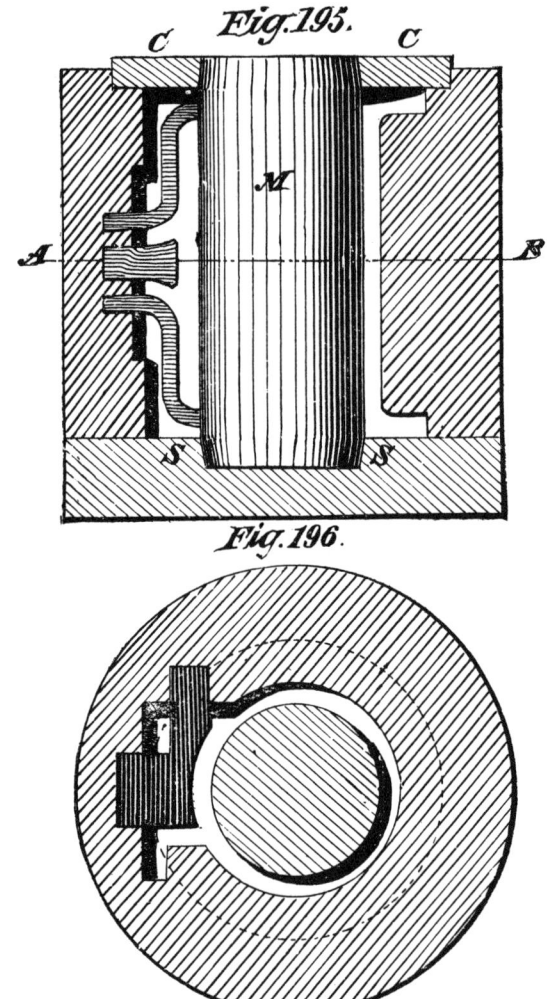

Fig. 195.

Fig. 196.

the same method, only varying the outline of the sweeps, a large class of circular work may be produced, including vases, speed cones, etc. Sometimes it is necessary to cast brackets, pipes, or other projections, upon the main piece; to do this, patterns must be made of those projections, and as many patterns as there are projections. The height at which it is required to bed in these brackets, etc., must be indicated to the molder by a small **V**, cut into the sweep; this will produce, as the sweep revolves, a line upon the mold. For the rest, unless simple directions can be given, the pattern maker usually visits the foundry, and assists in placing, or at least in verifying, the position of the pieces. When the mold is sufficiently hard, and before it is baked, these patterns are withdrawn.

A good illustration of the manner in which pattern work may be used in conjunction with sweeps, is furnished in the ordinary engine cylinder. Fig. 195 is a sectional elevation of a complete mold; Fig. 196 is a horizontal section of the same, on the line A B showing the outlet for the exhaust steam. This mold is composed of four parts that are swept or struck up—namely, S S, the seat; A B, the body; C C, the cope, and M, the main core. The latter may be struck upon a horizontal arbor, or formed in a box

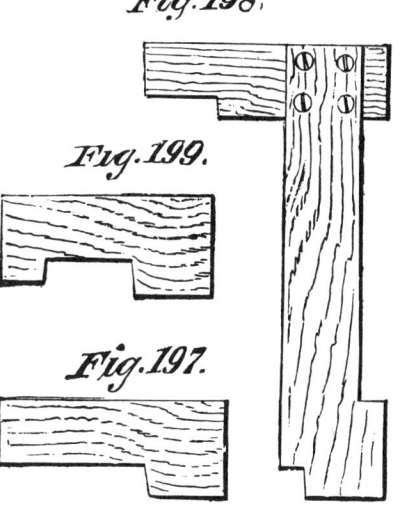

Fig. 198.

Fig. 199.

Fig. 197.

In addition to the parts above enumerated are the two steam port cores and the exhaust port core, all formed in core boxes. The procedure is as follows: With a board, shown in Fig. 197, the seat S S is struck up; upon this, when dried, is placed a flange of wood. It is set centrally; the seat is also carefully beveled and set by the spindle. A pattern of the slide face, with the parts in which the steam and exhaust passages occur, is set in position on this flange; the top flange of wood is now added, and temporarily fixed to the slide face pattern, and shored up on the opposite side, so as to maintain it true and level. With the board, Fig. 198, is formed the body A B; the shape of the exterior of the mold is not important; it is left rough, but some mark must be made so as to be able, after removing it from the seat, to restore it to the position as before. When the body has dried sufficiently, the pattern flanges and slide face are withdrawn, the body being lifted from the seat for this purpose by means of bolts passing through it, and terminating in a cast annular plate at the bottom. The projecting flanges on the slide face are attached by wires and dovetails; otherwise the piece would be locked in the mold. The side print for the exhaust port is attached also by a loose wire. Fig. 199 is a board for sweeping up the cope, C C. The whole of these boards are represented as carried to the center of the spindle; allowance must, therefore, be made for the spindle and bracket. For very large cylinders, wood flanges are not used, the sweeps being made to a shape to perform the whole of the work.

CHAPTER XIV.

We now approach a class of work in which the fullest amount of care and attention on the part of the pattern maker, for the attainment of accuracy, is exceedingly desirable. Patterns for wheel work, clumsily constructed, may be positively worthless, or may at least give rise to great loss of time in the fitting shop, in correcting the defects in the castings taken from them. It is not our purpose to enter into the various methods of arriving at the proper form or curvature that is to be given to the teeth, as that is a subject quite extensive, and a study in itself. What more particularly concerns us, is the general construction of the patterns from designs furnished.

Gear wheels are of two kinds, spur and bevel; the former for transmitting motion when the shafts are parallel, and the latter to be used when the shafts are inclined to each other. When the teeth of a bevel wheel are inclined at an angle of 45° with the axis, that wheel is called a miter. Skew bevels are wheels suitable for shafts that are inclined to each other, and are not in the same plane. Pinion is a distinctive term, applied to the smaller of a pair of gear wheels, when there is a great disparity between them; or it may mean generally a small gear wheel.

Fig. 200 is a plan and section of the pattern of a spur wheel and pinion, such as is usually supplied to workmen. The plan exhibits the form of the teeth and pitch, with the size and number of arms. The sectional view shows the breadth of face, depth of hub, and ribs on the arms. In the construction of gear wheel and pinion patterns, the particular method to be adopted, as also the material to be used, will depend upon size and the service expected to be got out of the patterns.   Mahogany, dry and straight grained, is an excellent material for wheel patterns; but for large work it is too costly.   In some cases the teeth are worked in mahogany and fixed to a pine body; in the majority of cases, however, pine is the only material used. The pinion may be carved out of one piece, or it may have the teeth attached to a hub; and if the latter, then the teeth may be held by dovetails, or they may be simply glued or nailed.   If the pinion is so deep in proportion to its diameter as to be strong enough, and not more than 5 or 6 inches diameter over all, it may be cut from the solid. In this case, the grain of the wood must lie in the direction of the teeth.   For turning the piece we must use a chuck or face plate, smaller than the pinion is at the bottom of the spaces, so as to be able to trace circles on both sides by the motion of the lathe; if such a face plate is not at our disposal, we may bore a hole in the piece to be turned, and fit to it an arbor of hard wood.   Having turned the pattern, trace upon it very fine circles to indicate the pitch line, the line for the roots of the teeth, and (if required) circles for the centers used in tracing certain peculiar forms of teeth.   All these circles are to be traced on both sides of the pattern, and draft is to be allowed by making the circle for the roots of the teeth a little smaller on one side than on the other, and also by turning the piece slightly taper.   The pinion is now to be pitched out, on one side, very accurately; this is sometimes a matter of no small difficulty, for, having passed round with the compasses a few times, the points are liable to slide into previous impressions, giving rise to error. For this reason the pattern maker does not allow the points of his compasses to fall where he intends the center of the teeth to be, until he has obtained the correct division, which is known by the compass point, after having made the tour of the circle, falling exactly into the starting point.   He now proceeds to lay down the centers of the teeth, and to delineate their size and form; then, by squaring across the face, the points of the teeth are transferred to the other side; the

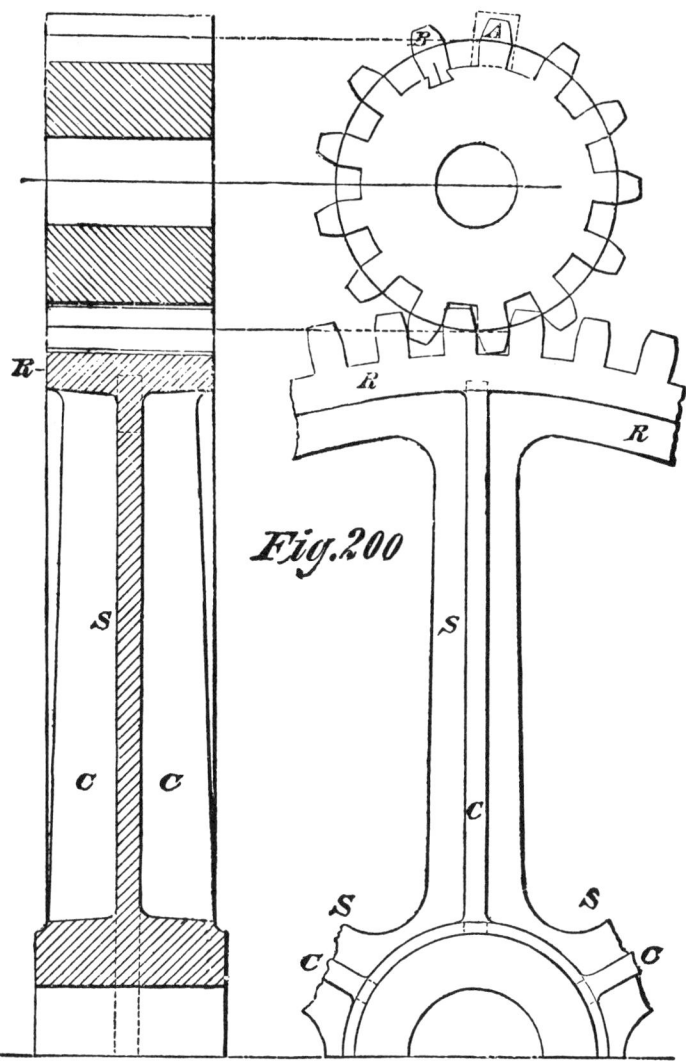

Fig. 200

teeth are then outlined on that side, and the intervening spaces cut away exactly to the lines.

9*

For a large-sized pinion, the usual method is to build up a hub or body with quadrants, breaking joint at each course or layer; the body is then turned, and the circumference pitched off to the required number of teeth. Blocks of hard or soft wood, planed nearly to the size of the teeth and hollowed on the side that goes next the body, are to be glued on and set to the lines made on the surface of the body when it was pitched off (see tooth marked A, Fig. 200). When the glue has properly set, the whole is replaced in the lathe and turned off, the same as for a solid pinion; the lining-in will also be a repetition of the process above explained. Another method is to fix the teeth on dovetails, as at B, Fig. 200; but as this is very seldom adopted for spur pinions, it will be more in place to describe it when dealing with bevel gear.

We now proceed to the construction of the wheel which, in our illustration, has six spokes or arms, marked S; the rim, R, must of course be built up in segments; and when we have reached to the height of the top of the flat arms, we should turn the inside to the finished size, and cut in the arms, as shown in Fig. 200, the rest of the building can then be proceeded with. To avoid here useless repetition as to the details observed in building or in preparing the arms, the reader is referred to Figs. 132, 133, 134 and 135. Having turned the body of the wheel, both inside and out, we proceed to attach, on each side of the arms, a hub, so as to form the whole hub, as in Fig. 200; the ribs, C, are then fitted, and lastly we complete the body by filleting the corners. For the teeth there is but one method that is usually adopted, and that is to form them in a box as follows:

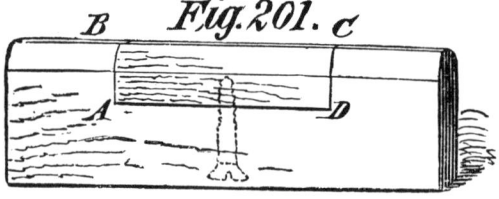

Fig. 201.

Plane a piece of hard wood, as in Fig. 201, some five or

six inches longer than the teeth, and about three inches wider; the thickness is not to be less than that of the tooth at its thickest part. The ends of this piece must also be planed; from the edge, B C, gage the line, A D, the required depth of tooth. Lay off, about in the center of the piece, the distance B C, equal to breadth of face of the wheel, and make two saw cuts, B A and C D. Let this piece be now let into a piece of planed board, Fig. 202, which is an inch or so longer than the radius of the wheel at the tops of the teeth. This piece is to fit tightly into the mortise, which is made equally on each side of a center line on the board. Take now in a trammel the radius of the wheel at the top of the teeth, and mark off, from the outer edge of the hard wood box, the distance E F on the center line of the board. The point F represents the center of the wheel. Take the radius of the wheel at the pitch line, and also at the roots and points of the teeth; and with these distances describe the arcs G G, H I, J K, and such other arcs as may be necessary, on which to take the centers for describing the correct form of the tooth. Complete the delineation of three teeth, or at

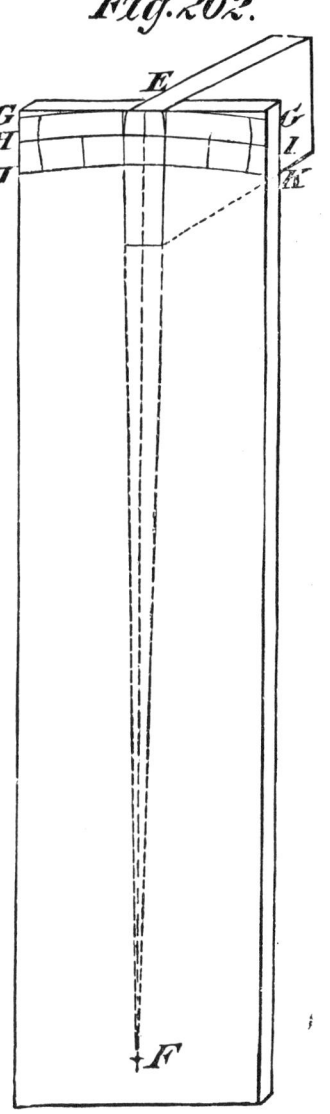

Fig. 202.

least the center one, which will be upon the hard wood box;

reverse now this box, and draw the outline of the **tooth**
upon the other end of it; remove the piece from the mortise, and plane off to the shape of the tooth as drawn; remove the portion B A D C, Fig. 201, and the box is ready
for shaping teeth in.   Such teeth during the process are
held by the screw shown.

Select for the teeth, lumber very straight in the grain,
and rip off a number of strips about two or two and a half
feet long, of a width and thickness (when planed) slightly
fuller than the required teeth, and hollow one edge to fit
the curvature of the rim of the wheel. Saw the strips into
pieces a trifle longer than the teeth, and plane the ends
so that, when finished, the length of the pieces is exactly
equal to the breadth of the rim. This latter process is most
rapidly performed by placing some eight or ten side by
side in a frame, and, if necessary, tightening them by a
wedge and nipping in the vise (see Fig. 203). The frame

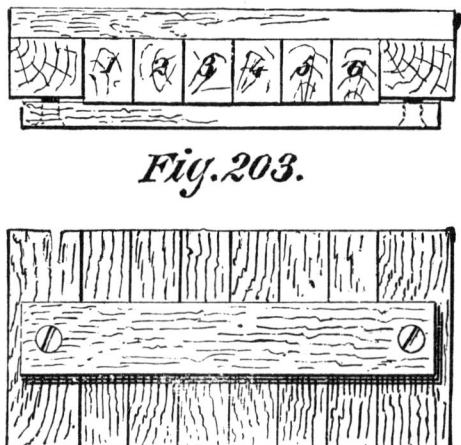

Fig.203.

must be equal in width to the length it is required to
make the pieces, and care must be taken not to diminish this width, as is sometimes done.   In planing a number of teeth, it perhaps is as well to black-lead the frame
where it is apt to be planed; this will at least show when

damage has been done. The blocks are now severally shaped to the proper contour in the box, Fig. 201, particular attention being paid not to shave away the box in shaping the teeth; for this reason it is well to have an extra plane, very finely set, to finish with. The rim of the wheel having been divided according to the number of teeth required, and lines squared across its face at *a*, Fig. 204, the finished teeth are glued on exactly to the lines. Only a few spots of glue should be applied, so that little or none may exude and hide the line that we pose the teeth by; when the glue has perfectly set, the teeth should be additionally secured by nails. If the above processes are followed up with proper care, the teeth will all be found evenly set around the wheel; nevertheless, it is only right to verify their position with a pair of calipers, while the glue is yet soft.

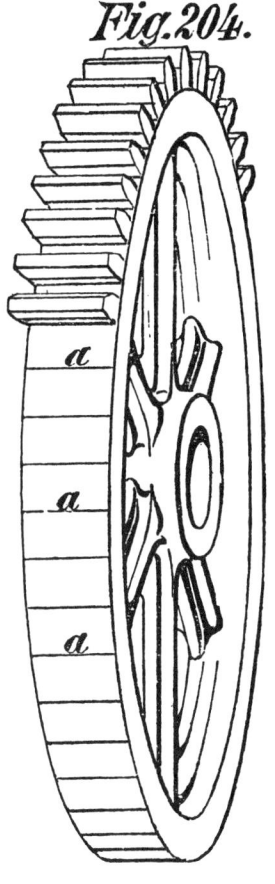

Fig. 204.

Very large wheels, or even those of moderate size, when difficulties of transportation are anticipated, are made by bolting together a number of sections. A section usually consists of an arm and two equal portions of the rim, one on each side of it, so as to have a joint midway between each pair of arms. However this may be, one thing must be strictly observed, namely, to have the joints always in the center of spaces; therefore it is sometimes necessary to employ unequal segments or sections, in which case the pattern is made to the longer segment; and when these

are cast, the flange is moved to suit the shorter one, and
the superfluous teeth are stopped off in the sand. This
saves cutting the pattern, which remains good for other
wheels, when required. The extremities of the arms,
which are to be screwed to the hub, are provided with
flanges for this purpose, the hub being flattened to
accommodate them. A great deal of nicety is required
in constructing wheels on this principle, as the spaces
between the teeth at the joints must be neither wider nor
narrower than at other parts.

BEVEL WHEELS.

" He who can make a good bevel wheel is a good pattern maker." That was once the saying; but the system
that divides a trade into specialties is now growing to be
the general custom, and it has robbed the expression of
half its truth, for there are many good pattern makers
who have been engaged all their lives in specialties remote from bevel wheel making. We give the saying,
however, merely to show the importance that has always
been attached to work of this kind, not undeservedly. A
pair of bevel wheel patterns, fresh from the workman's
hand, especially if of mahogany and nicely varnished,
excite general admiration. It is a job easy enough to do;
but you must know the way: that way is what I shall endeavor to elucidate.

Fig. 205 is a sectional elevation and plan of a bevel
pinion; the construction of the body does not differ mate-
rially from that of a spur. We may commence building up,
if the pinion is of such size as to require building, from the
small side, A B, for the reason that it is desirable and convenient to turn the part, where the teeth are to be, last,
when the building is completed; or if it is a solid piece,
we begin by turning off to the line, D C; then reverse on

the chuck and turn A B, making a slight recess for the
core pivot; set a bevel
to the angle, A B C, on
the drawing, and turn
the circumference to it
and at the same time to
the required diameter,
making it perfectly true
and straight for the re-
ception of the teeth.
Very little, if any, sand-
papering is to be done on
this part—it destroys the
evenness of the surface.
With a fine tracing
point, and while the
lathe is in motion, mark
a line near to D C on the
circumference, or, properly speaking, the face.
Upon this line the pitch-
ing or dividing is made,
to determine the position
of the teeth; divide this
line into as many parts
as it is desired to have
teeth. It often happens
in performing this divi-
sion that, having passed
the compasses around
the piece, we do not fall
exactly into the starting
point, but yet are so near
that we cannot shift the
compasses, even if they

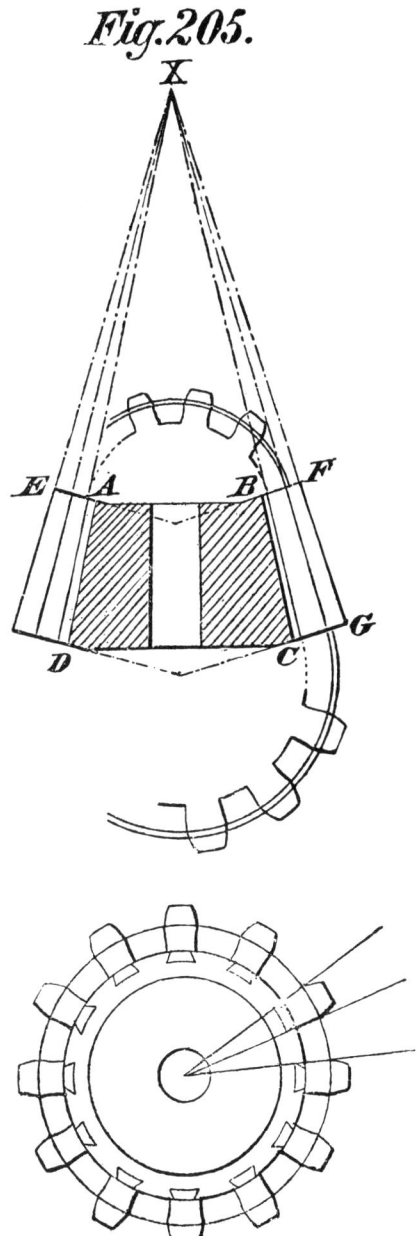

Fig.205.

are furnished with slow-motion screw, without **making**
the error greater. The usual way of overcoming this
difficulty is to give the compass points a few slight
rubs upon the oilstone, inside or out, according as we
wish either to enlarge or diminish the distance between
them.

When a pair of bevel gears are geared together, all the
teeth on each wheel incline towards a single point; this
point is where the axial lines of the shafts would meet if
produced. In order to give this direction to the teeth of a
bevel wheel or pinion, we must set them square; but to
an article of the shape we have produced, an ordinary
square cannot be applied in this case, and the workman
calls to his aid one of the simplest problems in practical
geometry—namely, to erect a perpendicular to a given
line. This is illustrated in Fig. 206, where the whole outline
is supposed to represent the turned body of the pinion.

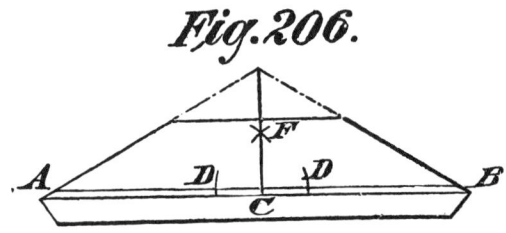

Fig. 206.

A B is the line passing around it, of which we have previously spoken. In it take any point, C; it may be one of
the points already made in pitching off. With C as a center, and at any distance convenient, mark D and D; with
D and D as centers, and at any suitable distance, mark
the arcs which intersect at the point F. Join F C; it is the
perpendicular line required. As it would be too troublesome to go through this operation for every tooth on the
wheel or pinion, a square has to be made, such as shown
in Fig. 207; the back is generally a piece of pine gaged

to fit the edge of the rim or face; a hard wood blade is screwed to it, so that, when the back is applied to the rim, the blade may be made to coincide with the perpendicular line F C; all the rest of the perpendiculars required at the points of division are traced by this square. Another method, even more simple, is to plane a piece of thin wood to lie upon the hand-rest of the lathe, so as at the same time to coincide with the perpendicular drawn by the aid of the compasses; it is then correct for tracing the others. This arrangement is shown in Fig. 209.

Fig. 207.

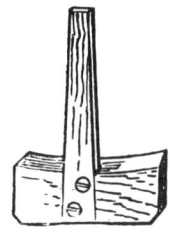

If we intend simply to glue and brad the teeth, we proceed to make blocks, a little larger every way than the

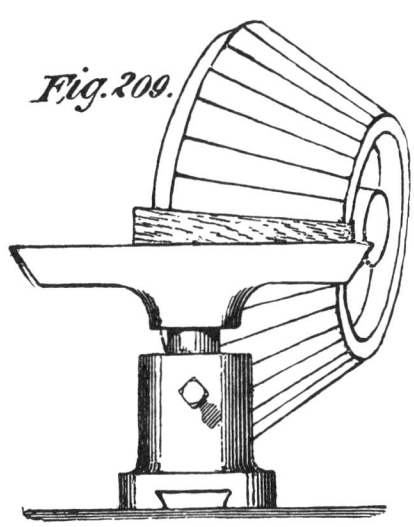

Fig. 209.

teeth require to be, hollowing out one side to fit the cone of the body of the pinion. These blocks are glued on to the lines; and when the work is set, it is returned, this

9**

time setting the bevel to the angle E F G. A pitch line must be traced on each side; redivide and draw in the outline of the teeth on the larger side; then, by the methods already described for making perpendiculars, transfer the points of the teeth to the small side; then complete the outline, following out the same principle adopted in tracing the large side—that is to say, taking corresponding centers and distances proportionate to the diminished size of the small side of the cone, as shown in Fig. 205, where the large and small ends of three teeth are set out.

When the subject of spur pinions was under consideration, I deferred making any remarks upon the attachment of teeth by dovetails, until bevel gear should be treated on. Let us now consider the advantages and disadvantages, if any, of this mode of fixing the teeth. We have long ago mentioned the property which wood has of altering its size according to the dryness or humidity of the atmosphere, which alteration, though considerable across the grain, is very slight in the direction of its length. Hence, when teeth are glued to a body, the grain of which crosses that of the teeth, there will be a movement between the two when the pattern is subjected to a change in dampness or dryness; the dovetail allows freedom for any movement from these causes, retaining the tooth in its position under all circumstances. Should the mold happen to break down in the act of withdrawing the pattern, it may be restored to a considerable extent by knocking out a few teeth, placing them in the damaged impressions left by the pattern, and bedding up the sand around them. It sometimes happens that the teeth of a bevel wheel or pinion will be too much undercut to leave the mold without damaging it; this method will admit of the teeth being withdrawn in detail, after which the pattern can be lifted without difficulty. To counterbalance these advantages must be mentioned the extra cost inseparable from this method of fixing the teeth. This, however, is really a small matter when dealing with pinions; and, therefore, bevel pinions usually have their teeth attached by dovetails, excepting those of small size. If it is decided to use dovetails, we proceed as follows: The body of the pinion has been turned and divided, and the perpendiculars all finely drawn in. Cut out of thin wood a piece of the size which the dovetails are intended to be, which is such that a small margin of tooth may be left on each side; set the piece on the rim, at a distance from a perpendicular equal to the margin allowed; set it by the square, shown in Fig. 207, as the dovetail must have such a taper that its sides may both tend towards the point X, before alluded to, namely, the intersection of the axes of the shafts. This will be the case if, when one side of the dovetail template has been set square, the other is square also. By this template, lines for all the dovetails are scribed on the face; the depth is laid off on the drawing by lines tending toward X; and from this the depth of each end of the recess may be gaged on the pattern. No curvature is given to the bottom of this; it is pared out flat with the chisel. The dovetails are now fitted, and left projecting above the face; they are driven moderately tight; the projecting parts are then turned off level with the rim.

We have now to go through the same process as before described for making and attaching teeth. When the glue is well set, each should be knocked out, numbered, and the dovetail bradded. Fig. 208 is a section and half plan of a bevel wheel. In the latter the shape of the teeth is not shown, but merely their thickness at the pitch line; in the sectional view, a few teeth are laid out in profile upon arcs struck from the centers, A and B, which are the points of intersection of perpendiculars from the ends of the teeth (at the pitch line) and the center line. In the section on one side is shown a series of rectangles, numbered from 1 to 5; these represent the segments of which the rim is composed. It is true that they might be made more nearly to approximate to the shape of the rim by sawing them to a bevel, but a machine suitable for this is not in every shop; and when it is considered that the segments themselves are

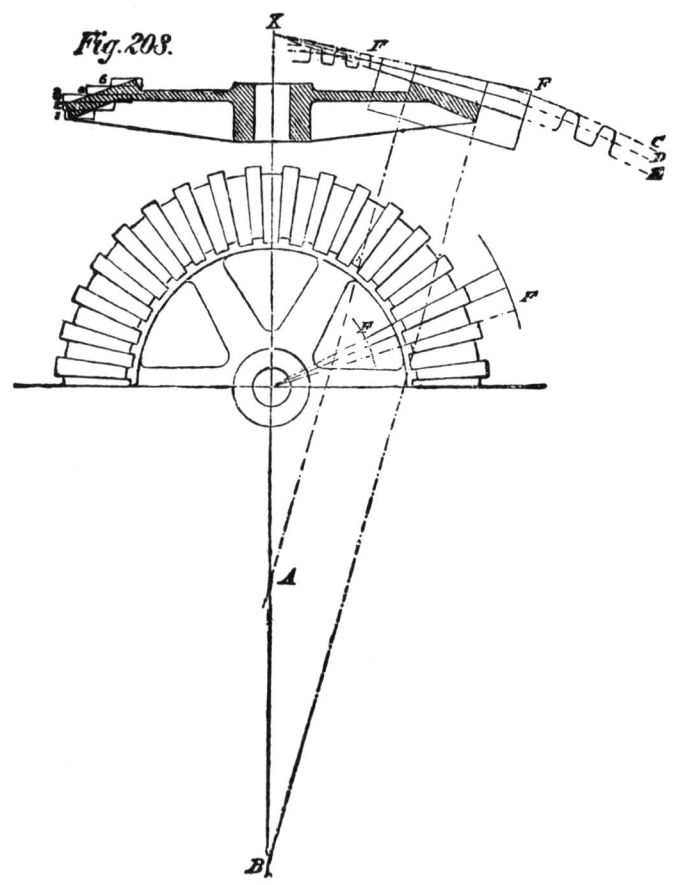

Fig. 208.

usually not more than $\frac{5}{8}$ inch in thickness, it will be seen that the additional complication counterbalances the saving in lumber and time in turning. If, however, the wheel is very large, or where thick segments are employed, we may advantageously saw the segments to a bevel. The method described for turning the bevel pinion is exactly suitable for the wheel; the arms will be checked together, but need not be built into the rim, unless we desire an exceptionally strong pattern; the obliquity of the rim enables us to get a good purchase, by means of screws through the end of each arm into it. Care must be taken to have the ends of the arms each to bear properly on the rim; otherwise the rim will be thrown out of true in screwing.

It will be remembered that, in treating upon the spur wheel, we had, in forming the box for shaping the teeth, simply to draw out on each end the natural size of the tooth, that is, if we except a slight diminution towards one end for draught; but the conical form of a bevel wheel gives a little extra trouble. In Fig. 208 the tooth proper is of the length of the face of the wheel, as seen in section. Now all lines bounding the teeth must converge to the point X; so if we take F F to represent the length of the box, we must strike out upon the large end an enlarged, and upon the small end a diminished tooth; then by planing to these lines we shall have formed such a box that any piece shaped in the gap formed in it, will be of the proper size and shape for a tooth. It would confuse our engraving too much were we to attempt to show the enlarged and diminished tooth on the ends of the box; but the principle is easily understood, as we have but to follow out whatever method has been adopted on the drawing for producing the tooth curves.

THE WORM, OR ENDLESS SCREW.

A worm pattern, when cut by hand, involves a slow and tedious operation; and even with the utmost care we can scarcely expect to produce an article so perfect as it would be if cut in a screw-cutting lathe. But however well adapted the screw-cutting lathe may be for producing good screws in metal, it will not be found to give such good results when wood is the material to be operated upon; this may be accounted for by reason of the high speed required to make a clean job with wood in a lathe, which is altogether incompatible with the working of the gearing necessary for cutting screws, at least of such fast pitches as are usually required for worms. Besides, special tools must be made for use in the lathe, conforming to the shape of the tooth; for a worm is really one long tooth wound about a cylinder. There are a few other minor difficulties attending the cutting of a wooden worm in a screw-cutting lathe; and when all are considered, it is doubtful if there is much gain over the old-time hand method. We will, however, describe both:

Let Fig. 209 represent the complete pattern. To make it in either way, take two pieces, each to form one half of the pattern; peg and screw them together at the ends, an excess of stuff being allowed at each end for the accommodation of such screws or dogs, if the latter are more convenient, as

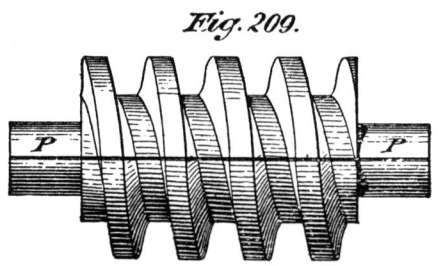

Fig. 209.

they might be in a large pattern. Turn the piece down to the size over the top of the thread, after which the prints, P P, are turned. Supposing it to be determined to cut the thread in a lathe, we must have ready a few tools adapted for the work; the first of which is the parting tool, very similar to a parting tool for brass, Fig. 210—namely, flat and level on the cutting face, but with a great deal more bottom rake, as strength is not so much an object, and the

Fig. 210.

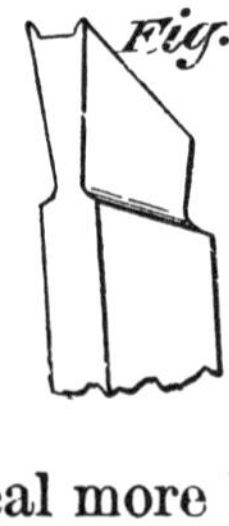

tool is more easily sharpened. We have also in addition a little projection, like the point of a penknife, formed by filing away the steel in the center; these points are to cut the fibres of the wood, the severed portion being scraped away by the flat part of the tool. We must not forget to give a side rake to the tool corresponding to the pitch we have to cut; and the width of the tool is to be a shade narrower than the space in the worm at the narrowest part, which is generally at the root of the tooth. Having suitably adjusted the change wheels to the pitch required, we drive down the parting tool until the leading points are on a level with what is to be the bottom of the spaces; a parting tool without cutting points is now adjusted, and the space made of the required depth. We now have cut a worm with a square thread; and it remains to finish to the required form of tooth. To do this, some have essayed a tool such as shown in Fig. 211; but this will not work, for the reason that it is end wood which we have to cut. Were we cutting across the grain—as, for instance, in making the groove with the parting tool— then the one shown in Fig. 211, which is nothing but a scraper, would act very well. The tool shown in plan and section, Fig. 212, has a keen edge imparted to it by piercing a hole through

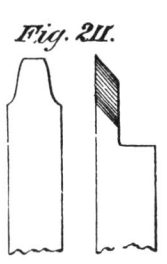

Fig. 211.

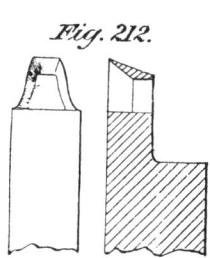

Fig. 212.

the steel and filing to a bevel; it must then be nicely oilstoned. The only objection to this tool is the difficulty of sharpening it. We ought not to suffer both sides of the tool to cut at once; in fact, the tool itself should not be made quite so wide as the space it has to finish. Furthermore, if the pattern is very large, it will be necessary to have two tools for finishing—one to cut from the pitch line inwards, and the other to complete the form from the pitch line outwards. It is advisable to use hard wood.

If it is decided to cut the thread by hand, then—the pattern being turned as before—separate the two halves by taking out the screws at the ends; select the half that has not the pegs, as being a little more convenient for tracing lines across. Set out the sections of the thread, A, B, C, and D, Fig. 213, similar to a rack; through the centers of

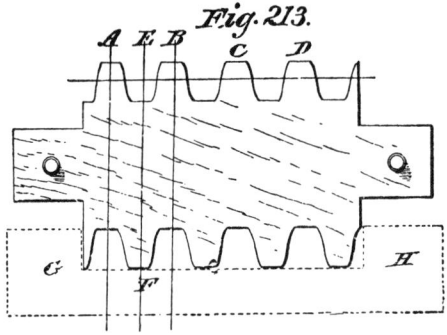

Fig. 213.

A, B, C, and D, square lines across the piece. These lines, where they intersect the pitch line, will give the centers of spaces on that side; or if we draw lines, as at E, F, through the centers of the spaces, they will pass through the centers of the teeth (so to speak) on the other side. In this position complete the outline on that side. It will be found, in drawing these outlines, that the centers of some of the arcs will lie outside the pattern. To obtain support for the compasses we must fit over the pattern a piece of board, such as shown by dotted lines at G H.

We have now to draw in the top of the thread upon the curved surface of the half pattern. For this purpose we take a piece of stiff card or other flexible material (see Fig. 214), we wrap it around the pattern and fix it temporarily by tacks, trim off the edges true to the pattern, and mark upon the edges of the card the position of the tops of the thread upon each side; we remove

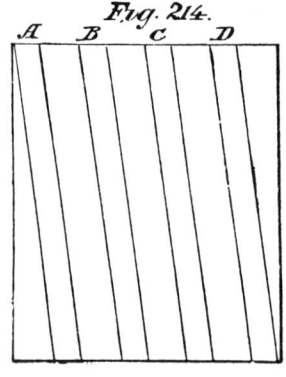

Fig. 214.

the card and spread it out on a flat surface, join the points marked on the edges, as in Fig. 215, replace the card exactly as before upon the pattern, and with a fine scriber we prick through the lines. The cutting out is commenced by sawing, keeping of course well within the lines; and it is facilitated by attaching a stop to the saw, so as to insure cutting at all parts nearly to the exact depth. This stop is a simple strip of wood and may be clamped to the saw, though it is much more convenient to have a couple of holes in the saw blade for the passage of screws. For finishing, a pair of templates, Fig. 215, right and left, will be found useful; and finally the work should be verified and slight imperfections corrected by the use of a form taking in three spaces, as shown in Fig. 216. In

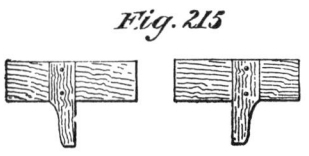

Fig. 215

drawing the lines on the card, we must consider whether it is a right or left handed worm that we desire. In the engravings, the full lines are those suitable for a right, and the dotted lines for a left handed thread.

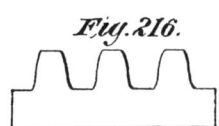

Fig. 216.

Having completed one half of the pattern, place the two halves together; and trace off the half that is uncut, using again the card template for drawing the lines on the curved surface. The cutting out will be the same as before.

Another and very quick method of making a worm pattern is to turn down the body of the pattern to the diameter of the bottom of the thread or worm, and to then turn up some rings whose bore must be the same in diameter as the bottom of the worm. Now, suppose we cut one of these rings in four quarters, and fasten one section to the body of the pattern, then put on the next section, not fair with the first but as much to one side as the pitch of the thread requires, and continuing this process the thread may be fas-

10

tened to the body.   It is obvious, however, that the thickness of the washers must be greater than the thickness of the thread, but what their thickness requires to be depends on how many sections it is intended to cut them up into.   It is best to so regulate the thickness, however, that the corner of each section on one side shall represent the exact pitch of the worm, so that the corners will act as a guide in cutting the thread.

The accompanying illustration (Fig. 217) represents a

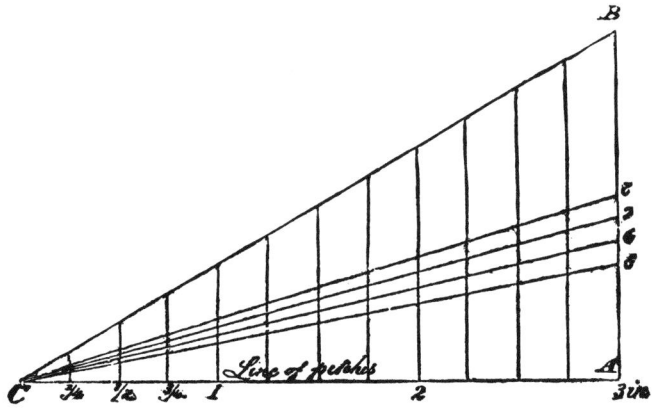

very serviceable article for those who may be called upon to lay out gearing.   It is not new to the mechanical world, but as the author never happened to meet with but one man who actually had made himself a scale of this kind, he considers it will prove a novelty to a large class of pattern makers.

Draw the lines A B and A C at right angles to each other.   Make A B equal to three inches; the line A C may be any convenient length, say six inches, as by observing this proportion the scale will be in addition a very useful set square, with the angles, at B and C, 60° and 30° respectively.   Join B C; divide A B into 15 parts; from C draw lines to the fifth, sixth, seventh and eighth parts, as in the figure. Divide A C into as many parts as there are inches in A B, number the divisions, and erect perpendiculars to A B. These are for the even inch pitches. To make the scale serviceable for the fractional parts, divide and subdivide again, and erect a perpendicular at each division. This process in our figure is carried out to quarter inches. It may, however, be further extended, if desired; but inasmuch as it is so little trouble to draw a perpendicular at any time for any fractional pitch required, it may be preferred by some that the scale should not be overcrowded with lines.

Brass is probably the most suitable material, as it takes the lines readily, does not oxidize, and is sufficiently hard to stand considerable wear.

The method of using this scale will be clear from the following example. Let O, Fig. 218, be the center of a tooth

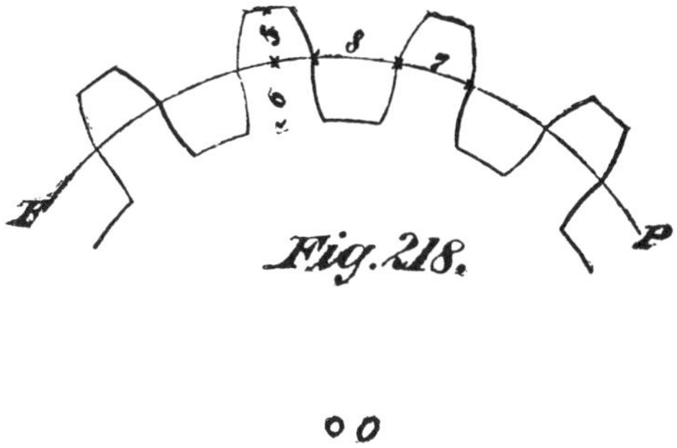

Fig. 218.

wheel or pinion, and F P the pitch circle, which we will suppose already divided off, and that the pitch is one inch; on the perpendicular marked take with the compasses the distance up to line 5, and set this off outside the pitch for the tops of the teeth; on the same perpendicular take the distance up to line 6, and mark this inside the pitch circle for the roots of the teeth. With center O, and the points so found as distances, describe circles.

Make the thickness of the tooth equal to the distance on the scale up to line 7; the width of the space will then be equal to the distance up to line 8—all, of course, measured from the base line, A C.

Scales upon this principle may be made to accommodate any preferred proportions of the teeth of wheels.

CHAPTER XV.

For the sake of durability, patterns for pulleys are generally made of cast iron. For convenience in molding it is usual to make them in halves, as shown in Fig. 220, A B being the line of division. The hubs are of wood, as they frequently have to be changed to suit different sizes of shafts.

We may commence by building up a wooden pattern for half of the rim, making it of such a size as to allow for its being turned by the machinist after being cast. Two castings having been taken from this pattern, they are bored

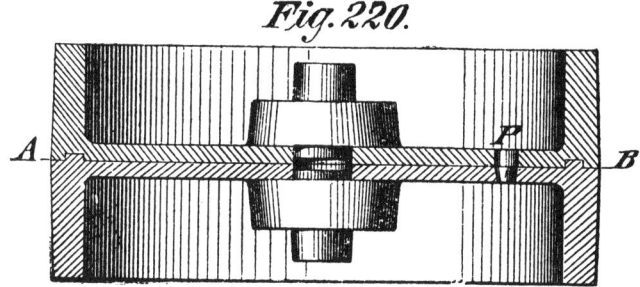

Fig. 220.

and turned to equal dimensions, the proper draught for molding being given in the process. A slight projection is turned upon one half, fitting into a recess on the other, as shown at B. When placed together, the two halves form the whole rim. The cast iron arms may be made either the full thickness or in halves. If made the full thickness, they will be fixed to one of the half rims. As half the thickness of the arms is made to project beyond the half rim, it will form a guide to keep the two rims central, so that in this case the projection, shown at B, need not be made. The arms are fitted to the ring by turning, and at the same time a hole is bored through the center to form a guide for the hub, as shown at P in the cut. When the arms are cast in two halves, and a half fitted in each rim, the pattern is easier to mold, as a level parting is secured. The rims must not only be kept central but be prevented from turning one on the other; hence the necessity for the hole to contain a pin, as shown at P. For convenience in drawing the pattern out of the sand, a couple of holes may be bored and tapped three eighths or half an inch, or larger if thought necessary, near the rim, diametrically opposite each other.

Occasions often occur when it is inexpedient to go to the expense of a pattern for making a pulley, especially if the pulley be large and only one or two castings required. In this case we may make use of the following contrivance, though it must not be expected that as well shaped castings can be made with it as from a finished pattern.

Fig. 221 illustrates by two views the apparatus as made

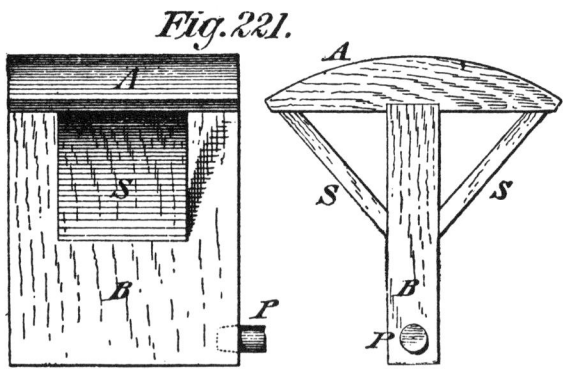

Fig.221.

wholly of wood. A is a piece shaped to the circle of the pulley. It is supposed to be large enough to extend at least about a sixth of its circumference; the depth of A is **equal to the width of the rim.** B forms a connection between it and the center, where the print, P, is fastened. S S are simply braces to stiffen the frame, the use of which will presently be described.

A core box must now be made, embracing a section of the interior of the pulley. If the pulley is to have six arms, the core box will take up a sixth of the interior; if four arms, a fourth. We will suppose the pulley is to have six arms. The core is made as shown in Fig. 222. A B

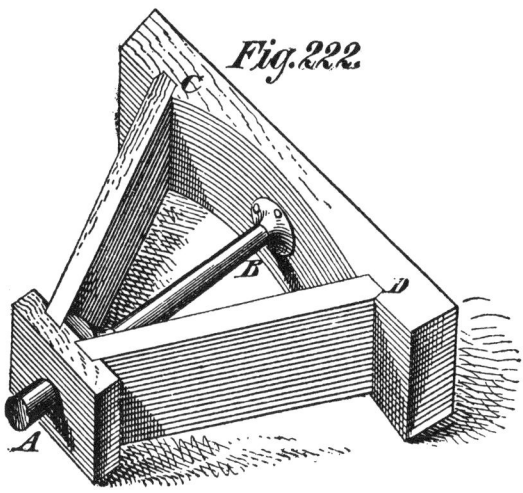

Fig.222.

represents the arm of the pulley passing through the center of the box; from C to D is exactly a sixth part of the inner circumference of the rim. A sixth part of the hub is fixed in the other corner. The piece C D is loose at the joints, as it is necessary to take it off to get out the core. The arm also is loose. When the core is made in this box, the arm A B is first pulled out; then the piece C D is removed, and afterward the other pieces. The hollows around the ends of the arms may easily be formed by the core maker, or they may be formed in the box, as seen in Fig. 222. The hollow or fillet at the end of the arm near the center must be worked out solid with the arm itself, while that which is at the circumference is worked in a piece fixed to C D, the arm being diminished so as to center this piece without making a feather edge. A plain straight arm, oval in section, is the cheapest and most convenient for pulleys made in this way. It may, however, be curved like the arc of a circle, but not made S-formed, as it could not then be drawn out from the solid core.

The molder, having prepared a level bed, places upon it the frame, Fig. 221, allowing the print to impress itself in the sand; a weight is then placed upon the frame to keep it in position while the sand is piled around the curve and made level at the full height of the same. The frame is then shifted, and the sand molded in again. This process is repeated until the circle of the pulley is finished. Into the mold so prepared must now be placed six cores, made in the box described in Fig. 222, and also the core to make the hole for the shaft. The whole is then covered with a level cope, and prepared for the casting.

CHAPTER XVI.

COGGING.

The term cogging is applied by pattern makers and wheelwrights to the process of furnishing wooden teeth to iron wheels, in the rim face of which are cast mortises to receive the wooden cogs. The term cog is applied to the piece of wood out of which the tooth is formed. This includes the shank fitting into the mortise, together with the tooth projecting from the face of the wheel. The term tooth denotes the part forming the tooth independently of the part fitting into the mortise.

The object of using cogged wheels is to avoid the jar and noise incidental to the use of large cast gear wheels, which it is found impracticable to cast true. If the wheel is cast from a wooden pattern, this pattern is liable to warp. Furthermore, the rapping of the pattern in the mold tends somewhat to destroy the truth of the mold. Even if these elements of error are eliminated in making the mold by using a molding machine, the unequal shrinkage of the casting induces untruth. After a gear wheel is cast, the face is then to be turned true. While in the lathe a circle may be made for the bottom of the teeth, and another for the pitch line. Other circles may be made as are deemed necessary as guides for adjusting the instrument used to form the outlines of the teeth. The wheel may be marked off as carefully as can be, and the teeth, after marking, may be chipped and filed to the lines; but it is not found in ordinary practice that by any such means a degree of truth, sufficient to avoid jar and noise, is attainable. This is especially the case with large wheels, and cogging is resorted to. It is usual to cog the large wheel of a pair that run

10*

together, and to make the wood teeth thicker across the pitch line than the iron one. If two cast wheels are made to run together, there is usually given a certain amount of clearance between the spaces and the teeth; whereas, when a cogged wheel is employed, this clearance is dispensed with, and back lash is avoided. The woods generally used for cogging are hornbeam, hickory, buttonwood or sycamore, maple, and locust. The blocks for the cogs should be cut out and kept, so as to thoroughly season before being used. There should, when there is likely to be a demand for them, always be kept a spare set of cogs, so that they will be ready for use, well seasoned and less liable to shrink, and thus come loose in the mortises.

When the cast wheel arrives from the foundry, it is taken to the machine shop, bored and turned across the face. The mortises receive a little attention, burrs and sprue fins are removed, the rough places leveled, etc. If it should

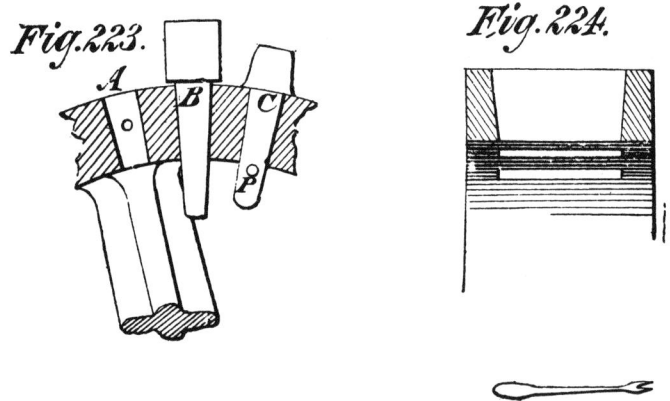

Fig. 223.   Fig. 224.

be found that any of the mortises are "blind," that is, stopped by the arms of the wheel, as shown at A, Fig. 223, a circumstance which is avoided as much as possible in the designing of the wheel, a small hole must be made through the rim to admit of the passage of a wire or screw. The first step taken toward getting out the wood teeth is to obtain the exact size and shape of the mortises. For this purpose, if the wheel is a spur, we must cut out two pieces of thin wood, as templates to fit the mortise, one representing the length of the mortise, as in Fig. 224, and the other its width. The templates must be tried in several holes, so as to insure their being the correct size. $a b c d$, Figs. 225 and 226, represent one of these templates. From it we get the size of the rough cogs. Add above $b c$ the height of the finished tooth, and from a quarter to half an inch more, according to the size of the wheel, to allow for turning off. Make a good allowance in this direction, as also at the other end of

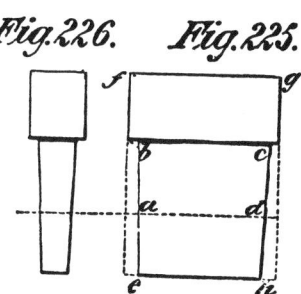

Fig. 226.   *Fig. 225.*

the piece, for the wood may be bruised by the hammer in driving the cogs in and out. The size of the cog is shown at $c f g h$, the length $f g$ being that of the finished tooth, and not less than $\frac{1}{8}$ inch allowed on each side for turning. To obtain the thickness, take that of the finished tooth, shown at C, Fig. 223, at the thickest part, and allow about $\frac{1}{8}$ inch of a side for trimming.

Having now the full size and thickness, cut out the number of cogs required, with three or four spare ones, as some may be split or possess some defect. To avoid damaging the teeth, a broad, flat-faced, heavy hand-hammer should be used to drive them with.

It is taken for granted that a circular saw bench is accessible, for without this cogging is made with difficulty. Have the saw in good order, and mount upon it a simple contrivance for shanking the cogs. It is composed of a box and two guides. These are illustrated in Figs. 227, 228, and 230, the parts throughout being marked with the same letters.

Make A C perpendicular with E F. Let E F be the height the saw stands above the table, which should be

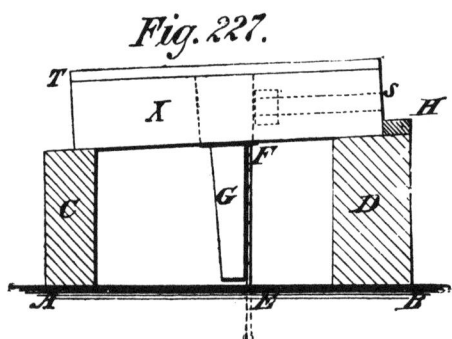

Fig. 227.

a little higher than the length of the shank of the cog. To the line E F apply the form or template, *a b c d*, of the width of the shank. Produce the top line of this form, and it is the top of the guides. Make the guide C at such a distance from the saw as to admit of the passage of the cogs the widest way. Make a box composed of two pieces, one piece being of sufficient thickness to take in the whole rough tooth of a cog in a mortise cut through the center of it, as indicated by the dotted lines in Figs. 231 and 232, and shown in full in Fig. 234. The thin piece T forms a backing to stop the cog in the mortise; it also, by being placed with the grain in an opposite direction to that of the box and screwed firmly, adds much to the strength of the box, and enables it to resist the strain of the binding screw S, by which the cogs are held while being sawed. Having the thickness of the box, lay it off upon the opposite side of E F, and draw the guide D; if, as at G, in Fig. 234, the size of the top of the shank be laid down, then the distance from it to the sides and ends of the box must be equal to E F, the height of the saw above the table. Having the size of the box, we can now mark the position of the guide H.

Eight movements with the box over the saw shanks the cog; two movements, as in Fig. 231, make slits through the width of the stuff and bring it to the right thickness; at Fig. 232, two movements, with the box held in the direction shown, bring the shank to the width. The box is now to be held with one of its edges on the table and passed between the guide, D, and the saw. It is to be passed through four times. A slab is detached each time.

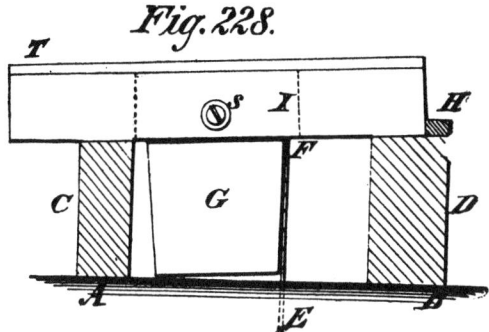

Fig. 228.

Figs. 229 and 230 illustrate two of these positions; and after turning the box upside down, the other two movements may be performed.

Having now completely shanked one cog, it must be compared with the templates and tried in the mortises.

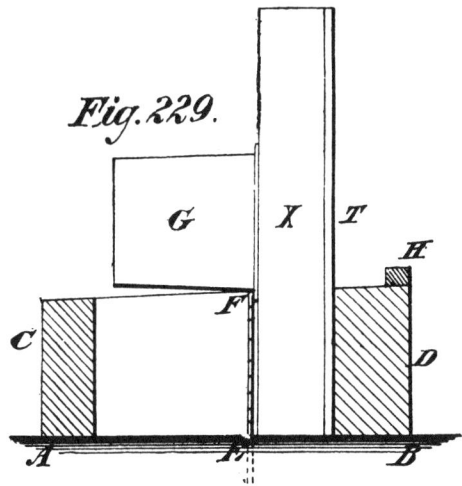

Fig. 229.

Care and patience at this time may save hours of labor in fitting. Proceed now to fit the cogs to the mortises, as at B, Fig. 223, driving them tightly, and leaving them with their shoulders, say, $\frac{1}{8}$ inch above the rim at the **widest** part. Use raw linseed oil to lubricate the surfaces while driving. All the cogs being now driven into their places, take a little instrument, shown in Fig. 224, called a fork scriber, and with this trace a line upon the shoulder of each cog by allowing one prong to travel along the turned face of the wheel while the other is pressed against the wood. The shanks of the cogs must also be marked with a common scriber where they project through on the under side of the rim.

Number all the cogs with a pencil, and number two of the mortises with a center punch or stamp, to show the direction of the numbering. Now drive out all the cogs and "shoulder" them, that is, dress the shoulders to the fork-scribe line, so that, when driven in, the shoulders will fit

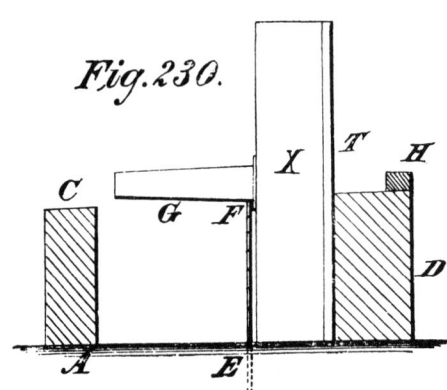

Fig. 230.

the face of the wheel. This being done, mark a mark on the shank; into this mark on both edges of the cog insert the fork scriber, and scribe a line parallel to the first but nearer up to the shoulder. This line shows where the under side of the rim will come when the cog is next driven in, for of course it will be driven just as much further as the distance between the two points of the fork scriber. In Fig. 223 observe the pin, P, the top of which lies against the rim; so in finding the center of the hole for the pin, we must place it nearly one half the diameter of the wire below the fork-scribe line. Make this nearly so as to have a little draw on the cog, and insure that the wire pin shall touch the rim. Then when the cogs shrink and become loose in their mortises, as they often will, the pins will at least keep the shoulders in contact with the rim. Cogs in blind mortises are made to fit at the first drive and not removed, unless from some oversight it is inevitable. Carefully examine the hole and remove lumps or cut away the wood to escape them, and gage the size and depth of the hole. Do this to avoid the unpleasantness of having to draw the cog when once driven in.

The cogs may now be bored for the pin. This is most rapidly performed by running a boring bit in the lathe. The ordinary pin bit will do, but let it be so pointed as not to run away from the center mark made with a center punch. It should be lubricated with tallow or beeswax very frequently, or the temper will be drawn, because the material is so hard and the speed so high. It takes too

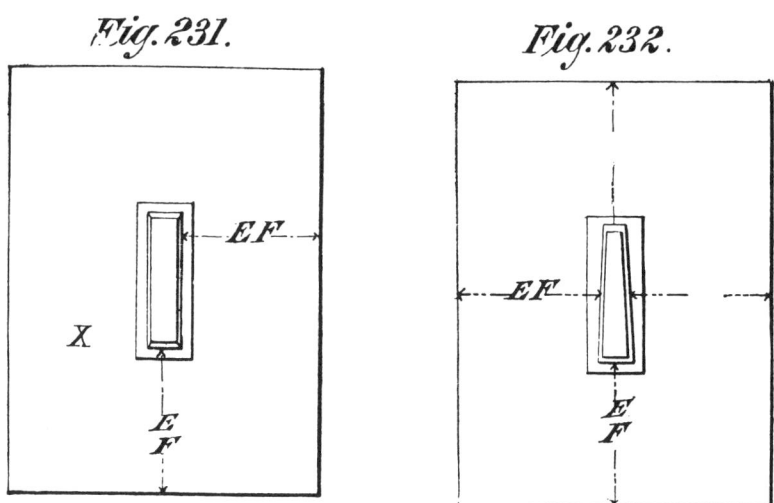

Fig. 231. *Fig. 232.*

much time to run the lathe mandrel back and forth by means of its screw; therefore, to remove the cap and wheel, fit a wooden knob or handle on the end of the screw and work the mandrel by hand. This will be clearly understood by turning the attention to Fig. 233. R is the running head with bit held by a chuck G, the cog T, tail-

stock W, the knob of wood. This method bores the cogs
rapidly and straight. The cog when bored half way may
be reversed and the rest of the boring completed from the
other side.

The next process is to saw the shanks off to an equal
length, measured from the shoulders which have been
dressed. In Fig. 234, S is the circular saw, F a guide
strip, B a planed board, H a handle, T a stop. The cog
G is shown with its shoulders resting against the edge of
the board and its side against the stop. In this position

Fig. 233.

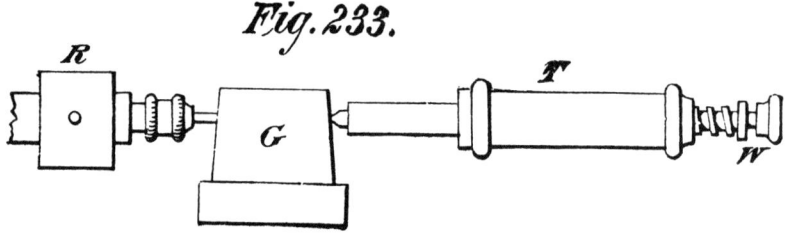

it is held firmly by the left hand, the right hand seizes the
handle and pushes toward the saw. A second stop is
shown at O; it is fixed to the table to prevent the board

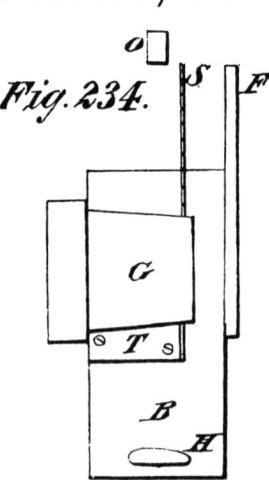

Fig. 234.

by any inadvertence from being
pushed too far. The ends of the
shanks may now be rounded at the
corners, or chamfered to give them a
presentable appearance, and the
cogs are ready to be again driven
into the wheel. A mixture of white
lead and boiled linseed oil is to be
made, of the consistence of thick
paint. This, with a piece of stick or
brush, is applied to that part of the
shank which remains in the rim.
Each cog is then driven into the
mortise, to which it was fitted, and which may be known
by the number marked on it. Insert the pins—pieces of

strong wire, pointed like a center punch; these are in length somewhat less than the rim is wide, but longer than the tooth. The wheel now goes to the turning shop, where the teeth are turned to the proper size and the pitch lines marked. Upon its return it is divided off, the outlines of the teeth drawn on both sides, and the excess of stuff removed with chisel and gouge. If it is possible to remove a portion with a good sharp hand-saw, that may be done, as much time may be saved thereby. When the teeth are all formed, filed, and sand-papered, they may receive a few good soakings of raw lin-seed oil.

In bevel wheels the mortise is narrower at one end than at the other, as shown in Fig. 235. It follows that the shanks of the teeth must be made to fit; therefore an extra template must be made, so as to have one for each end of the mortise. The shape of the mortise, or in other words, the top of the shank and its size, is to be laid down as in Fig. 232, and the distance E F (the length of the top of the circular saw from the saw to the table) laid off

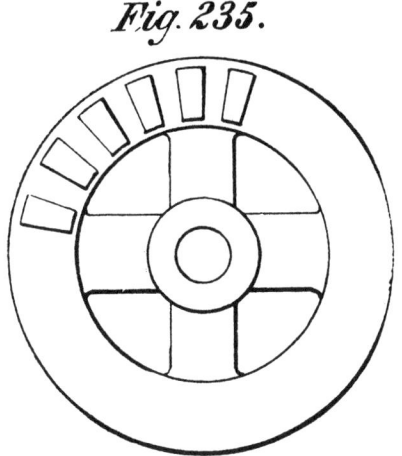

Fig. 235.

on all sides, so that the box will assume a shape corre-sponding to that of the shank, the guides remaining the same. In this way the outer edges of the box form a gage to saw the cogs.

10**

CHAPTER XVII.

Pattern making being a process for originating, it is obvious that the use of special tools in the same is out of the question; and there is at the present day no branch of woodworking in which power-driven tools or machines are so little used as in pattern making. In some pattern shops a lathe only is to be found; in a great many a lathe and jig-saw complete the complement. The lathes are in a majority of cases of simple, if not crude, construction, without any slide rest or self-acting feed motions — those shown in Figs. 45 and 55 being a fair representation. It must be conceded that from the desultory nature of pattern work and the fineness of finish required, hand work possesses many advantages, because in so many cases the work can be done by hand in about as much time as it would take to set a machine for the purpose. Furthermore, a hand plane can be sharpened on an oilstone in less time than it would take to stop a machine and take the planing cutter out. A pattern, when commenced, is worked upon by the workman or workmen until finished; and in any case each man does his own marking out, sawing, planing, boring, turning, etc.; and as each job must be, in the main, done in certain order, no part of his work can well—as a general rule—wait until a machine is unoccupied. Notwithstanding all this, however, there is no doubt that much work is done by hand that could be advantageously done in a machine, providing the latter does not occupy too much shop space, is not too heavy, is designed to perform several operations, and to be set for either of them readily and easily. As an example, core boxes and the segments for building up cylinders, etc., may be noted. A well constructed lathe device would bore a core box in a fraction of the time it requires by hand. A pattern maker's lathe having a friction straight and cross feed, and very light parts, would be a desirable tool, because of the facility with which facing up work and cutting out core boxes could be done. In facing up work, a large porportion of the time is spent in testing the straightness of the face. Core boxes could be bored out rapidly by fastening them to the light lathe saddle by a handy fixture designed for the purpose—the cutter being adjustable in a bar revolved between the lathe centers.

Of the few power tools or machines designed for pattern makers' use, a few of noteworthy examples are shown in the following engravings :

In Fig. 236 is shown a pattern maker's face lathe. The hand rest, it will be noted, is supported by an arm pivoted at one end, and supported by a leg at the other end, so that it can be adjusted to suit the work.

The reason for making the cone pulley of wood is, that its momentum when in motion being less than if of iron, it will stop and start more quickly ; and this is a valuable consideration, when the lathe requires to be so often stopped and started, to try the work. The box frame is provided to prevent the excessive vibration to which lathes, supported upon legs, are subject under high speed.

In Fig. 237 is shown a smaller face lathe for turning hubs, bosses, core prints, and similar work, than can be done without the use of a back center.

In Fig. 238 is represented a lathe head and tailstock for mounting on either wooden or iron shears, as may be preferred. Iron shears keep more true, and the tailstock is more easily moved and kept in line or set over, as the case may be ; the only objection to them being that they are apt to damage the edges of tools carelessly laid down; and wood may be made of large proportions, to avoid tremor where lathe shears and legs are used, as in this class of lathe.

It will be noted that each end of the cone spindle is provided with a face plate.   The extra one is for use upon

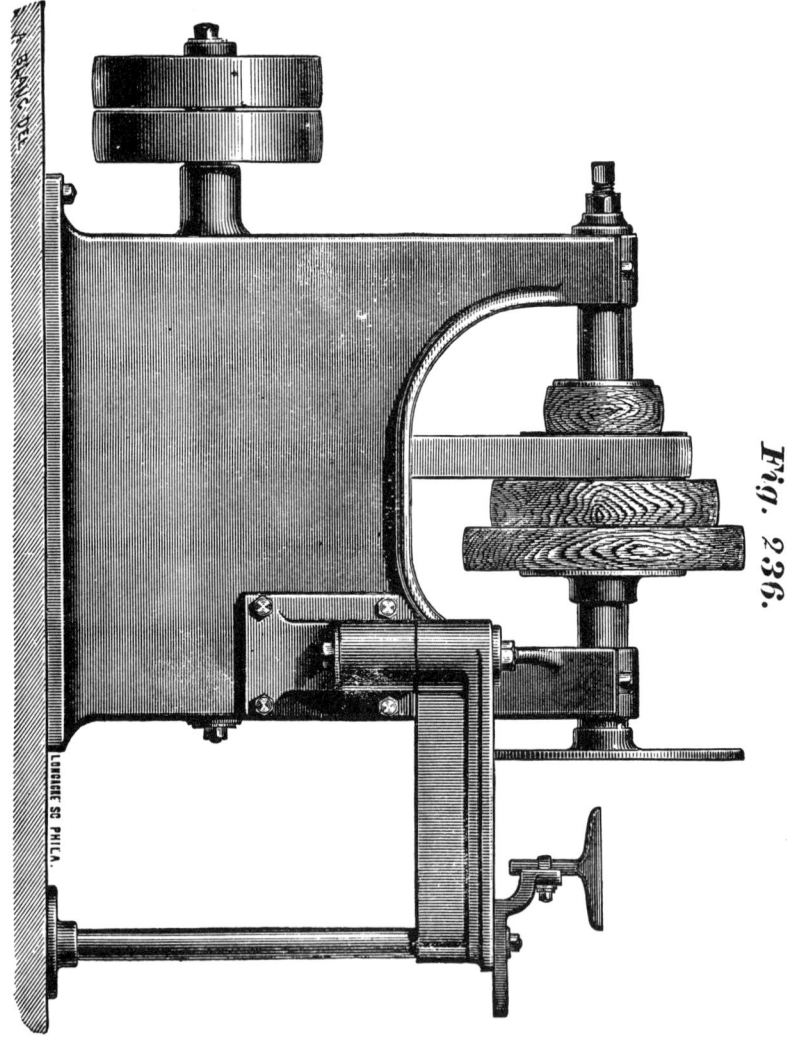

Fig. 236.

work too large to go between the lathe centers; in which case a movable hand rest — after the style shown in Fig.

47 — becomes necessary. This provision is very handy, but is not so good as the large face lathe shown in Fig. 236.

Fig. 237.

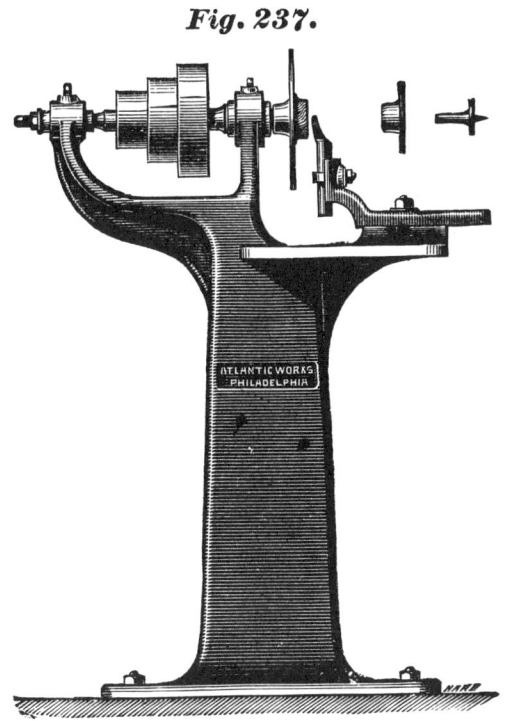

Fig. 238.

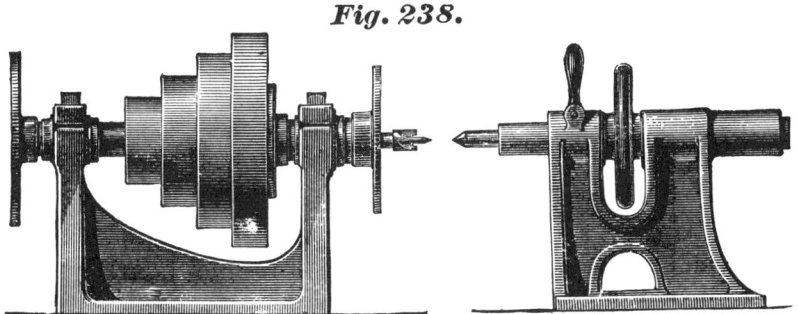

Next to a lathe, a jig saw is the power tool most commonly found in a pattern shop. It is indeed a very useful tool to the pattern maker, notwithstanding the noise and jar that usually attends its use. Its small expense and lightness, as compared to a band saw, are no doubt the con-

Fig. 239.

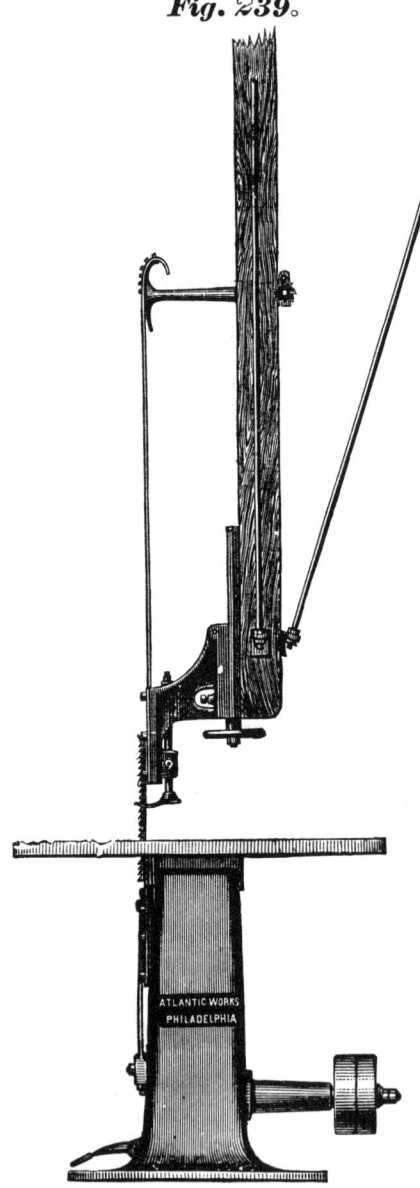

siderations which cause it to be preferred, because the band saw is an infinitely superior machine, except it be in cases where an area surrounded by solid wood requires to be cut out, in which case the jig saw can be detached, passed through the work, and attached again — thus performing a duty peculiar to itself. In the jig saw, shown in Figs. 239 and 240, the table is planed true and pivoted, so as to cant over, for sawing bevels, or to give the pattern the necessary draught. The crank is provided with a conical schiele bearing at the front, adjusted by nuts at the end of the shaft. To stop the saw instantly, a friction brake is provided, and the sliding head or stock is adjustable in a long planed bearing upon the front of the column. The top guides are adjustable vertically, to suit different lengths of saws, and pivoted to regulate the

Fig. 240.

amount of rake given to the saw. The machine is also provided with a rotary fan, to remove the sawdust from the lines upon the work, and keep the latter visible.

The band sawing machine, shown in Fig. 241, is a very valuable machine for pattern making, because it will perform its duty with great truth as well as great rapidity,

Fig. 241.

answering also the whole purpose of a circular saw, and very nearly the whole purpose of a jig saw. Among these qualifications, however, that of cutting true and exact to line is the most valuable, especially in the case of the teeth

for wheels, segments, etc. The table is made adjustable
for cutting bevels or draught.

The circular saw, as used in pattern making, is mainly
applied to roughing-out purposes. More stuff being left
for finishing by hand, than would be the case were the
work sawn with a band or a jig saw. The circular is a
very useful saw, however, especially for roughing out rab-
bets and similar work. The table for pattern maker's use

Fig. 242.

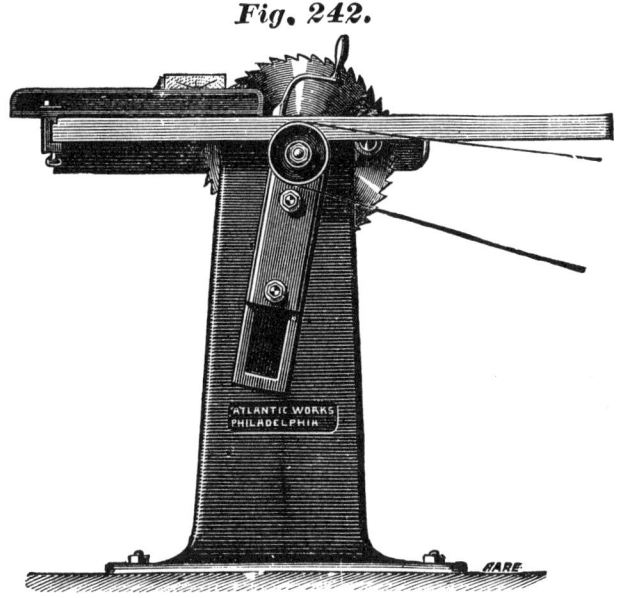

should adjust to saw at a bevel, and should rise and fall
adjustably at one end, so that the saw may project more
or less above the surface of the table; the height of the top
of the saw, from the table surface vertically beneath it,
regulating the depth of the groove the saw will cut. The
same saw being used for slitting and cross-cutting purposes, the teeth are filed slightly pointed, and thus answer
both purposes. The circular saw, shown in Fig. 242, is designed for pattern maker's use; the gage being operated
by a screw operated by the handle shown.

11

Roller feeding planing machines are not properly adapted for pattern making, because the pressure of the roller springs the work out of true. They may, it is true, be used upon work too thin to be held in other planers, but there being in any case no assurance of truth (that great desideratum for pattern makers) their employment, even for

Fig. 243.

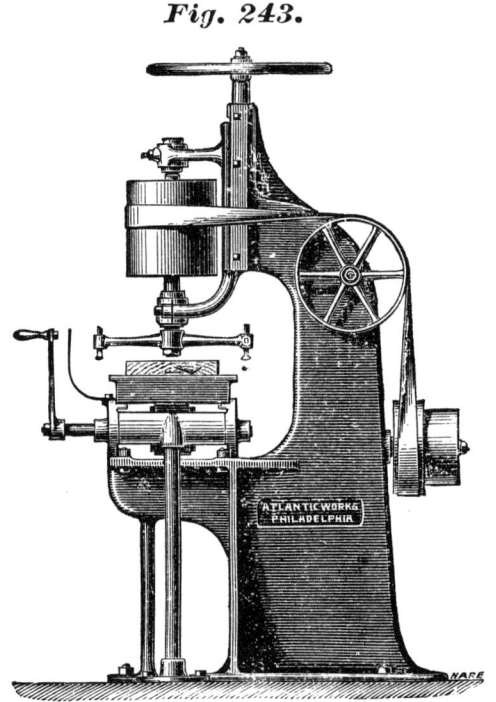

thin work, is not advisable. A traverse planing machine, however, is a very useful tool, especially upon segment work; hence such a machine is shown in Fig. 243. The frame is boxed, to secure rigidity with compactness and lightness. The feed is a hand one, as is preferred by all pattern makers, because it admits of rapid manipulation. The framing being open at the front, gives easy access to the cutters, and admits work of greater width.

In every pattern shop hot glue is a primary necessity, and steam is by all means the best medium of keeping the same heated ready for use. In Fig. 244 is shown a steam glue heater; the outer casing containing the water, there being a glue pot on each side of the upper face, and a pot for hot water in the center. In the absence of steam, the ordinary glue pot, heated by gas or a spirit lamp, is employed.

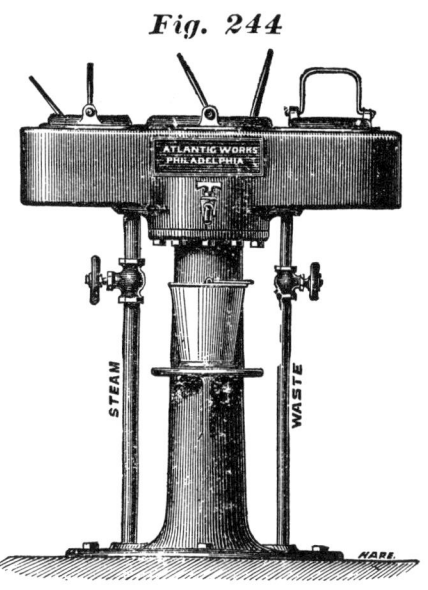

Fig. 244

The glue used in pattern making must be of the best quality, well boiled, and applied properly hot; because, notwithstanding the varnish, patterns are affected by the moisture of the molding-sand, and from rapping the pattern to loosen it in the mold. Defective gluing — or in fact any but the best executed gluing — will rapidly show itself, and impair the value of the pattern.

CHAPTER XVIII.

SHRINKAGE IN CASTINGS.

To allow for the shrinkage in castings, the pattern is not infrequently made in form and size to meet the requirements of any known case. Suppose, for example, that the surface of a large casting is found to be hollow, then that surface upon the pattern will be made sufficiently rounding to allow for the shrinkage, thus giving a casting with the desired flat surface. In large bodies of metal the shrinkage is always sufficient to demand an allowance therefor by the pattern maker; and it always takes place in the largest mass of the metal. The directions of this shrinkage are thus given for particular forms by Mr. ALFRED C. WATKINS:

SOLID CYLINDERS.

In the case of a shaft, or other solid cylinder, it will be noticed that the surface of the casting at the ends will be slightly depressed. This is occasioned by the surface of the cylinder being cooled by the walls of the mold first, and setting, while the central portion yet remains fluid or soft. In a few moments more the central portion cools, and in shrinking draws in the ends of the cylinder, the outer crust acting as a prop or stay to the atoms of metal adjacent to it. If this theory be correct, the depression should take the form of an inverted cone, owing to the gradual checking of the shrinkage as it approaches the outer crust. In practice this will be found the case—the obtuseness of the angle being greater or less, according to the nature of the iron to shrink.

GLOBES.

In the case of solid globular castings, the heart or central point within will usually be found hollow or porous, owing to the following causes: The walls of the mold cooling off the outer surface, causes it to set immediately; the interior, cooling from the exterior inward, endeavors to shrink away from the outer crust, which resists its so doing; hence, the interior is kept to a greater diameter than is natural, and there being but so much metal in the entire mass, the atoms are drawn away from the central point toward all directions, to supply the demand made by the metal in shrinking.

DISKS.

In the case of flat round disks or plates, they will usually be found hollow on the top side, although in some cases the hollow is on the bottom side. This is owing to the following causes: The top and bottom faces, together with the outside edge, become set first through contact with the mold, leaving the center yet soft. When the center shrinks a severe strain is put on the plate by an effort to reduce its diameter, which the outer edge resists. Now, if the cop be thin, the heat will radiate rapidly in that direction, causing the outer or top side to set first; the under side, setting later, will drag the top side over with it, causing it to round up on top and dish in the bottom. Or if the pattern be not perfectly true in every direction, the strains first spoken of will cause any curved portion to become more exaggerated. If the pattern be perfectly true, cop and drag of the same thickness, and both rammed evenly, there is no reason why the plate should not come out perfectly true, the strains being all self-contained in the same plane and balanced. If the plate, however, have an ogee molding projecting downward around the edge, it will likely be depressed on the top surface when cast. This is due to all the surfaces being set alike and at the same instant, excepting the metal within the corners, which, containing the most metal in a mass, will shrink last of all. When this does shrink, its tendency is to pull over the top side of the molding toward the plate, which being soft, although set, will be forced downward at the edges, giving a chance for the strains within the plate, as above described, to aid in the distortion.

ROUND AND SQUARE BARS.

These strains are similar in both, and are already treated of under solid cylinders. There is another feature, not before spoken of, which is rather curious. If two bars of the same dimensions and mixture of iron be heated to the same temperature, the one allowed to cool in the mold, the other plunged while hot into water, the latter will be found to have shrunk the most. This is due to the particles about the surface having been enabled, by the softness of the interior metal, to get closer to each other than they could have done if the material had cooled slowly.

RECTANGULAR TUBES.

These are usually cast with a core, which has a tendency to retain the shape of the casting; still the flat sides will show a tendency to bulge up slightly at the middle. This is due to much of the same causes—the outer surface is cooled instantly by the wall of the mold, and is set; the inner surface is not cooled quite so rapidly, owing to the core being of harder material, and not so good a conductor of heat. When this does cool it will pull inward the outer skin of the casting, forming a slight curve; each side acting for itself, will produce the same effects.

GUTTER, OR U-SHAPED CASTINGS.

These are usually made thinner at the edges than at the middle, because the pattern has been made with draught. When castings of this shape are taken from the mold, they will be found rounded over in the direction of their length, the legs being on the curved side. This is explained by the mold cooling and setting the legs first; then when the back or round shrinks, it pulls upward the two ends of the casting.

WEDGE-SHAPED CASTINGS.

In parallel castings of any length, having a cross section similar to a wedge—or similar to a "knife" in paper-mill work—the thick side will invariably be found concave and the thin edge curved. This is due to the same causes as explained above. The thin edge is set as soon as cast; the thick edge, cooling later, shrinks and draws the ends of the casting upward, and with them the thin edge, which acts as a pillar to resist further shrinkage.

RIBS ON PLATES.

All ribs have a tendency to curve a plate, if they be thicker or of the same thickness as the plate, owing to the fact that whatever shrinkage strain they possess is below the general plane of the shrinkage of the plate itself. If the ribs be thinner than the plate, they will cool first; and by resisting the shrinkage of the bottom of the plate, cause it to curve upwards, or "dish" on top.

GENERAL LAWS REGARDING SHRINKAGES.

The most metal in a mass always shrinks last; hence if a casting be composed of irregular thickness, it will be liable to be broken by the forces contained within itself. It is, therefore, especially necessary that columns and castings supporting or resisting great pressures, should be so designed as to prevent this great error. Moldings on columns are often so badly designed with regard to this matter, that the columns are excessively weak where they should be the strongest. As a rule, moldings should seldom be cast on a column, but rather bolted on. Much of the irregularity of flat castings and those of irregular shapes, could be remedied by a proper attention to cooling the castings while in the mold. To be sure, this is done to a certain extent, though few molders know why they do so. They know that by removing the sand from a particular casting, it will straighten in the shrinking. This is but the result of experience, not of thought, or any attempt to know why they so act. It is useful to know, also, that all shrinkage takes place while the casting is changing from a red to a black heat.

SHRINKAGE OF CASTINGS.

In locomotive cylinders......................$\frac{1}{16}$ inch in a foot.

In pipes ....$\frac{1}{8}$ "   "

Girders, beams, etc...................$\frac{1}{8}$ "   15 in.

Engine beams, connecting rods ....$\frac{1}{8}$ "   16 in.

In large cylinders, say 70 in. diameter, 10 ft. stroke,
   the contraction of diameter is about...........$\frac{3}{8}$ " at top.

     "   "   "   "   ....$\frac{1}{2}$ " at bottom

   Shrinkage of length is...................$\frac{1}{8}$ " in 16 in.

In Thin brass...........................$\frac{1}{8}$ "   10 "

" Thick brass ....$\frac{1}{8}$ "   12 "

" Zinc ....$\frac{5}{16}$ "   12 "

" Lead ....$\frac{5}{16}$ "   12 "

" Copper ....$\frac{7}{32}$ "   12 "

" Tin ....$\frac{9}{32}$ "   **12** "

TO CALCULATE STRENGTH OF PIPES OR OTHER THIN CYLINDERS.

RULE :—Multiply the inside diameter of the pipe or cylinder in inches by the pressure in lbs. per square inch that is to act inside of it, and divide the product by 10,000. To this result add a sufficiency to insure a good casting, and to enable the pipe to stand handling; and this will give the total thickness.

NOTE :—The amount to be added varies with the diameter of the pipe.

On a 4″ pipe, and under, allow $\frac{3}{16}$
6   "   over 4″   " $\frac{1}{4}$
8   "   "   6 allow $\frac{5}{16}$
12   "   "   8   " $\frac{3}{8}$
30   "   "   12 " $\frac{1}{2}$
48   "   "   30 " $\frac{5}{8}$
70   "   "   48 " $\frac{3}{4}$
100 "   "   70 " $\frac{7}{8}$

EXAMPLE :—What must be the thickness of a 25 inch cylinder for a steam engine, so that it may stand 60 lbs. per square inch ?

$25 + 60 = 1500 \div 10000 = \frac{3}{20}$ or $\frac{5}{32}$ of an inch; add to this $\frac{3}{8} = \frac{1}{4}$ inch $+ \frac{1}{32}$. Add another $\frac{1}{4}$ for reboring.

———

MOLESWORTH'S RULE for calculating the necessary thickness of metal for cylinders or pipes, is as follows:

RULE :—Multiply the inside diameter of the pipe or cylinder by the pressure in lbs. per square inch it is to bear, and divide the product by 4000. The last product to be increased one half.

It is to be noted, however, that the rules for calculating the necessary thickness of a cylinder to withstand a given pressure, do not give the thickness that the pattern maker requires, because the number of times allowed for reboring the cylinder, its situation as to its being subjected to oxidation, and other similar considerations, have caused the existence in actual practice of greater thicknesses than those given by any of the rules; and in a general way specific kinds of cylinders are made to conform in thickness to that which practice has demonstrated to suit the requirements of the duty; this latter term including more than mere strength.

TO CALCULATE THE THICKNESS OF METAL FOR CYLIN-DERS FOR HYDRAULIC PRESSES.

RULE:—Multiply the constant number given below for the material of which the cylinder is to be made by the pressure in tons per square inch, and by half the internal diameter of the cylinder.

EXAMPLE:—A 10-inch cylinder is to bear a pressure of 3 tons per square inch; what must be its thickness in cast iron ?

$$
\left.\begin{array}{ll}
\text{CONSTANTS:} & \\
\text{Cast iron} & \cdot41 \\
\text{Gun metal} & \cdot22 \\
\text{Wrought iron} & \cdot14 \\
\text{Steel} & \cdot06
\end{array}\right\} \cdot41 + 3 = 1\cdot23 + 5 = 6\cdot15 \text{ or } 6\tfrac{1}{8}.
$$

EXAMPLE:—A steel cylinder of 5 inches internal diameter is to bear a pressure of 35 tons per square inch; what must be its thickness ?

$$0\cdot6 \times 35 = 2\cdot10 \times 2\cdot5 = (Ans.)\ 5\cdot25,\ \text{or } 5\tfrac{1}{4}\ \text{inches.}$$

TO CALCULATE THE WEIGHT OF RIMS FOR FLY WHEELS.

RULE:—

$$
W = \frac{2542FS}{n^2x^2f}
\left\{
\begin{array}{l}
F = \text{Constant force in pounds, or mean force on piston;} \\
S = \text{Stroke in feet;} \\
W = \text{Weight in pounds of fly wheel;} \\
x = \text{Radius of center of gyration in feet;} \\
n = \text{No. of revolutions per minute;} \\
f = \cdot05.
\end{array}
\right.
$$

Multiply the area of the cylinder by the mean pressure on the piston in lbs. per square inch, by the stroke in feet, and by 500, and divide by the product of the number of revolutions per minute, multiplied by the radius of the fly wheel, measured at the inside of the rim.

11*